READING

The Eve of St. Agnes

READING
The Eve of St. Agnes

The Multiples of
Complex Literary Transaction

Jack Stillinger

New York   Oxford
Oxford University Press
1999

Oxford University Press

Oxford   New York
Athens   Auckland   Bangkok   Bogotá   Buenos Aires   Calcutta
Cape Town   Chennai   Dar es Salaam   Delhi   Florence   Hong Kong   Istanbul
Karachi   Kuala Lumpur   Madrid   Melbourne   Mexico City   Mumbai
Nairobi   Paris   São Paulo   Singapore   Taipei   Tokyo   Toronto   Warsaw

and associated companies in
Berlin   Ibadan

Copyright © 1999 by Jack Stillinger

Published by Oxford University Press, Inc.
198 Madison Avenue, New York, New York 10016

Oxford is a registered trademark of Oxford University Press

Library of Congress Cataloging-in-Publication Data
Stillinger, Jack.
Reading The eve of St. Agnes : the multiples of
complex literary transaction / Jack Stillinger.
p.   cm.
Includes bibliographical references and index.
ISBN 0-19-513022-7
1. Keats, John, 1795–1821. Eve of St. Agnes.
2. Literature—History and criticism—Theory, etc.
3. Authors and readers.   4. Canon (Literature)   I. Title.
PR4834.E83S75   1999
821'.7—dc21   98-46402

1 3 5 7 9 8 6 4 2
Printed in the United States of America
on acid-free paper

I have worked on *Kubla Khan* for thirty years and I do not know if it is a poem about poetry or politics, or is in three sections or five, or is satirical or celebratory, or whether it makes different sense if you are a lesbian or a royalist. I could speculate about whether it is a complete poem or a fragment, but answers to the questions I described would be negotiable.

J. C. C. Mays

Poetry is like shot-silk with many glancing colours. Every reader must find his own interpretation according to his ability, and according to his sympathy with the poet.

Tennyson

I still think the business of criticism is interpretation. I just no longer believe that interpretive criticism is transparent, or that it sees the world steadily and sees it whole. Nor is interpretation properly "supplementary" to its object, like reader's guides and *Cliff Notes*. I believe instead that interpretation is always partial, that it never "fills up" its object, and that its "partiality" needs to be interpreted in its turn.

Michael Bérubé

> The earth tilts and spins around. A thing
> is true one time and then another is.
> Proverbs all have equal opposites.
> Believe everything; one time it's true.
> Many other meanings is what it means.
> William Bronk

I think I shall be among the English critics after my death.

Anon.

PREFACE

JOHN KEATS (1795–1821) WAS THE youngest of the currently canonical
British poets writing in the early years of the nineteenth century. Practically
all the other major British writers lived two or three times longer than Keats, and
it is a fact of literary history that not one of them, if they had stopped writing as
early as Keats did, would be known or read today. Keats also had the shortest literary career on record, hardly more than three and a half years. For the first two
and a half years of this brief span, he was not a distinguished poet. In his final
year of writing—actually, his final nine months of writing—he suddenly (and
unexplainably) began producing, one after another, a sizable number of what
are now the most admired works in standard English poetry: *The Eve of St. Agnes*,
Hyperion, *La Belle Dame sans Merci*, *Ode to a Nightingale*, *Ode on a Grecian Urn*,
Lamia, the ode *To Autumn*.

The year during which I wrote and delivered the lectures on which this book
is based, 1995, was the two hundredth anniversary of Keats's birth year, and
events were scheduled weekly to mark the occasion: conferences all over the
world, speeches, dedications, lectures, layings of wreaths, unveilings, commemo-
rative walks, musical celebrations, poetry readings. A John Keats rose was specially cultivated. A Keats coloring book and a Keats T-shirt were put on sale. A
comprehensive "Calendar of Events" issued by the Friends of Keats House in
Hampstead ran to ten legal-size pages of single-spaced entries.

What, one may ask, lies behind all this attention? Why are we still reading
and thinking about Keats two hundred years after his birth? What is it about
Keats that makes so many people think he is better than many other writers who
do not inspire international events to celebrate a significant anniversary and in
fact are totally unknown after such an interval? In short, what is so great about
Keats?

I have been reading and teaching Keats seriously for some forty years, and what increasingly impresses me is that a good Keats poem means something different every time I read it—and I speak from the experience of hundreds of teachings and thousands of readings. For a long time I just took this richness for granted, thinking how lucky it was that when I was in graduate school I decided to specialize in Keats instead of some other writer. Now I am making it a subject of scholarly investigation. I want to know (and then tell everybody else) how it is possible that Keats's texts—which never in themselves change from one reading to the next—can keep producing new meanings.

In this book I shall use *The Eve of St. Agnes* to make several points about Keatsian inexhaustibility. I am interested in three basic questions: how a Keats poem registers its effects on a reader; why the effects that are registered differ from one reading to another; and why we are still, in large numbers (for this kind of activity), reading and admiring Keats's poems two hundred years after his birth. The questions are of course related, and the answer to the last should follow from the answers to the first two.

These could be considered theoretical questions—the first implying or involving a theory of reading, the second a theory of interpretation, and the third a theory of canonicity. But I am above all concerned with the practical situations of real readers reading (they *do* such and such in the process of reading), real readers disagreeing with one another (students, teachers, critics *say* such and such to explain what they have read), and everybody, whatever the processes and results of their reading, in general agreeing about the quality of the poetry (Keats undeniably *is* in the canon). I am, then, reversing the more common sequence of theory followed by illustrative example (as, for example, in E. D. Hirsch's *Validity in Interpretation*). And although it is hardly possible to write about reading, interpretation, and canonicity without being theoretical, my primary aim here is practical improvement of the ways we read, teach, and write about literature.

The "multiples" of complex literary transaction have been a special interest of mine for the past several years. In older critical thinking, the standard transaction of author, text, and reader involved a single author creating a single text for a single reader (an imagined ideal reader, perhaps, or the teacher in a literature class, or the latest critic "performing" the reading in a book or an essay). More recently, several concepts of multiples are complicating this traditional thinking: a multiple of collaborative authors instead of just the one writer whose name is on the title page; multiple versions of a work rather than a single ideal text (whether the earliest, the latest, something in between, or an editorial composite); and, what is most obvious, multiple readers—and, as a consequence, multiple readings—everywhere one turns. My *Multiple Authorship and the Myth of Solitary Genius* (Oxford University Press, 1991) contributed to the complication of the authorship end of the transaction, and my *Coleridge and Textual Instability: The Multiple Versions of the Major Poems* (Oxford, 1994) to a similar expansion of the middle component of the transaction. The present work focuses on multiplicity at the reception end of the business.

If there is an opponent against whom all this is addressed, let it be Matthew Arnold, who, for all his wisdom in nearly every paragraph he wrote, bears a large responsibility for some of the worst aspects of our literary profession in the present century: the basic idea of literature as a substitute for religion, and the consequent ideas of texts as sacred documents, teachers and critics as priestly authorities, students and general readers as a lay audience incapable of understanding or evaluating a text without authoritative pronouncement from above (by the priestly keepers of the touchstones). Our ordinary practices in the classroom—teacher as lecturer, student as notetaker and examinee—follow from Arnold's fundamental thinking; and if, over the decades, most of the lecturers and examiners have been male, that is because criticism as an "old-boy" activity is inherent in the concept of critic as priest. All such authority is just now being called into question by multiple authorship, multiple texts, and multiple reading.

I believe in major authors and in major works by those authors. This makes me a conservative critic in today's culture wars. At the same time I believe that no poem or play or novel has a single correct interpretation, because the meanings of literary works reside in the activities of those who read them and no two people read in exactly the same way. This makes me a radical critic in today's culture wars. I want to show how these positions are compatible. My ideal is, in effect, interpretive democracy, and, like political democracy, it negotiates between individual freedom (as in the notion of "no-fault reading" introduced in the penultimate section of chapter 4) and some familiar restraints (in the form of factuality, comprehensiveness, and consensus).

The overall progress of my argument should be clear from a glance at the Contents. The Introduction expands on the ideas just mentioned—the literary transaction and the complication of multiples—and poses a preliminary question about the nature and whereabouts of "meaning" when we read a poem. Chapter 2 provides several kinds of background information about *The Eve of St. Agnes*, chiefly to make the point that all the different ways of reading the poem proceed from the same starting materials. Chapter 3 describes some of the numerous interpretations of *The Eve of St. Agnes* proffered over the past several decades, including recent readings that have followed from poststructuralist theory. Chapters 4 and 5 attempt to explain *why* there have been (and continue to be) so many different ways of reading this poem, examining first the creative activity of readers and then the more complex prior creativity of the poet, a multiple author within himself as a genius of internally contradictory tendencies. My Conclusion connects the multiple meanings of Keats's poems with his enduring status as one of the canonized English poets. The three appendixes provide a variorum text, a token list of "Fifty-nine Ways of Looking at *The Eve of St. Agnes*" (originally a handout at several of my 1995 lectures), and information about paintings and other illustrations related to the poem. But I am perhaps making my work sound overly comprehensive. This is not, I should emphasize, an exhaustive study of *The Eve of St. Agnes* but, rather, a study in the poem's continuous inexhaustibility.

MY GREATEST DEBT, as always, is to Nina Baym, who has been my muse and best practical helper for three decades now. Other individuals whom I wish especially to thank—for information, suggestions, encouragement, challenging skepticism—include Mike Abrams, Hermione de Almeida, Bob and Jane Hill, Mark Jones, Laura Mandell, Barbara Michaels, Matt Mitchell, Leslie Morris, Bryan Rasmussen, Julia Saville, Peter Shillingsburg, Stuart Sperry, Tom Stillinger, Charles Webb, and Jim Weil. I am also much obliged for the positive responses and questions of my lecture audiences celebrating the Keats Bicentennial at Loyola University of Chicago, the University of Texas at El Paso, the Clark Library in Los Angeles, Harvard University, Southwest Texas State University, and the University of Illinois. In connection with those lectures, I owe particular thanks to Steve Jones, Lois Marchino, Beth Lau, Paul Sheats, Ron Sharp, Bob Ryan, Allan Chavkin, and Nancy Grayson. Several parts of the book have appeared in earlier form in *Journal of English and Germanic Philology* (October 1997) and *The Persistence of Poetry: Bicentennial Essays on Keats*, edited by Robert M. Ryan and Ronald A. Sharp (University of Massachusetts Press, 1998). I am grateful to the editors and publishers for permission to use the materials again here.

Urbana, Illinois   J. S.
February 1999

CONTENTS

READING
The Eve of St. Agnes

ONE

INTRODUCTION

The Literary Transaction

T HIS IS A BOOK ABOUT how we read *The Eve of St. Agnes*. The "we" in this case is a large subject—no less than all the readers of the poem from the time it was first written, in 1819, until today. And one could carry this forward to all future readers as well. The poem has been read in many different ways, in whole and in each of the separate parts, and will continue to be read in more and more different ways in a continually expanding complexity of cumulative interpretation. I have written this book to argue that all of these different readings are justified, that all are in some reasonable sense "right" (as opposed to "wrong"), and that the abundance and variety of these readings are just what we should expect—the standard rather than the exception—when a piece of canonical literature is the object at hand.

I shall begin with some modest generalizations about what I call the literary transaction—the relations among author, text, and reader in the process of communication—to make clear where I think the various activities of creativity, reading, and interpretation take place. After this initial chapter, the focus will be more strictly on Keats and *The Eve of St. Agnes*.

Author—Text—Reader: Where's the Meaning?

In a long-established tradition—almost from the beginning until, say, yesterday—the literary transaction has been thought to involve three basic elements: a creating agency (the Author), an object of creation (the Text), and a receiving agency (the Reader). In one obvious model for these elements, the Author was God; the Text, depending on one's particular theological interest, was either nature (the world) or some divinely authored scripture (the Bible, the Torah, the

3

Koran, the Bhagavad-Gita, the Vedas); the Reader was all of humanity, individually or collectively. When priests became a part of this model, their job was to interpret God's creation—nature or scripture—to humanity. The inescapable parallel in literary terms is the Critic mediating interpretively between Text and Reader, and the transaction then involves four instead of three elements: Author, Text, Critic, and Reader. But let us stick with the simplicity of the original three for a while—a simplicity not unlike the fabled perfect unity of God, nature, and humans in medieval thinking.

The elements in the first part of my section heading ("Author—Text—Reader") constitute a blackboard diagram that I use for different purposes in virtually every course I teach these days. They identify three important areas of theoretical inquiry: how literature is produced (questions of origin); how literature exists (questions of ontological identity); how literature registers effects (questions of reception, affect, response, interpretation). They also are focal points of three continuing interests of teachers and practical critics: history (including biography of authors, historical contexts, the methods of textual production); formal analysis (including standard New Critical focuses such as theme, structure, plot, relation of theme to form, relation of theme and form to style); and reception (including original audience, history of reception, current reading and, again, interpretation). They reflect a succession of distinct cultures impinging on one another, and they are adaptable to other matter besides literature: art, architecture, music, food, clothing, gardening, and so on, where in each case the author-figure (artist, architect, composer, chef, designer, gardener) produces something corresponding to a text (a painting, a building, a sonata, etc.) for a class of spectators, listeners, or consumers. Each such scheme has its separable elements of creation, existence, and reception, and one can employ them to organize any number of theoretical discussions concerning production, modes of existence, structures of effect, and canons of value.

Conventionally used to describe the literary transaction, the blackboard diagram symbolizes a straightforward process in the direction of left to right: the author puts meaning in a text; the text contains or represents the author's meaning; and the reader goes to the text to learn what the author meant to convey. For a long time, in theory at least, there were no problems with such a scheme of communication—though the practical working of the scheme almost always depended on contextual clues that were not themselves part of the original three elements. If I leave an undated and unsigned note on the family bulletin board saying "I'll be home at 5:30," my wife knows perfectly well who wrote it and what it means in its entirety. But many practical communications are like Peter Shillingsburg's "This year's juice," an inscription on three containers of grape juice that Shillingsburg discovered in his freezer, with no indication of how many months or years the juice had been in the freezer (*Resisting Texts* 63–64). If I were to leave my same note—"I'll be home at 5:30"—beside a classroom door in our English Building, it would be virtually meaningless: no one would know who wrote it, which day (or even, in strict logic, which part of the day, A.M. or P.M.) the "5:30" refers to, or where "home" might be in such a case. These are not far-fetched examples. Inscriptions like "Back in 5 minutes" pinned or taped to an office or business door almost never indicate when the specified time period began or will have passed.

The precariousness of practical communication has sometimes led theorists, especially in the heyday of deconstruction, to abolish the idea of transaction altogether. Authors do not know what they mean anyhow (and with Barthes's and Foucault's proclaimed "Death of the Author" three decades ago, were stripped of their right to have opinions in the matter); the texts by themselves convey no determinate meanings; readers have no authority for the interpretations they construct. But still, in practical literary situations (as opposed to "This year's juice" and "Back in 5 minutes"), not only authors on their side but readers, critics, teachers, students, and anybody else on the recipient side collaborate as best they can in the working of the traditional scheme: the author writes, producing the text; the reader reads the author via the text; and the common goal is the reception of meaning.

Of course, the idea of "meaning" in a literary work may strike some readers of this book as woefully old-fashioned. We do not, these days, approve of translating or converting literature into some nonliterary other thing: the paraphrase, the bare statement of idea or moral, the author's message or "philosophy." A poem is not supposed to mean something but to be something—or, even better, to do something. Even so, in practical situations it is impossible to read without receiving or constructing meaning. A meaningless literary work has never existed. The most ordinary descriptions of what happens in works, no matter how brief or simplistic, constantly refer to their meanings ("Porphyro rescues Madeline in *The Eve of St. Agnes*"; "No, it is Madeline who rescues Porphyro"; "The *Nightingale* speaker wishes to die while the unseen bird pours forth its song"; "The speaker realizes that, having died, he will no longer be able to hear the nightingale"). Our basic critical activity is first and foremost interpretation; whatever else we do, whatever theory or theories we subscribe to, our day-to-day reading, teaching, and writing about literature center on questions such as "What is this work about?" "What kind of character is this?" "What does this word mean?"

The second part of my section heading poses the most important question usually raised about this blackboard diagram: "Where's the meaning?" Obviously, at least at the outset of the inquiry, there are three basic possibilities.

In the commonest and longest-established theory, the meaning of a work resides with the author, that is, in the author's mind. It is the task of the recoverer of authorial meaning somehow, usually (one supposes) by reading the text, to gain entrance to the author's mind and thereby discover the author's thinking. For many decades in our profession, the idea of the author's intended meaning was fundamental to the activity of critical interpretation; the universal standard for the "correctness" of a reading, or the superiority of one reading over another, was the better likelihood that it repeated or recreated what the author meant to convey. Similarly, until quite recently, the goal of virtually all scholarly editing was the fulfillment or "realization"—approximation, recovery, (re)construction—of the author's final intentions.[1]

But there are serious problems with lodging the meaning of a work with the author in these ways. Authors are often dead or otherwise unavailable. Even if they were available, there is still no guarantee that they would explain what they meant in a work, and—even more of a problem—there is no reason to think that they themselves would know what they meant. Authors write for all sorts of reasons and from all sorts of impulses. For many authors, their works, at least in first-draft stage, were for all practical purposes intentionless.

Keats is an epitomizing example of a writer in this "intentionless" category. The evidence includes his original draft manuscripts, records detailing circumstances in which he wrote his poems, and his own comments in letters and elsewhere concerning spontaneity in writing, as in his famous axiom, in a letter to his publisher John Taylor, that "if Poetry comes not as naturally as the Leaves to a tree it had better not come at all" (*Letters* 1:238–39). Discussing his "mode of writing" with his friend Richard Woodhouse, the poet explained "that he has often not been aware of the beauty of some thought or expression until after he has composed and written it down. It has then struck him with astonishment— and seemed rather the production of another person than his own. He has wondered how he came to hit upon it. . . . It seemed to come by chance or magic—to be as it were something given to him."[2] Remarks like these suggest that Keats did his best work when he wrote without a plan. They also suggest that the reader who reads in order to recover what Keats consciously meant to convey—that is, who wishes to base an interpretation on Keats's original intentions—is looking for something that may in fact never have existed.

In a second theory, the meaning of a work resides in the text and is always there for anyone who takes the trouble to read it. This is the old New Critical concept of the autonomous "text in itself," which was devised in the first place, in the later 1920s, to oppose the then-current academic overemphasis on authors' lives at the expense of their works. I. A. Richards's *Practical Criticism* (1929), probing his Cambridge University students' inability to read and understand even a short poem, was an important initial influence in turning the focus from author biography to textual analysis. The epitomizing theoretical statement seventeen years later, W. K. Wimsatt and Monroe Beardsley's "The Intentional Fallacy" (1946), maintained that both the meaning and the value of a literary work exist independently of the author's intentions and must be determined, therefore, from the text.

There has, however, been considerable subsequent argument both by theorists and by empirical researchers that texts cannot have meaning in themselves. In theory, it takes a human being—an author at one end or a reader at the other—to register meaning; there is no meaning possible without a human being to *think* it. Try to imagine a closed book containing *The Eve of St. Agnes* that nobody has written and nobody is reading. Can there be meaning in that closed book with no human presence on the scene? The commonsense answer is obviously no. Even to imagine such a book containing such a poem is to cast the imaginer as reader; there has to be a writer or a reader to *mean* something by the text.[3] And empirical evidence shows repeated disagreement concerning meaning in all but the simplest situations, even among experts. If the meaning really resided in the text, more people should agree about the text.

In the third theory, the meaning of a work resides in the mind of the reader, possibly the best position simply by default. If authorial intention is in fact unrecoverable apart from the texts that the authors produced, and if texts do not speak for themselves, the only remaining choice, if we cannot do without meaning, is the meaning produced by a reader's interpretation at the recipient end of the transaction. But this theory offers something more. Reader's meaning has the attraction of being practically attainable in ways that the other kinds (the author's meaning, the text's meaning) are not; it can be stated, repeated, refined, discussed, queried, and (if anyone wishes) gathered collectively and even treated statistically. This is the kind of meaning that seems the most promising for further investigation, and it is the main focus of the present study.

The Complication of Multiples

The simplicity of the blackboard diagram, showing three principal locuses of meaning and seeming to imply a unified entity for each of them, reasonably represents earlier thinking about the literary transaction. Although literary art itself involves both unity and disunity, literary criticism until a couple of decades ago emphasized the former, not the latter. We have been constructing unity in works, in groups of works, in single authors, in groups of authors, in whole periods and whole centuries, and making much of these unities, as if we had found them instead of constructed them. Thanks to the assumption that each work had a single author, a single text, and a single reader (usually each critic individually, positing himself or herself as the ideal reader), it followed that there was a single interpretation of the work, which was, of course, the critic's own reading.

In more recent thinking, each of these onenesses has been supplanted by a plural. We now have multiple authors rather than single solitary geniuses. We now acknowledge the existence of multiple versions of works rather than just one text per work. Instead of a single real or ideal reader, we have multiple readers everywhere: classrooms full of individual readers in our college and high school literature courses, journals and books full of readers in our academic libraries, auditoriums full of readers at our conferences. All of these readers are constructing interpretations as fast as they read. As one might imagine, for a complex work, the interpretations differ from one another as much as the readers do. It is not possible that only one of the interpretations is correct and all the others are wrong.

My own scholarship of the past decade has paralleled and contributed to this thinking. In a progression moving in the same left-to-right direction as the traditional transaction itself, I have been complicating this simple diagram by studying each of the three elements as a complex of multiples: multiple authorship, multiple versions of text, and multiple readership. In *Multiple Authorship and the Myth of Solitary Genius* (1991), which had its origins in textual work that I had done earlier on Keats, Wordsworth, and John Stuart Mill, I suggested that numerous works, including plays by Shakespeare, novels by Dickens, poems by Keats,

Wordsworth, and many others, have not just a single author but a multiplicity of collaborative authors: the nominal authors plus friends, spouses, ghosts, agents, editors, transcribers, translators, publishers, censors, printers—and in the case of plays and films, actors, producers, directors, and even audiences whose reactions led to revisions of the script.

My initial examples in that book were "Keats's" longish narrative *Isabella*, actually a product of Keats's original writing in combination with revisions, alterations, and further changes by his friend Woodhouse, his publisher Taylor, and the compositors of the 1820 volume in which the poem was first printed, and "John Stuart Mill's" *Autobiography*, again first drafted by the nominal author but extensively revised, censored, and simplified by the nominal author's wife, Harriet Mill—and then further altered by relatives, a friend, and the original printers. To these I added instances of other common situations of composite creativity: a writer revising earlier versions of himself (Wordsworth in *The Prelude*); a writer interacting collaboratively with his sources and influences (Coleridge and several plagiarized sources in *Biographia Literaria*); a younger writer being revised and trimmed down by a mentor (Eliot and Pound in *The Waste Land*); and the collaborative elements routinely at work in the production of commercial literature. A grandiosely titled appendix, "Multiple Authorship from Homer to Ann Beattie," offered a ten-page list of examples not discussed in the book.

The point of the study, which seems obvious now that it has been out and reviewed for several years, was to juxtapose my evidences of collaborative authorship against the prevailing notion of single-genius creativity, mainly in order to question our confidence in the existence of a unified mind, personality, or consciousness in (or behind) the texts that we interpret and edit. In *Isabella*, Keats initially wrote one kind of poem, and his helpers subtly changed it into another kind. In the *Autobiography*, John Mill had one kind of idea of himself and what he wished to tell the world about himself, and Harriet Mill had (and enforced) a different idea of what was appropriate. The young Wordsworth of the early *Prelude* manuscripts is certainly not the same person as the poet who read and revised himself in successive rewritings of the poem in his later years. In these paradigms of collaboration, if we lodge the meaning of the work with "the author"—that is, if our goal is to read, interpret, and edit according to authorial intention—we encounter a plurality of authors and conflicting intentions. In such cases, the answer to "Where's the meaning?" has to take account of several different authorial intentions. And if the intentions of one author are difficult or impossible to recover, how much more so are the intentions of several?

I addressed the plurality of texts, using Coleridge as the example, three years later in *Coleridge and Textual Instability: The Multiple Versions of the Major Poems* (1994). Coleridge was an obsessive reviser all his life. After studying numerous original drafts, holograph fair copies, transcripts, letter manuscripts, notebooks, successive printings, annotated copies, and other sources, I identified some eighteen distinct versions of *The Rime of the Ancient Mariner*, sixteen versions of *The Eolian Harp*, twelve of *This Lime-Tree Bower My Prison*, and similar numbers for the other best-known poems. This multiplicity of versions (as I explained in my preface) raises important and interesting issues, both theoretical and practical:

the constitution of the Coleridge canon (how many *Rimes of the Ancient Mariner* did Coleridge write?); the ontological identity—sometimes referred to as "mode of existence"—of any specific work in the canon (is *The Ancient Mariner* a single version of the work or all the versions taken together? and if it is all the versions taken together, is the work constituted by the *process* of its revisions, one after another, or by all the versions considered as existing simultaneously, as they might in a variorum edition giving in one place a complete account of the successive readings?); practical questions about the editorial treatment of Coleridge's works (most obviously, which version to choose for reprinting in a standard edition or an anthology when one may print only one version per title); and the ways in which this multiplicity of versions complicates interpretation of the poems as a unified, or disunified, body of work.

Keats, to bring this discussion closer to home, is not one of the famous revisers of English poetry. The brevity of his career precluded revision over a span of decades or succession of editions. But his practice and his comments about spontaneity make it seem unlikely that he would have revised radically even had he lived as long as Coleridge. Even so, virtually all of Keats's poems do in fact exist in multiple texts. For *Endymion* we have three principal authorial versions: the text of the original draft; the text of the revised fair copy that Keats wrote out for the printer; and the first printed text, representing the words of the fair copy, subsequent changes by the publisher John Taylor and the printers, and still further changes by Keats in reaction to those by Taylor and the printers. For each of the other complete long narratives—*Isabella, The Eve of St. Agnes,* and *Lamia*— there is the same array of draft, fair copy, and first printed text. For *La Belle Dame sans Merci*, we have two principal versions in manuscripts by Keats and his friends and the first printing of the poem in Leigh Hunt's *Indicator*. For *Ode to a Nightingale* and *Ode on a Grecian Urn*, there are the first published versions in a magazine (*Annals of the Fine Arts*), the next published versions in Keats's *Lamia* volume of 1820, and still other versions that differ from these in authoritative manuscripts. For the one hundred poems and fragments that were first published posthumously, there are almost always variant versions in the surviving sources—for example, two quite different endings of the *Bright star* sonnet, where in one the speaker lives on forever and in the other the speaker dies.

Thus, even though Keats was not an obsessive reviser, still he—sometimes he and his helpers—created multiple texts of his poems. We are becoming increasingly sophisticated about these texts. We have long known about the two main versions of *La Belle Dame*, and recently Elizabeth Cook in her Oxford Authors *John Keats* printed an alternative text of *The Eve of St. Agnes* in an appendix. Nicholas Roe in his new Everyman *Selected Poems* of Keats is well aware of the existence of competing versions and makes some interesting departures from the standard.

This multiplicity of versions raises the same kinds of question for Keats as for Coleridge. How many *Eves of St. Agnes* should we say Keats actually wrote? What *is* Keats's *Eve of St. Agnes* when there are several different versions and Keats (or Keats and his helpers) authored all of them? It certainly complicates the business of interpretation, as when critics expound composite rather than discrete versions of a work, or cite one version to help interpret another (an earlier text to explain a later, or vice versa). It enters as well into matters of basic communication, as when critics arguing about significant details in a work are using different versions and therefore may be said to be actually talking about different works.

Above all, the existence of multiple versions makes more problematic the notion of the autonomous "text in itself." Any residual theorizing about interpretation on the basis of the text alone must address and resolve the additional question of *which* text or texts we seek to interpret. If we attempt to settle on the text most representative of the author, we have abandoned the autonomous text theory entirely. If we accept all versions of a work, we inevitably arrive at many different interpretations.

The complicating multiple of the third element, the reader, is familiar to every teacher. A class of students will produce multiple readings any time they are allowed to voice their own opinions. The multiple is also familiar to every trained critic whose prized interpretation provokes a chorus of objections from other trained critics. Indeed, some people in our profession regard the multiple interpretations that multiple readers necessarily construct as a situation calling for remedy: some authority-figure—a teacher or a critic—is needed to separate the "correct" from the "wrong" readings and reduce the unshapely multiplicity to a manageable conformity. I think we should, instead, welcome the unshapeliness. A main point of this book is that canonical works have not just one but a great many different meanings, and that these meanings exist not serially—one does not replace another, giving us *a* meaning or *the* meaning of the work at any one time—but in some ideal sense simultaneously, with all the multiple meanings potentially together at once. And the principal locus of these meanings is the collective readership of the work.

Reader's meaning is not without its problems. Questions arise about "validity" in interpretation: how can there be right and wrong interpretations if the meaning lies in the responses of individual readers? And there are related questions about authority: how can the teacher or critic tell other people what something means when the teacher or critic is just another individual reader? These problems are serious but not insurmountable. While allowing for the most divergent of multiple readings, one can apply standards of factuality (including, where it can be determined, factuality of textual detail), comprehensiveness, and, in some matters, at least, consensus. Even interpretations that fail these standards—what we used to call misinterpretations—can be of practical use. I shall return to these matters toward the end of chapter 4.

At this point, our blackboard diagram has been complicated by multiples; it consists now of three plurals, Authors—Texts—Readers, so that answering the question of "Where's the meaning?" requires expanding to contain these additional possibilities. In the long run, all three elements of the diagram, whether viewed as singular or plural, are part of any literary transaction: with no author(s), we have no work in the first place; with no text(s) we have no embodiment of the work; and with no reader(s) we have no reading or interpretation. But still the best answer to the initial question concerning the locus of meaning is some formulation pointing to the reader's end of the scheme. Reader's meaning—that is, interpretation constructed by the individual reader—is both the only kind of meaning that is practically attainable and the only kind that, taken collectively, reflects the genuine complexity of the canonical works that we read over and over and celebrate for their inexhaustibility.

The Legitimacy of Audience

My section heading comes from the conclusion of a recent essay by Morris Eaves subtitled "Speculations on the Authority of the Audience in Editorial Theory." Eaves's persuasive point in the essay, which marshals examples from, among others, Blake's illuminated books, *Hamlet*, Stephen Crane's *Maggie*, Dreiser's *Sister Carrie*, the restoration of the Sistine Chapel frescoes, and the colorization of films, is that all of our various practices of editing, preservation, and reproduction—ranging from strict fidelity concerning the minutest details of a unique original source, on the one hand, to eclectic construction of some ideal form, on the other—are theorized and carried out according to our own present intentions rather than those of the author, artist, or culture that produced the work in the first place. And not only is this the way things are; in Eaves's view, this is the way things should be. "Here, then, is an unacknowledged axiom of textual criticism: the granting of legitimacy to the audience, and hence to its editorial decisions, must precede all acknowledgment of the legitimacy of the author's claims—even when the audience, through its editorial representative, wants that authority only in order to return it straightaway to the author" (97).

Eaves's essay, published in a book entitled *Cultural Artifacts and the Production of Meaning*, a collection of essays that treats audience in practically every piece, is a product of the historical shift of critical focus from the author, around the beginning of the twentieth century, to the text, in the 1920s through the 1960s, and then on to the reader, since the 1970s. The current situation is much different from, and in my view a considerable improvement over, the thinking that prevailed when I was a graduate student at Harvard in the middle 1950s. In those days, nobody doubted the fixed reality of historical authors or the objective existence of their works; authors and works alike (the authors contained in the works, of course) had certain qualities such as form, theme, style, and structure that could be objectively described and compared with qualities of other writers and works, and there was a guarantee of stability about the works in that they were always reliably there, when one returned to them, and always the same. Our professional models as graduate students were the likes of Douglas Bush, Harry Levin, and Perry Miller, and our goal was to learn to read the way they did, because that was the right way to read. The unspoken assumption was that Milton wrote his poems for Bush, Shakespeare his plays for Levin, and the Puritans their sermons for Miller. What matter that we did not know the Greek and Roman classics by heart, as Bush did, or sixteen different modern literatures, as Levin did, or the forty thousand Puritan documents that Miller managed to read in his spare time. Our aspirations were ardent and unambiguous.

If that kind of innocence now seems ridiculous, it is because a number of alert critics in the late 1960s and early 1970s began speaking out against this same objectivity of works on the grounds that it takes two sides to complete an act of communication, the author side and the reader side, and that while the author side may be forever fixed in history (Keats and his helpers are all dead), the reader side, constituted by innumerable separate individuals, past, present, and future, is constantly changing.

Stanley Fish's "Literature in the Reader: Affective Stylistics" (1970) was a major early stimulus. For the usual interpretive question "What does this sentence mean?" Fish urged the substitution of "What does this sentence do?" The rationale was that reading is a temporal activity: the words succeed one another in a certain order and register effects according to that order (a condition that critics entirely lose sight of, routinely reading a work over and over in the process of interpretation); meaning is not a property of texts as such but a series of events in the reader's mind. Walter Slatoff's *With Respect to Readers* (also 1970) was another powerful acknowledgment of the importance of the reader end of the transaction. Slatoff based his work (as David Bleich did a little later in *Readings and Feelings*, 1975, and *Subjective Criticism*, 1978) on students in his own classes and the enormous discrepancies between their experiences of a work and those of professional scholars writing about the same work in the standard criticism. One of the arguments is that professionals had no adequate critical methods for dealing with most of what he and the students considered important in a work: "We have developed elaborate vocabularies for classifying and anatomizing literary works; we scarcely know how to talk about their powers and effects. We have an immense accumulation of knowledge about authors, periods, movements, and individual texts; we know almost nothing about the process of reading" (187–88).

Around the same time, Norman Holland began his studies of literary audience by creating and then psychoanalyzing an entire culture of readers (the readerships of *Oedipus*, *Hamlet*, and other classics) in *The Dynamics of Literary Response* (1968)—then drastically reduced his scope, but greatly enhanced the potential validity of his results, by working with a handful of real readers in *Five Readers Reading* (1975), *Laughing* (1982), and other works. Wolfgang Iser and Umberto Eco made important contributions in the next wave of reader theory, and the 1980 collections of essays by Susan Suleiman and Inge Crosman (*The Reader in the Text*) and Jane Tompkins (*Reader-Response Criticism*) were also influential in making critics increasingly aware of readers. The movement soon got its label—reader-response theory, sometimes called reception theory[4]—and, although not very well organized or formalized (the theorists have never been able to agree on a definition of "reader" or any notion of a reader's proper relationship to meaning, authority, or value), it has been the most fruitful of the principal literary theories of the last three decades.

Considerably before any of this made much headway in university English departments, Louise Rosenblatt had written a blockbuster reader-response manifesto in *Literature as Exploration* (1938), emphasizing reading as a creative activity that depends on what the individual reader brings to the work and castigating the teaching profession for everywhere stifling that creativity: "Much of even the best literature teaching is analogous to typical American spectator sports.

The students sit on the sidelines watching the instructor or professor react to works of art" (57). The "transactional theory" of literature, more fully elaborated in Rosenblatt's *The Reader, the Text, the Poem* (1978), is present in this earliest work, as is her constant focus on the importance of each reader's separate experience; the statement that "no one can read a poem for us" recurs in one form or another in all of Rosenblatt's writings.

Though apparently unknown to Fish and the other reader-response heavyweights of the 1970s, Rosenblatt has been tremendously influential in the schools and has been cited everywhere by reading specialists in colleges of education for the last half-century. She has, in fact, something of the same luminary status among schoolteachers and writers on pedagogy as important Europeans such as Derrida, Foucault, and Lacan currently have among poststructural theorists.[5] But the two parallel lines, Rosenblatt in the schools and Fish and the rest in the universities, have at last converged. The Modern Language Association is the publisher of the fourth and fifth editions of *Literature as Exploration* (1983, 1995), the fifth with a foreword by Wayne Booth, and *The Reader, the Text, the Poem* has recently been reissued in paperback, so that it can be used as a course textbook.

So now, as a result of all this critical and pedagogical theorizing, one would suppose that the reader is well established as a reckonable entity in the literary transaction. In certain quarters this is demonstrably true. Any historicist investigation into the social contexts of literature and the conditions of literary production will necessarily take into account readers, reviewers, purchasers, sales figures, contracts, copyright, printing history, and numerous other aspects of the economics of authorship and publishing. "Literary marketplace" occurs repeatedly in the titles of recent scholarly studies, whether about individual authors or whole classes or periods, and in each such study the principal entity at the consumer end is the reader. We have sharper and sharper examinations of how people read in the past—discussions of the successive audiences of *Paradise Lost* or *Lyrical Ballads*, for example, or *The Ancient Mariner* in its incremental complexities during the course of Coleridge's revisions—and of how people read today. There is a keen interest in gender differences in readers, and increasing exposure of the fact that nearly all teaching and criticism of the past century, even the teaching and criticism done by women, has assumed a masculine point of view as the standard. More and more work focuses on the audiences that our standard and not-so-standard writers had in mind when they wrote, and on the discrepancies between the writers' ideas of their audiences and the real readership. Readers are often collaborators in the authorial phase of a work, as when they respond to a draft, a public reading, a serial installment, a first edition, a rehearsal, a first run, a first showing (and so on) in ways that cause the author and the author's helpers to make changes that otherwise would not have been thought of. Indeed, in almost no aspect of literary study these days can the reader/audience end of the transaction be safely ignored.

It is all the more remarkable, therefore, that the real readers closest to us in our profession—the readers whom we address in books and essays written with the aim of improving their reading, the auditors attending our lectures and papers, and above all the students in our classes—are hardly more legitimized as independent thinkers and responders than their counterparts were in the bad old days before reader-response criticism came along. Large numbers of writers in the journals continue to expound *the* meaning of a complex poem or novel, trying to persuade us that they have at last hit on the right answer to a problem that all previous critics of the work (and, by inference, all previous readers) had failed to solve. Textbook anthologies continue to explicate difficult works and passages in their introductions and notes; in many cases, the students are reading only the editorial explications, since these have the appearance of being more accessible, not to mention more authoritative, than the texts themselves. There is plentiful evidence—for example, in the recent Modern Language Association "Approaches to Teaching" volumes and numerous collections of essays on reader-response techniques in the classroom—that the teaching of literature continues, in spite of our best intentions, to be the spectator sport that Rosenblatt made fun of sixty years ago: the teacher performs the reading, as it were, and the students take notes on what moved the teacher the most. As faculty and teaching-assistant budgets shrink further and further, colleges and universities are reducing or abandoning altogether small discussion classes, substituting the large lecture format and even, in the most drastic circumstances, resorting to multiple-choice examinations on the lectures. (We are all theoretically in favor of multiples, but not when there is only one right answer!) Even in the small discussion classes, as we can see any time we visit a colleague's class (or, I regret to say, any time a colleague visits one of *my* classes), the main business at hand continues to be, more frequently than it should, what Dickens described in the first chapter of *Hard Times* as the filling of little vessels until they are full to the brim.

Human nature is part of the continuing problem. It is natural (as we say), when one has learned something, to want to tell other people about it; and in a teaching situation especially, whether in the classroom or in print, when one knows more than the students or the audience, it is difficult to resist the assumption of authority. But the reader-response theorists themselves have not been much help toward legitimizing real readers, whom they evade by constructing one or another kind of inimitable abstract super-reader in their stead: the "ideal reader," the "informed reader," the "competent reader," the "model reader," the consensus of an "interpretive community," and so on.[6]

None of the readers of *The Eve of St. Agnes* who figure in this book, professional or amateur, is an ideal or model reader. Some are not even very well informed. There is a question in each case as to their competence. And the "interpretive community," however constituted, cannot agree on interpretations of the poem. Nevertheless, these are, at all levels, the real readers with whom, precarious as it may seem, the "meaning" of Keats's poem has always been lodged—the guarantors, as it were, the custodians, and the performers through whom the work is being endlessly reenacted, and on whom it registers its inexhaustible effects. They are a vital group, these questionably competent readers. Whereas the author(s) and text(s) of *The Eve of St. Agnes* are historically determinate—there will be no new authorship and no new versions[7]—the readership is virtually limitless in scope, consisting not only of all past and present readers but an infinite possibility of additional readers in the future. To deny the legitimacy of their readings is tantamount to denying meaning to the poem.

Let us turn now to what they are reading. The next chapter takes up the origins, texts, and publication history of *The Eve of St. Agnes*. These are the starting materials on which, in varying degrees, all readers have based their interpretations.

TWO

THE STARTING MATERIALS

Texts and Circumstances

K EATS DRAFTED *The Eve of St. Agnes* during the last two weeks of January and perhaps also the first few days of February 1819, at the beginning of his so-called "living year," the nine-month period in which he wrote practically all of his most admired poems.[1] He revised the work in September, at the end of this period, and it was first published in June 1820, in his landmark volume of that year, *Lamia, Isabella, The Eve of St. Agnes, and Other Poems*. Essentially there are three authoritative versions: the text of Keats's original draft, the text of his revised manuscript, and the printed version of 1820. This last, a composite of original and revised manuscript readings plus further changes before and during the printing by Richard Woodhouse and John Taylor, has been the standard text of the poem in every kind of printing, scholarly and popular, ever since.

My purpose in this chapter is to give as complete an account as the known facts will allow of the creation of the poem by Keats and his helpers, the various states and relationships among the authoritative texts, and Keats's known comments on the poem while and just after he was working on it. These facts form the starting materials of modern readings of the poem. Some of them have only gradually come to light in Keats scholarship, especially the details deriving from letters and poetry manuscripts, and even now both trained and untrained readers vary in their acquaintance with them. But in general, even thus evolving and cumulative, they constitute a relatively stable body of materials—texts with an accompaniment of textual and biographical information—in striking contrast to the instability of the wide range of interpretations that readers have based on them.

Composition, Revision, Publication
of *The Eve of St. Agnes*

At the beginning of 1819, Keats's career as a poet took a decided turn for the better. Two years earlier, in March 1817, when he was twenty-one, he had published a first volume, titled simply *Poems*, that, as he remarked in the draft of a preface to his next book, "was read by some dozen of my friends, who lik'd it; and some dozen whom I was unacquainted with, who did not" (*Poems* [1978] 739). He had spent much of the rest of 1817 and the first three months of 1818 writing and revising the 4,000-line narrative *Endymion*, which appeared as his second book toward the end of April 1818; and at about the same time that he was revising and reading proofs of *Endymion* he had drafted his next substantial poem, *Isabella*. Seven weeks of the summer of 1818 were occupied in a walking tour through northern England and Scotland with his friend Charles Brown, but Keats had caught a cold, then developed an ulcerated throat and a fever, and had to return home before the end of the tour.

Back in Hampstead, he met and fell in love with Fanny Brawne (perhaps as early as the end of August); coped with the effects of two savage reviews of *Endymion* that appeared in *Blackwood's* and the *Quarterly Review* (September); thought intermittently about writing an epic titled *Hyperion* (October–December); turned twenty-three (on 31 October); and took care of his eighteen-year-old brother Tom, who had been ill with tuberculosis for more than a year. Tom died on 1 December, and a few days afterward Keats moved to different lodgings in Hampstead, to share part of a double house, Wentworth Place (now the Keats House), with his friend Brown. There followed six weeks of accelerated social activities as friends attempted to console Keats (and he attempted to console the youngest of his siblings, the only member of his immediate family left in England, the fifteen-year-old Fanny, who lived with their guardian a few miles away at Walthamstow). On 18 or 19 January 1819, he rode the coach to the cathedral town of Chichester, seventy miles southwest of London, and a few days later walked the dozen further miles to Bedhampton, in both places visiting friends and relatives of Brown, and then returned to Hampstead around 2 February. The decided turn for the better in his career occurred during this trip: he took some paper with him specially for the purpose and, as he told his surviving brother and sister-in-law, George and Georgiana, now living in America, "wrote on it a little Poem call'd St Agnes Eve" (*Letters* 2:58).

The draft that he produced at Chichester and Bedhampton is the earliest of four extant manuscripts of the poem, and the sole version in Keats's handwriting. The initial leaf, containing the first eight stanzas (lines 1–63 plus a stanza subsequently deleted at 27/28), has disappeared, but the rest is safely housed in the Harvard Keats Collection in the Houghton Library and can be examined at second hand, without a trip to Cambridge, in the complete set of facsimiles included in *John Keats: Poetry Manuscripts at Harvard*.[2] The surviving portion consists of nineteen pages on five leaves—meaning that Keats folded each leaf once, vertically, to make four surfaces to write on, front and back, each roughly 8 inches high by 5 inches wide, and completed the draft on the nineteenth of the extant pages, leaving the twentieth page blank. It is the messiest and most fragile of Keats's poetry holographs, for several reasons.

The principal reason is the elaborateness of the form that Keats had decided on, the nine-line Spenserian stanza rhyming *ababbcbcc*. The two *a* rhymes could be managed easily enough, and even the three *c* rhymes, when Keats got to the end of a stanza; but the four *b* rhymes, in the second, fourth, fifth, and seventh lines of each stanza, were a killer. It is difficult for nonpoets (most of my students, for instance) to contrive four *b* rhymes for just a single stanza; in the draft text, which is a stanza longer than the final version, Keats had to devise *forty-three* sets of *b* rhymes. As a consequence, there are false starts, backtrackings, cancellations, and rewritings in the margins and above and below the lines everywhere in the manuscript. For stanza 26 (to give a single brief example), describing Madeline undoing her hair and jewelry and stepping out of her clothes, Keats took twenty-five or more lines on two successive pages to arrive at a set of *b* rhymes that would work.

To complicate the messiness, the paper that Keats used for the draft is unusually thin, a batch that his friend William Haslam gave him for letters to be sent overseas. Keats wrote his journal letter to George and Georgiana of 16 December 1818–4 January 1819 on this paper, and he mentions it a second time, in the next journal letter, specifically in connection with *The Eve of St. Agnes* (*Letters* 2:6, 58). The thinness of the paper allows the writing from the back of the sheet to show through on the front, and thus the deletions and interlineations on one side further fill the spaces between words and lines on the other side. In addition to the original fragility of the paper and Keats's heavy revising on both sides of the sheets, a further general blurring and fading resulted from mildew and subsequent repair and silking for preservation after a freak accident in March 1920, when the manuscript was in the possession of Amy Lowell and a forgetful servant left a pail of water overnight in the airtight safe in which it was kept (see Damon 528).

The next two surviving manuscripts of the poem, also in the Harvard Keats Collection, are by Richard Woodhouse, a close friend of both Keats and his publishers and legal and literary adviser to the firm. Since the fall of 1818, convinced that Keats was a genius who one day would be classed with Shakespeare, Spenser, and Milton among the most highly regarded English poets, Woodhouse had been collecting and copying Keats's unpublished poems from every available source including the poet himself. By the spring of 1819, he and Charles Brown were the two main transcribers of the poems, and their manuscripts frequently became the principal authorial versions as Keats gave away or discarded his drafts after they had made their copies.

The two extant Woodhouse transcripts of *The Eve of St. Agnes*, in the Harvard notebooks that Keats scholars routinely refer to as W^2 and W^1, reproduce the text of Keats's draft, but neither was made directly from the holograph. Instead, Woodhouse first wrote out the poem in a now-lost shorthand transcript, "from J.K's rough M.S. 20 Ap[l] 1819," as he noted in the W^2 notebook.[3] He then made the W^2 longhand copy from the shorthand, and sometime afterward recopied the W^2 text in W^1. The two extant Woodhouse transcripts are our only source for the readings of the first eight stanzas in Keats's draft—the contents of the now-missing first leaf—and W^2 contains some important notes that Woodhouse made later from Keats's revised manuscript of the poem (see just below). If, as I have suggested elsewhere (*The Texts of Keats's Poems* 39), the W^1 transcripts were a safekeeping set of duplicates that Woodhouse wrote out for Keats's publishers, then the W^1 copy of *The Eve of St. Agnes* probably played a part in the construction of the text published in 1820.[4]

The next stage of composition, Keats's revision of his draft text, dates from early September 1819. In terms of outward events, nothing very extraordinary had happened in his life since he returned home with the draft of the poem at the beginning of February. He remained in Hampstead, making frequent trips into the city to meet friends, see plays and exhibitions, and conduct business with his guardian and his publishers, until the end of June, when he went to Shanklin, on the Isle of Wight. He spent July and the first two weeks of August at Shanklin and then moved to Winchester in order to be near a library. Financial problems were a recurrent concern in the day-to-day activities of this period; at one point, near the beginning of June, Keats was desperate enough to consider becoming a surgeon on a merchant ship in the India trade. Fanny Brawne and her family had moved into the other half of Wentworth Place in April, and unquestionably Keats's worry over money was intensified by his deepening relationship with Fanny and the hope that they could soon be married.

Keats produced steadily and impressively all through these months: *The Eve of St. Mark* in the middle of February; most of the *Hyperion* fragment probably in March and April; *La Belle Dame sans Merci* and *Ode to Psyche* in late April; *Ode to a Nightingale* in May (and perhaps *Ode on a Grecian Urn* and *Ode on Melancholy* near the same time); *Lamia* in early July (part 1) and late August (part 2); the five-act tragedy *Otho the Great* also in July and August (much of it drafted between the first and second parts of *Lamia*); and still another long work, the recasting of *Hyperion* as the dream-vision *Fall of Hyperion*, also in the summer months, between the end of July and the third week of September. Keats was, in fact, piling up a sizable number of substantial works, with the aim, as he told his sister on 17 June, of "try[ing] the press once more . . . with all my industry and ability" (*Letters* 2:121). His revision of *The Eve of St. Agnes*—turning draft into revised fair copy, as he had earlier done with *Endymion* and *Isabella* and was just then in the process of doing with *Lamia*—was a part of this astonishing productivity. In a letter to Taylor on 5 September, Keats mentions finishing *Otho* and *Lamia* "and am now occupied in revising St Agnes' Eve" (2:157). He brought the revised manuscript with him when, on receiving some worrisome news from his brother George in America, he was "hurried to Town" on financial business on 10 September; and next day he called on Taylor's publishing partner, J. A. Hessey, with a proposal (as Woodhouse reported to Taylor, who was away in the country) "to publish the Eve of St Agnes & Lamia *immediately*." Unfortunately, immediate publication was out of the question: "Hessey told him it could not answer to do so now" (2:160, 162).

The revised holograph of September 1819 has not survived, but we have considerable information about its text from two reliable sources. With the fussiness characteristic of a modern textual scholar, Woodhouse collated the revised manuscript against his transcript of the draft text, painstakingly noting Keats's "alterations" above the lines, in the margins, and on the facing versos of the W^2 notebook. Our other source for the revised text is the fourth of the extant manuscripts of the poem, a transcript by George Keats, made from this same lost holograph, in a notebook now in the British Library (MS. Egerton 2780). George, who is known to have been an unusually precise copyist, paying close attention to the punctuation and spelling as well as the words of a text, transcribed *The Eve of St. Agnes* during a visit to London on business during the last three weeks of January 1820. Woodhouse's "alterations" were recorded earlier, sometime between September, when he first learned about Keats's revision, and January, when George took his copy. The consensus of the two documents—Woodhouse's notes and George's transcript—is a fair representation of the most significant textual content of the lost holograph. There are, to be sure, discrepancies between the two records, most often where George has a revised reading not noted by Woodhouse; and it is not always clear whether a difference between them should be interpreted as an oversight by Woodhouse when he noted the variants in W^2, a further revision by Keats after Woodhouse saw the holograph, or a transcribing error by George. In my discussion of the principal versions of the poem in the next section, as well as in my simplified apparatus in Appendix A, I have relied mainly on the consensus of Woodhouse and George Keats—and on the latter where the former is silent—for my reconstruction of the revised text.

Keats read his new version of the poem to Woodhouse on 12 September, and some of his revisions—most notably his alteration of lines 314–22 to make the sexual consummation between Porphyro and Madeline more explicit—shocked his lawyer friend and drew an emphatically negative reaction from Taylor. Both Woodhouse's anxious letter to Taylor on 19 September and Taylor's response a week later deserve lengthy quotation, because they offer revealing commentary on several important matters: Woodhouse's understanding of the action of the poem; Keats's, Woodhouse's, and Taylor's various ideas about the likely audience for the poem (and for Keats's and his contemporaries' poetry more generally); the moral constraints hedging the relationship between author and publisher; the influences that shaped the further revisions that produced the text of the poem published in 1820.

Here is Woodhouse's account of what he considered the most notable changes in the revised version:

> [Keats] had the Eve of St A. copied fair: He has made trifling alterations, inserted an additional stanza early in the poem to make the *legend* more intelligible, and correspondent with what afterwards takes place, particularly with respect to the supper & the playing on the Lute.—he retains the name of Porphyro—has altered the last 3 lines to leave on the reader a sense of pettish disgust, by bringing Old Angela in (only) dead stiff & ugly.— He says he likes that the poem should leave off with this Change of Sentiment—it was what he aimed at, & was glad to find from my objections to it that he had succeeded.—I apprehend he had a fancy for trying his hand

at an attempt to play with his reader, & fling him off at last. . . . There was another alteration, which I abused for "a full hour by the *Temple* clock." You know if a thing has a decent side, I generally look no further—As the Poem was orig[y] written, *we* innocent ones (ladies & myself) might very well have supposed that Porphyro, when acquainted with Madeline's love for him, & when "he arose, Etherial flush[d] &c &c (turn to it) set himself at once to persuade her to go off with him, & succeeded & went over the "Dartmoor black" (now changed for some other place) to be married, in right honest chaste & sober wise. But, as it is now altered, as soon as M. has confessed her love, P. winds by degrees his arm round her, presses breast to breast, and acts all the acts of a bonâ fide husband, while she fancies she is only playing the part of a Wife in a dream. This alteration is of about 3 stanzas; and tho' there are no improper expressions but all is left to inference, and tho' profanely speaking, the Interest on the reader's imagination is greatly heightened, yet I do apprehend it will render the poem unfit for ladies, & indeed scarcely to be mentioned to them among the "things that are."— He says he does not want ladies to read his poetry: that he writes for men—& that if in the former poem there was an opening for doubt what took place, it was his fault for not writing clearly & comprehensibly—that he sh[d] despise a man who would be such an eunuch in sentiment as to leave a maid, with that Character about her, in such a situation: & sho[d] despise himself to write about it &c &c &c—and all this sort of Keats-like rhodomontade. (*Letters* 2:162–63)

Taylor replied to Woodhouse on 25 September:

This Folly of Keats is the most stupid piece of Folly I can conceive. . . . I don't know how the Meaning of the new Stanzas is wrapped up, but I will not be accessary (I can answer also for H[essey] I think) towards publishing any thing which can only be read by Men. . . . As it is, the flying in the Face of all Decency & Discretion is doubly offensive from its being accompanied with so preposterous a Conceit on his part of being able to overcome the best founded Habits of our Nature.—Had he known truly what the Society and what the Suffrages of Women are worth, he would never have thought of depriving himself of them.—So far as he is unconsciously silly in this Proceeding I am sorry for him, but for the rest I cannot but confess to you that it excites in me the Strongest Sentiments of Disapprobation—Therefore . . . if he will not so far concede to my Wishes as to leave the passage as it originally stood, I must be content to admire his Poems with some other Imprint, & in so doing I can reap as much Delight from the Perusal of them as if they were our own property, without having the disquieting Consideration attached to them of our approving, by the "Imprimatur," those Parts which are unfit for publication. (*Letters* 2:182–83)[5]

Woodhouse and Taylor together exerted considerable influence, whether for good or not, on the final authoritative version of the poem, the text that appeared in Keats's third volume, *Lamia, Isabella, The Eve of St. Agnes, and Other Poems*, published by Taylor and Hessey at the end of June 1820. Keats had persisted in his attempts and by 20 December 1819, as he told his sister, was "very busy . . . especially the last Week and shall be for some time, in preparing some Poems to come out in the Sp[r]ing" (*Letters* 2:237). Progress toward the new volume was frequently interrupted by Keats's worsening health, the biggest setbacks coming with a severe hemorrhage in the lungs early in February and several attacks of "palpitations at the heart" in March. But he and Brown worked on the manuscripts in the intervals, as when Brown wrote to Taylor, around the middle of March, that "Keats . . . wishes his Poems to be published as soon as convenient to yourself,—the volume to commence with St Agnes' Eve. He was occupied yesterday in revising Lamia" (2:276). Toward the end of April, the entire manuscript was in the hands of the publishers. Keats read proofs of the volume as it was printed and corrected some errors in *The Eve of St. Agnes* in an extant letter written on or about 11 June (2:294–95).

What has survived of the printer's copy for the volume—Keats's revised fair copy of *Lamia* (at Harvard), Woodhouse's W^1 transcript of *Isabella*, the W^1 transcript of *Hyperion* (in this instance made by two of Woodhouse's law clerks), and a fair copy in Keats's hand of *Song of Four Fairies* (Harvard), a shorter work that was not finally included—shows that the volume was put together from a variety of sources. We have no information about printer's copy for *The Eve of St. Agnes*. Probably it was the same now-lost revised holograph that Keats produced in Winchester and read to Woodhouse in London in September and that first Woodhouse and then George Keats collated and copied between September and the following January.[6] But the revised manuscript text was further altered by Taylor and Woodhouse before it was given to the printer. Woodhouse explains in a note opposite the beginning of his W^2 transcript:

> This Copy was taken from K's original M.S. [i.e., the draft]—He afterwards altered it for publication, & added some stanzas & omitted others.—His alterations are noticed here. The Published Copy differs from both in a few particulars. K. left it to his Publishers to adopt which [readings] they pleased, & to revise the Whole.

The published version resulting from Woodhouse's and Taylor's editing is a composite of draft and revised holograph texts plus new readings that do not occur in any manuscript. It seems certain, especially in the light of the exchange between Woodhouse and Taylor quoted above, that some of the editorial changes were made by the publishers against the poet's wishes.

The Textual Versions

In the larger perspective, there have been many more versions of *The Eve of St. Agnes* than the three singled out in my account of the drafting, revision, and production of the poem in 1819–1820. All scholarly editions without exception base their texts of the poem on the printing of 1820, yet no two of them have exactly the same text. H. W. Garrod's Oxford English Texts edition, *The Poetical Works of John Keats*, which served as the academic standard from 1939 through the 1970s, departs from its source, not always intentionally, in half a dozen lines. Miriam Allott's *The Poems of John Keats* (1970) modernizes the 1820 spellings and punctuation; her several hundred changes affect more than 190 lines of the poem. My own Harvard edition of 1978 emends 1820 capitals and punctuation in eight lines and drops opening quotes, where 1820 repeats them at the beginning of lines within quotations, in seventy-three other places (*Poems* [1978] 707). Similar variances of one sort or another appear in every other scholarly edition that I have checked. And popular texts are no different from scholarly in this respect, although the departures from their sources may more often be mistakes than emendations.

Such traditionally nontextual matters as book design, page size and format, typography, the color(s) of the ink, the appearance and feel of the paper, the character of the binding, and the general quality of the printing and production are also distinguishing features among versions. Illustrations, if there are any, are an additional element in the overall presentation of the poem, an inescapable influence on a reader's interpretation of the action and many other textual components. Context, in the sense of Paul Magnuson's recent focus on the question of where a text appears and who put it there, is another important variable.[7] The 1820 text is one thing in its original setting in Keats's *Lamia* volume, pages 81–104; another thing, even though the text is reproduced photographically, in a facsimile of this same book; still another in the Harvard *Poems* or somebody else's scholarly edition; still another in the *Norton Anthology of English Literature*; and so on. *Lamia* was a brand-new volume of poems at the bookseller's in the summer of 1820, and 180 years later is a venerable rare book. A facsimile reprint conveys additional ideas that will be different for each user (for example, the antiquity of the work being reproduced, the historical, cultural, and aesthetic importance of the work—since nobody makes facsimiles of unimportant books— and even, for some users, the spectacle of the modern publisher of the facsimile hoping for quick returns from sales to would-be research libraries). The scholarly edition, especially one with an elaborate textual apparatus at the foot of the page, makes clear that this is a significant work (and also, it sometimes seems, a work very much in the hands of scholars, who may or may not let the reader have a clear view of it). The inclusion of the poem in the *Norton Anthology*, alongside selections from other famous writers, emphasizes the author's and the work's canonicity (and, again, there is the accompaniment of foot-of-the-page editorial material to remind the reader that professors are near at hand with ready explanations).

These variations in the text as such, in combination with variations in the nontextual elements of physical presentation and context, produce a situation of almost limitless potential for difference, and hence the possibility of an infinite number of versions. The result is a strong likelihood that no two printed texts of *The Eve of St. Agnes* have been exactly alike in the entire history of its publication and, further, that no two will be exactly alike in the future as well.

Having made this point, however, I wish to bring the discussion back to where I left off with the publication of the poem in 1820. The important versions are those that Keats had some direct hand in: the draft, the revised manuscript text, and the first printing. All three tell the same story, regardless of how one reads it (see the first section of the next chapter), and the main differences among them do not concern large elements such as plot, character, and theme, but instead Keats's (and his narrator's) manner of telling the story and numerous specific details of description and tone.

Version 1: The Draft

The version contained in Keats's draft, titled "Saint Agnes' Eve," amounts to 387 lines, the equivalent of the forty-two stanzas of 1820 plus a stanza following line 27 that Keats seems to have canceled before reaching the end of his manuscript (see *Poems* [1978] 630). The poem is not quite finished in this version: Keats had not finally settled on the name of his hero—he consistently first wrote "Porphyro" in the dozen places where the name occurs but then substituted "Lionel" in four of them, leaving the others unchanged—and five of the lines are incomplete (see the apparatus in Appendix A for lines 123, 136, 161, 189, and 322). Even so, the draft shows the final (1820) wording of the poem in 275 lines, close to three-quarters of the whole, and the proportion would be even higher if one calculated the percentage of final *words* (rather than complete lines) that Keats arrived at in this first-draft stage.[8]

The draft is the most sentimental and innocent of the three versions, just as we should expect. The canceled stanza at 27/28 recalls the artifice and stilted apostrophizing of some of the later stanzas of *Isabella*, completed nine months earlier. This comes at a point where Keats wishes to move us along from the sensations and the bare feet of the Beadsman, in the first three stanzas, to a different set of ears, eyes, and feet of the revelers elsewhere in Madeline's castle:

> But there are ears may hear sweet melodies,
> And there are eyes to brighten festivals,
> And there are feet for nimble minstrelsies,
> And many a lip that for the red wine calls.—
> Follow, then follow to the illumined halls,
> Follow me youth—and leave the Eremite—
> Give him a tear—then trophied banneral,
> And many a brilliant tasseling of light,
> Shall droop from arched ways this high Baronial night.

The narrative voice here seems uncomfortable, almost giggly with embarrassment, rather in the manner of "O Melancholy, linger here awhile! / O Music, Music, breathe despondingly! / O Echo, Echo" and so on in *Isabella* lines 433–48, 481–88. The same stiffness of transition appears a little later, when the narrator, having brought in the "argent revelry" with plume, tiara, and "all rich array," directs the reader's attention to Madeline:

> Ah what are they? the idle pulse scarce stirs,
> The muse should never make the spirit gay,
> Away, bright dulness, laughing fools, away,—
> And let me tell of one sweet lady there.
>
> (lines 39–42)

Obviously the draft lacks the (arguably) more telling words that Keats substituted here and there in revising. Perhaps the flattest line of the entire manuscript is Porphyro's practical advice to Madeline when they are about to leave the castle and go out into the storm: "Put on warm cloathing, sweet, and fearless be" (line 350). But the draft, though it may seem relatively simple in comparison with what followed, is not lacking in the leering overtones that complicate Porphyro's action and motives in the later versions. His situation of "covert" when he hides himself in the closet of Madeline's bedchamber is "panting covert" in the draft (line 188), and toward the end of the narrative he calls Madeline a "Soft Nightingale" and says he will "keep [her] in a cage" (lines 341–42).

Version 2: The Revised Holograph

The text of Keats's now-lost revised manuscript—recoverable via Woodhouse's notes and George Keats's transcript—is the same length as the draft and has the same title.[9] An inserted stanza near the beginning adds further details about the old-wives' ritual that Madeline is practicing and prepares the reader for the elaborate feast that Porphyro sets out for Madeline later in the narrative. The new version also has physical details of the sexual consummation between hero and heroine that do not appear in the draft, as well as changes in descriptive phrasings all through the poem. In general terms, the revised text is less innocent, less idealized than the version of Keats's draft.

Here is the added stanza, which is introduced by "They [the "old dames"] told her how . . ." and a list of the requirements of the ritual in lines 46–54, and then is followed by the narrator's skeptical comment—"Full of this whim was thoughtful Madeline"—in line 55:

> 'Twas said her future lord would there appear
> Offering, as sacrifice—all in the dream—
> Delicious food, even to her lips brought near,
> Viands, and wine, and fruit, and sugar'd cream,
> To touch her palate with the fine extreme
> Of relish: then soft music heard, and then
> More pleasures follow'd in a dizzy stream
> Palpable almost: then to wake again
> Warm in the virgin morn, no weeping Magdalen.

"More pleasures . . . in a dizzy stream" and the irony of "Warm in the virgin morn," called a "whim" by the narrator in the very next line, could have helped prepare Woodhouse, when he heard Keats recite the new version, for what was coming in the revision of the consummation at lines 314–22:

See, while she speaks his arms encroaching slow,
Have zoned her, heart to heart,—loud, loud the dark winds blow!

For on the midnight came a tempest fell;
More sooth, for that his quick rejoinder flows
Into her burning ear: and still the spell
Unbroken guards her in serene repose.
With her wild dream he mingled, as a rose
Marrieth its odour to a violet.
Still, still she dreams, louder the frost wind blows. . . .

Though some of the draft's physical details describing Porphyro at this point have been discarded ("flush'd, and like a throbbing star" in line 318), other details that were substituted in their place in the new version add complications not in the original: Porphyro's "rejoinder" flowing into Madeline's "burning ear," the odd juxtaposition of "serene repose" with "wild dream," and the instant presence of the storm ("louder the frost wind blows"). But above all it was the explicitness of Porphyro's slow-encroaching arms *zoning* Madeline, "heart to heart," that disturbed Woodhouse. For the first time (even though he had transcribed the draft text on three different occasions earlier), the genial lawyer discovered that Porphyro and Madeline have sex, and *before* they are married.[10]

All told, Keats revised his wording in some ninety lines in this new version. Most of the changes will strike sympathetic readers as improvements, for it is easy to reason that a revised reading is more accurate, or more logical, or more pictorially or texturally effective than the original it replaced. "Chill" is a better word than "cold" in the first line, because it avoids the repetition of the draft's "bitter cold . . . was a-cold" in lines 1–2; "woolly fold" describing the huddled sheep in line 4 has a more physical (tactile) effect than the draft's mainly abstract "sheltered fold"; the revised "incense from a censer" in line 7 is more accurate than the original "incense in a censer"; "Rough ashes" in line 26 seem a more uncomfortable penance for the Beadsman than "Black ashes"; and so on. The new lines that replaced the draft's lines 39–42, quoted above to illustrate the narrator's (and Keats's) stiffness in a transitional passage, contain thematic material not present in the original, mentioning "triumphs gay / Of old romance" and continuing, "These let us wish away"—in effect, thus early in the poem, seeming to invite attention to the antiromantic aspects of the action to follow. Some of the revisions quietly correct earlier miswriting—Porphyro's swearing not to "displace" Madeline's ringlets (line 148), for example, rather than, as in the draft, "misplace" them. Others add to the already powerful pictorial effects by introducing still more visual imagery—Porphyro kneeling "with joined hands" (line 305), for example, instead of the draft's "with an aching brow."

The conclusion of the poem in the revised text is something of a mystery. Woodhouse told Taylor, after hearing Keats recite the new version to him, that the poet had "altered the last 3 lines to leave on the reader a sense of pettish disgust, by bringing Old Angela in (only) dead stiff & ugly" (*Letters* 1:162–63). But all known texts "bring in" both Angela and the Beadsman at the end, and it is probably best to suppose that Woodhouse simply misunderstood what he heard, or else that Keats read him only part of the conclusion. The final couplet of the revised version gives the Beadsman a more abrupt, as well as more openly sardonic, death: "The Beadsman stiffen'd—'twixt a sigh and laugh, / Ta'en sudden from his beads by one weak little cough." But the original last line of the draft, suggesting that no one ever discovers the Beadsman's corpse ("for aye unsought for"), may seem more grotesque than the revision.

Version 3: The Published Text of 1820

The composite version that appeared in *Lamia, Isabella, The Eve of St. Agnes, and Other Poems*—a text of forty-two numbered stanzas, made up of parts of the original draft and parts of the revised manuscript, with editorial tinkering and bowdlerizing by Woodhouse and Taylor—departs from Keats's revised text in title ("The Eve of St. Agnes"), in the omission of the added stanza at 54/55, and in the wording of some sixty lines. Many of these departures—a little over half the total—represent a return to the wording of the draft text, which Woodhouse and the publishers had available in Woodhouse's transcripts. A handful of others we know originated with Woodhouse, because they occur first in one or another of his copies, sometimes as a tentative revision penciled opposite Keats's text. Still another group, about a third of the total, are readings that show up for the first time in the printed text.

In general, we do not know who was responsible for the reversions to the draft text or for the entirely new words in 1820. Some of those in the latter category that now seem perfect choices for their contexts—"regardless" in place of the earlier versions' "uneager" in line 64 (in the description of Madeline's "vague, regardless eyes"), "on fire" instead of "afire" in line 75 ("Porphyro, with heart on fire"), "Flushing" instead of "Heated" in line 137 ("Flushing his brow"), "quick" instead of "still" in line 325 ("quick pattereth the flaw-blown sleet")—we should of course like to attribute to Keats. But others that are similarly a permanent part of our experience of the poem are almost certainly the work of Keats's helpers in the publication, Woodhouse and Taylor.[11] We owe to Woodhouse, for example, the alteration of "quickly" to "slowly" in line 182: "The lover's endless minutes slowly pass'd." Unable to grasp how something that was "endless" could pass "quickly" (the reading of both the draft and the revised holograph), the literal-minded lawyer substituted the less blatantly opposite concept and, probably inadvertently, produced a better joke out of this wry characterization of Porphyro's loverly impatience.

The letters quoted above between Woodhouse and Taylor in September 1819 show that they were almost certainly responsible for the removal of the stanza that Keats added at 54/55 and for the return to the draft's more innocent description of the lovers' union in lines 314–22. Several other alterations that eliminate religious references from the manuscript versions were probably their doing as well: Angela's "Mercy, Jesu" in the manuscripts is reworded "Mercy, Porphyro" in the printed text (line 98); "O Christ" becomes a characterless "Go, go" (line 143); and Porphyro's swearing by Saint Paul in lines 145–47 ("'I will not harm her, by the great St Paul,' / Swear'th Porphyro: 'O may I ne'er find grace / When my weak voice shall unto heaven call'") is turned into a more general appeal to "all saints" and "last prayer" in the final version. Woodhouse apparently authored most of the alterations in these five lines, penciling suggestions and trial revisions opposite the text in W^1. Probably Woodhouse and Taylor worked together over these passages, putting Keats's revised holograph and the W^1 transcript side by side and inserting draft wording (from W^1) and some, at least, of the additional changes into the holograph for the printer. As Woodhouse noted cryptically in W^2, "K. left it to his Publishers to adopt which [readings] they pleased, & to revise the Whole." Keats's letter to Taylor of mid-June 1820 (*Letters* 2:294–95) is clear evidence that he saw the final version in proofs and requested (and got) correction of passages that he thought were altered by mistake. There is, however, no record of his participation or concurrence in the bulk of the changes.

The approximate dates of composition and revision have been known since 1848, when passages of Keats's letters to his brother and sister-in-law and to Taylor of February and September 1819 were made public (from transcript sources quoted in R. M. Milnes's *Life* of Keats). But it was several decades later, and only gradually, that the manuscript versions of the poem became available. Details from the holograph draft initially appeared in 1883, when Harry Buxton Forman, issuing the first of a long series of scholarly editions, *The Poetical Works and Other Writings of John Keats*, recorded variant readings from the manuscript (minus the first leaf), lent to him by its then-owner, Frederick Locker. Readings of the remainder of the draft text—the missing first leaf—followed soon after, when Sidney Colvin, having acquired Woodhouse's W^1 notebook from a relative of Taylor (to whom Woodhouse had bequeathed his collections), published draft variants for the first seven stanzas in his English Men of Letters Series *Keats* (1887), enabling Forman to include these in his reissue of the *Poetical Works* in 1889.

The text of Keats's revised holograph was the next to come to light, via George Keats's transcript, which had made its way from the United States to Australia sometime after 1840 and then was brought to England in 1892 and acquired by the British Library in the following year. Distinctive readings from George's transcript were incorporated into Forman's apparatuses beginning in 1900. Woodhouse's W^2 transcript was the last of the significant manuscripts of the poem to surface, having been purchased from a Taylor relative around 1912 or 1913 by the Marquess of Crewe (R. M. Milnes's son) and then purchased from Lord Crewe by Arthur A. Houghton, Jr., in the 1930s and deposited at Harvard in 1941. Woodhouse's alarmed letter to Taylor of 19–20 September 1819 describing Keats's revisions was acquired by the Morgan Library (with the rest of Woodhouse's scrapbook of miscellaneous Keats materials) in 1906; the main contents of the letter were first published by Amy Lowell, along with Taylor's reply, which she had acquired on her own, in her biography of Keats in 1925.

In sum, we have had the first published text since June 1820, the draft version since the middle 1880s, and a version of the revised holograph text since 1900. For much of the twentieth century, however, *The Eve of St. Agnes* has continued to be the version of 1820. The two commonest beliefs in textual theory over the years are first, that there should be a single "best" or "most authoritative" text of each of an author's works (an idea that necessarily elevates one version above all the others that might have a claim) and, second, that the best or most authoritative text of a work is some form of "final" version (most often the latest printed during the author's lifetime, presumed to be the last over which the author had personal control). These two principles have kept the manuscript versions of Keats's poem relegated to foot-of-the-page apparatuses in scholarly editions and out of sight entirely in popular and textbook printings.[12]

More recently, however, textual thinking has expanded to encompass several alternative ideas about the identity or constitution of a literary work, including competing theories about what is "best" and "most authoritative."

The draft version (in Woodhouse's transcripts for lines 1–63 and the Harvard holograph for the rest), even though it is not quite finished, would be, or theoretically should be, the choice of anyone who believes that the most authoritative version of a work is the earliest. This view dominates the ongoing Cornell edition of Wordsworth's poems, for example, and has been championed in American literature by Hershel Parker. The basic premise is that works deteriorate in revision, even when the reviser is the original author; in Parker's (unrevised?) words, "revising authors very often betray or otherwise blur their original achievements in ways they seldom intend and seldom become aware of" (*Flawed Texts* ix). If the Cornell editors were producing a multi-volume Keats on the same principles, or if Parker were in charge of a standard edition, the main text of *The Eve of St. Agnes* would be the draft, and Keats's revisions that we know about from Woodhouse's notes and George Keats's transcript, as well as the later changes appearing for the first time in 1820, would be subordinated to the apparatuses. In an essay on the state of Wordsworth's texts a few years ago, I described this kind of thinking—the preference for earliest over revised versions—as "textual primitivism." But the first-draft text of *The Eve of St. Agnes* clearly has its own legitimacy. It is the version closest to the "magic" of spontaneous creativity that Keats referred to when he was telling Woodhouse how he composed his poems. And he read the draft to Charles Cowden Clarke shortly after he wrote it (Rollins, *Keats Circle* 2:151), he let Woodhouse make a copy of it a few weeks after that, and for several additional months it was the only version in existence.

The text of the revised manuscript, largely recoverable from Woodhouse's notes and George Keats's transcript, would be the choice of anybody who believes that the best version is the author's final text before it is subjected to changes by interfering, "nonauthoritative" agencies such as editors and printers. Essentially this is the position of the Greg-Bowers-Tanselle school that dominated editing and textual criticism from the 1950s on into the 1980s. In their scheme, the ideal version of *The Eve of St. Agnes* would be Keats's final manuscript handed over to the publishers, or, since the manuscript is lost, an editorial reconstruction of it via Woodhouse and George Keats. Since George's manuscript is thought to be the later witness, his text can be reasonably taken to represent Keats's manuscript just a short time, perhaps only a matter of weeks, before he and Brown prepared the poems for the printer of 1820.

A third view, sometimes called the "social contract" theory of literary production and associated in Romantics studies with Jerome McGann, beginning with his *A Critique of Modern Textual Criticism* (1983), is that the creation of literature is a social and institutional activity involving not just authors but publishers, editors, designers, printers, illustrators, binders, advertisers, booksellers, purchasers, readers, reviewers, critics, teachers, and students, among others—and not just at some point in the past but in a continuous progression of events right up to the (continually advancing) present. In this view, the 1820 text is clearly the most important of the versions, not, this time, because it is the "latest that the author could have had a hand in" but because it represents the complex collaborative efforts of Keats, Woodhouse, the publishers, the printers (and so on) to create a work that in fact could never have been accomplished if only Keats, or only Woodhouse, or only the publishers, or only the printers were responsible. And, just as important, it is the version that everybody has known, read, assigned, discussed, and written about for the past 180 years—the subject of the myriad critical interpretations surveyed in the next chapter.

Still other views of an ideal or "best" text are possible—for example, an editorially constructed combination of readings from 1820 with readings from what we know of Keats's revised holograph. The ostensible aim of such a composite would be to discriminate between peculiarities of the 1820 version that we think Keats initiated himself, or at least accepted (which the editor would retain), and those that were forced on him against his wishes (which the editor would replace with others more "authoritative"). The problem in this case is that we have no way of knowing what Keats approved or did not approve in the published text. In an essay of 1963, I argued for an eclectic version that would consist of 1820 readings generally but incorporate readings of Keats's revised manuscript in lines 98, 143, 145–47 (passages where I thought Woodhouse and Taylor had altered troublesome religious references), 314–22 (the more explicit details of the physical union of the lovers), and the added stanza following 54 ("More pleasures . . . Warm in the virgin morn," and so on); and I repeated this suggestion when the essay was reprinted in 1971 and again in *The Texts of Keats's Poems* in 1974. But when I had to settle on a single (standard) text for the Harvard edition of 1978, I decided that the "subjective eclecticism" I had earlier so breezily recommended would be just as likely to distort as to fulfill Keats's "final intentions," for it would produce a new version far different from any that Keats could actually have had an opinion about.[13]

I have, in the two decades since then, evolved into an advocate and theorist of multiple versions, with, however, the general provision that the better texts are those which at one time or another existed intact, embodied in historical documents, and which carry a measure of "authorial" authority: not necessarily the nominal author's alone but some kind of agreement among the principals who collaborated in the production of the work. But that may be just my own prejudice. Each of the competing views of what constitutes the "best" text of *The Eve of St. Agnes*, and therefore of what constitutes the poem itself, is arguable and reasonable. And any one of the versions I have described has a claim to be designated "Keats's poem about the Eve of St. Agnes," though the exact title will vary according to whether we choose Keats's own wording (the manuscripts' "Saint Agnes' Eve") or the wording that Woodhouse and Taylor preferred instead for 1820 ("The Eve of St. Agnes").

It is worth noting, however, that for at least the past three or four decades critics have been combining versions of the poem in their interpretations, in effect creating instant eclectic texts of their own. Intent on explaining the version of 1820, they have drawn freely on readings from both the draft (for example, the images of "panting covert" at line 188 and caging at line 341) and the revised manuscript (for example, "Warm in the virgin morn, no weeping Magdalen" at 54/55) to "clarify" events in the printed text. This practice is common and in literary scholarship has long been one of the principal justifications for recovering and recording variants from other texts besides the standard "most authoritative" version being examined. In such a procedure, *The Eve of St. Agnes* has to be considered all the versions of the work taken together simultaneously. If we did not have Keats's manuscript revision of lines 314–22, along with Woodhouse's and Taylor's exchange of letters calling special attention to what was (shockingly) different in the new version, some of us, at least, like Woodhouse when he was copying and recopying the draft text (and, for that matter, like Woodhouse and Taylor together subsequently, when they approved the original more innocent version of the passage for publication), might never suspect a sexual union in the poem.

Keats's Comments on the Poem

We have very little comment by Keats himself on *The Eve of St. Agnes*. When Woodhouse reacted so strongly against the revised version, saying that Keats, in showing Porphyro embracing Madeline in her bed, had now made the poem "unfit for ladies, & indeed scarcely to be mentioned to them among the 'things that are,'" Keats responded (either angrily or jokingly, it is not possible to tell) that "he does not want ladies to read his poetry: that he writes for men—& that if in the former poem [the original version] there was an opening for doubt what took place, it was his fault for not writing clearly & comprehensibly" (*Letters* 2:163). Woodhouse's account of this incident confirms that Keats meant to describe sexual intercourse—at least in the revised manuscript—and one could infer from it something about Keats's idea at the time of a proper readership for the poem, if only one could be sure (as we cannot) that he was serious when he said that he wrote only for men.

The rest of the poet's comments are similarly problematic. Describing the subject matter, he tells his friend Benjamin Bailey, in a letter of 14 August 1819, two or three weeks before he began the revision, that the poem is "on a popular superstition" (*Letters* 2:139). This is a possible clue to what Keats himself thought was important in the poem. (Woodhouse says, in a note opposite the W^2 transcript, "The Poem was written on the suggestion of M^rs [Isabella] Jones," a friend of Taylor and others among Keats's circle. But we do not know what Woodhouse meant by this—maybe the "popular superstition" that Keats mentions, but maybe also, or instead, another more specific element of plot, setting, or theme.) In a cryptic remark to Woodhouse, 22 September 1819, about the simplicity and sentimentality of his earlier narrative poem *Isabella*, Keats muses in an aside that he perhaps entered too much into the feeling of the characters in *The Eve of St. Agnes*: "If I may so say, in my dramatic capacity [in *Isabella*] I enter fully into the feeling: but in Propria Persona I should be apt to quiz it myself— There is no objection of this kind to Lamia—A good deal to St Agnes Eve—only not so glaring" (*Letters* 2:174). This presumably is an authorial comment on an aspect of style in connection with narrative stance in the poem. In another letter, this time to Taylor, 17 November 1819, he mentions a wish "to diffuse the colouring of St Agnes eve throughout a Poem in which Character and Sentiment would be the figures to such drapery" (*Letters* 2:234). Probably "colouring" and "drapery" are, again, primarily matters of style. The final comment before the poems were set in type comes in a note from Brown to Taylor around the middle of March 1820: "Keats . . . wishes his Poems to be published as soon as convenient to yourself,—the volume to commence with St Agnes' Eve" (*Letters* 2:276). As published, the poem was in third place in the volume, following *Lamia* and *Isabella*. It is not known who—Keats, or Woodhouse and the publishers, or all of them working together—determined the final arrangement.

For later readers, these comments provide very little interpretive guidance. Keats does not tell us how to read or interpret the action or characters or theme or even any particular detail,[14] but instead simply launches the poem into the world, leaving the reading and interpreting to his readers. (His seeming casualness, outside the texts, contrasts sharply with the example of Wordsworth, who, in his repeated attempts to guide readers in the direction he wished them to take, represents a quite different relationship between writer and audience. Wordsworth is famous for irrepressible, lengthy pronouncements on the meanings that he thought he intended in his poems, though his statements have had, over time, very little effect. Readers from his own day to the present, even those dedicated to the recovery and preservation of authorial intention, have regularly set them aside in favor of other, more complicated meanings that he somehow neglected to mention.)[15] It is possible that Keats's most pointed indications toward interpretation were his revisions in the second manuscript—the added stanza at 54/55, the rewriting of lines 314–22, and the revised lines near the beginning about "triumphs gay / Of old romance" (lines 40–41). But these are *inside* the poem (in one version or another), and to read them thus is merely one more act of interpretation. The chief responsibility for understanding the poem continues to lie with the reader, where Keats lodged it from the beginning.

Thus, from 1820 to the present we have had a stable text of *The Eve of St. Agnes* or, rather, a stable array of versions (three of them), with no subsequent text having the "authority" of those of 1819 and 1820. And we have from Keats himself, outside the poem, only a handful of incidental remarks. These, then, are the texts and authorial commentary that have been available to readers and critics for at least most of the twentieth century. Every idea of what this poem is—what it is about, what it means, and what it does—is the product of readers and critics working with one or another combination of these same starting materials.

THREE

THE MULTIPLE READINGS

A MAIN POINT OF THIS BOOK, developed at length in the next chapter, is that every individual reader's experience of a complex literary work is different from every other reader's. Many hundreds of thousands have read *The Eve of St. Agnes* in the 180 years since it was drafted, revised, and published in 1819–1820, creating an enormous accumulation of different experiences, understandings, and interpretations of the poem. Obviously there is no way to check this out empirically. I am familiar with many of my students' responses, in classroom discussions and various kinds of writing, and with responses written up as opinions in the existing criticism—to which I can of course add my own experiences over the years (only some of which appear in the "existing criticism"). Yet other readers have just read and responded inside their heads and nervous systems, *silent* readers (analogous to Wordsworth's reiterated description of "silent poets") about whom we can only speculate.[1]

In this chapter on multiple readings, I mainly treat the written responses that have contributed to the ongoing discussion in print. These are, in general, the opinions of literary professionals—teachers and scholars—but I intend to use them, for the sake of argument, as representative of nonprofessional readers' responses as well. I am primarily interested not in the rightness or wrongness of a reading (or even which ones are "better" and which less so) but rather, more simply, in the impressive multiplicity of responses that the poem has stimulated. For such a demonstration, the relative handful of readings in the critical literature—hardly more than a few hundred—offer plentiful variety.

The first section presents a brief, initial look at the main elements of the plot, or plots, of the narrative—the characters and actions that readers have responded to in their experiences of the poem. The next section recounts some of the earliest ways of reading the poem, the beginnings, as it were, of the multiple reading process that seems now to be permanently established in the existing criticism. Then comes the main business of the chapter, a lengthy, but nevertheless "token," account of different ways of interpreting the poem.

The Stories of the Poem

There are several ways of telling the story of *The Eve of St. Agnes*. I shall present three of them as separate versions of the plot, one of them more innocent than the other two. In the more innocent version, Keats's heroine, whose name is Madeline, is practicing a St. Agnes' Eve ritual according to which, if she goes to bed supperless and prays to St. Agnes, she will dream of the man who will become her husband. The hero, Porphyro, who is an enemy of Madeline's family, comes from his home across the moors, enters Madeline's castle, makes his way to Madeline's bedroom, and, just when she is dreaming about him as her future husband, awakens her, declares his love, and takes her out of the castle and back to his home to be his wife.

This version of the plot combines the *Sleeping Beauty* motif—Madeline is Sleeping Beauty, and Porphyro is the Prince Charming who awakens her to a joyous, love-filled reality—with elements from *Romeo and Juliet* and any other story or myth that involves enmity between families and rescue of a maiden from imprisonment or a spell. It is, in effect, *Romeo and Juliet* with a happy ending.

The second and third versions are not so innocent. Two minor characters add religious and moral complications. One of these is an old Beadsman who figures in the first three stanzas—a religious person hired to pray for the people who live in Madeline's castle. The Beadsman has renounced all the joys of life and is practicing a ritual that parallels Madeline's action as the plot unfolds, a ritual involving renunciation of every pleasurable aspect of earthly life in favor of imagined bliss in another world: heaven for the Beadsman and a dream-world for Madeline. The Beadsman exits the poem at the beginning of the fourth stanza, but then reappears at the end as a corpse lying in his cell, undiscovered, unburied.

The other minor character is Madeline's not-so-trusty nurse, an old woman named Angela, who helps Porphyro avoid discovery by Madeline's kinsmen, leads him to Madeline's bedchamber, and hides him in a closet so that he can secretly watch Madeline undress. Angela too is killed off at the end of the poem, dying a grotesque death, "palsy-twitch'd, with meagre face deform" (line 376). The only other human characters in the poem (apart from the narrator) are Madeline's kinsmen and a throng of revelers invited to the castle on St. Agnes' Eve. These characters, at the end, are in a drunken stupor, suffering nightmares about witches, demons, and coffin worms.

My second version of the plot, played out against this ominous background of self-deprivation, grotesque dreams, and death, is the story of *Porphyro's Stratagem*. Early in the action, Porphyro proposes a "stratagem" (line 139) that involves spying on Madeline as she undresses, then climbing into her bed and, while she is still asleep (and unaware of what is actually happening), in effect raping her. Madeline awakens to find a real Porphyro in her bed instead of the lover she was innocently dreaming about, and she is astonished and dismayed. One might take this to be bad behavior on Porphyro's part, because it is connected in the poem with various images of witchcraft, sorcery, peeping Tomism, seduction, and rape.

My third version of the plot focuses on *Madeline's Dream-Ritual*. Madeline is totally engrossed in a superstition known as "fasting St. Agnes' Fast," according to which, by following certain practices, she hopes to see her future husband in a dream, make love with him, and awaken still a virgin. Angela thinks this ritual is a foolish amusement (lines 124–26); Porphyro sees it as the perfect occasion for the working of his stratagem (lines 136 ff.); the narrator calls it an old-wives' tale and a whim and describes Madeline as hoodwinked with faery fancy, metaphorically both blind and dead (lines 45, 55, 70).

If we combine all three of these versions of the plot, the innocent tale of young lovers plus Porphyro's stratagem and Madeline's dream-ritual, we have a Romeo and Juliet story in which the Romeo character is a peeping Tom and cowardly seducer and the Juliet character renounces life in favor of a foolish ritual. And this story is framed by images of freezing cold and death. The opening stanzas describe the bitter chill of St. Agnes' Eve and the suffering of animals and humans and even the "sculptur'd dead" in the chapel connected to Madeline's castle (line 14). The closing stanzas describe an icy storm, nightmares, and the deaths of both Angela and the Beadsman. These elements *ought* to give a decidedly unpleasant tone to our originally innocent story of Sleeping Beauty, Prince Charming, and happiness ever after.

The Three Bears and Single Meanings

For the first 130 years after it was published, readers viewed *The Eve of St. Agnes* mainly as a series of pretty pictures, a rich Romantic tapestry, as critics sometimes called it, beginning with Leigh Hunt in Keats's own time.[2] The pretty pictures were the Beadsman praying in his chapel, Porphyro entering the castle, Porphyro and Angela sitting by the fireplace, Madeline and Angela meeting on the stairs, Madeline undressing in her bedchamber, Madeline praying before she gets into bed, Porphyro setting out the banquet, Porphyro and Madeline tiptoeing out of the castle. The poem is also replete with cinematographic effects, starting in the first stanza with an overview of the wintry scene outside the castle, including owl, hare, and silent flock of sheep, followed by quick zoom into the chapel to focus on the Beadsman's fingers. Keats's contemporaries could easily appreciate effects like these—a frame at a time, as it were—without knowledge of our movie technology. The pictures were increasingly admired as the principal content of the poem for the rest of the nineteenth century and the first half of the twentieth.

Then in 1953 appeared Earl Wasserman's brilliant and provocative reading of the poem as a metaphysical allegory, based on two passages in Keats's letters (*The Finer Tone* 97–137). The first of these passages compares the imagination to Adam's dream of the creation of Eve in *Paradise Lost*: Adam "awoke and found it truth" (to Benjamin Bailey, 22 November 1817, *Letters* 1:183–87). This is a type of dreaming, or visionary, imagination, and for Keats it prefigures an earthly happiness repeated spiritually in a finer tone somewhere else. In Wasserman's application, Madeline is having just such a prefigurative dream when she practices her St. Agnes' Eve ritual: she dreams of the lover she will marry, then awakens, and there he is in truth. The other passage that Wasserman uses from the letters is the famous simile comparing human life to a "Mansion of Many Apartments" (to John Hamilton Reynolds, 3 May 1818, *Letters* 1:275–83). In Wasserman's interpretation, Madeline's castle represents human life, and Porphyro, passing upward to a closet adjoining her bedchamber and thence into the bedchamber itself, is progressing from apartment to apartment in the mansion of life, on a spiritual journey to join Madeline in some kind of higher (transcendental) reality.

There seemed at the time to be a number of mistakes in Wasserman's interpretation, and I launched my own career as a Keats critic by pointing them out in an essay first published more than thirty-five years ago called "The Hoodwinking of Madeline." Madeline, when she awakens, is not happy to find a real Porphyro in her bed. Porphyro has been sneaking around the castle like a peeping Tom. Rather than experiencing spiritual repetition in a finer tone, leading to a higher reality, the two principals seem to be having sex with only one conscious of what is going on. And the narrative is full of echoes of bad happenings in earlier works: the rape of Philomel, Satan seducing Eve, Lovelace raping the unconscious Clarissa Harlowe, and others. My essay went on in considerable detail, and was well known for a while as the dirty-minded reading of *The Eve of St. Agnes*. When I republished the essay as a chapter in a book, a reviewer, Richard Harter Fogle, commented in verse in the Phi Beta Kappa *Key Reporter*:

> Alack for Madeline, poor hoodwink'd maid—
> By Porphyro then, now Stillinger betrayed.

A decade after "The Hoodwinking of Madeline" first appeared, Stuart Sperry published his fine essay entitled "Romance as Wish-Fulfillment," establishing Wasserman's and mine as two extremes of critical opinion on the poem, Wasserman's being too romantically metaphysical and mine being too anti-romantically realistic. Sperry's interpretation skillfully steered a middle course between these extremes, and so for the next two decades the standard opening for an essay on *The Eve of St. Agnes* was to recite a kind of "three bears" litany in which Wasserman was too high-flying, I was too down-to-earth, and Sperry, like the reiterated judgment of the third of the three bears, was "just right." This opening, however, was always followed by a "but": Sperry was "just right" in his way, *but* all previous critics, including Sperry, had overlooked such-and-such . . . which then led into yet another new reading.

Notably, each successive interpretation of the poem was intended to supersede all the previous interpretations. Wasserman made obsolete the idea that the poem is merely a rich Romantic tapestry; I explained that Wasserman's reading was "wrong" in all the major particulars; Sperry showed how both Wasserman and I were oversimplifying the important points. Each subsequent critic negated an ever-growing body of predecessors. This was the era of single-meaning interpretation, and to some extent it continues today.

A Token Fifty-nine Interpretations

After Sperry, whose essay was first published in 1971, a great many readings have appeared in print. Not all of them, to be sure, are single-meaning interpretations, but most of the writers have some "Lorenzo's head" to propose as Keats's or the poem's central preoccupation that ties together and explains the various parts, and most offer their explanation as correction and improvement of our current understanding.[3]

In what follows, I shall briefly summarize fifty-nine interpretations of the poem. (My starting point is a list, reproduced in Appendix B, that I devised for some lectures connected with the Keats Bicentennial in 1995.) These by no means exhaust the interpretive possibilities, and in any case the list and my summaries are simplifications of more complicated arguments. Even so, the array will certainly convey the variety of approaches and responses of trained readers. And it is, as I shall emphasize more than once, just a token array, from whose vantage point *The Eve of St. Agnes* appears as the stimulus and, to some extent, corrective for an interactive process of interpretation. This activity may be both what *The Eve of St. Agnes* is ultimately about and what its survival as a work of literature amounts to.

THE FIRST EIGHT OF THE "fifty-nine ways" form a group under the heading Love, Sex, Marriage.

1. *Human love (celebration of love over all obstacles).* In the most common of the older thematic readings, *The Eve of St. Agnes* is a celebration of romantic love. It is, to quote a handful of representative critics from the 1940s to the 1980s, an "imaginative projection of young love" (R. H. Fogle, "A Reading" 328). "Keats discovered a seemingly happy alternative [to *Isabella*, *Lamia*, and the darker odes linking the ideal with death or failure]. Madeline and Porphyro consummate their secret love and boldly escape the decaying castle" (Arthur Carr 238). "There can be no other way of reading the poem than as a great affirmation of love—of an intense, happy, achieved love that makes it the antithesis of *Isabella*"; it is an expression of "unquestioning rapture," "a day-dream of happy, fulfilled love" (E. C. Pettet 212, 245, 297). "Critics are nearly unanimous in agreement that the major theme of *The Eve of St. Agnes* is celebration of human love" (Gerald Enscoe 125). The poem "is, quite simply, a finely wrought dramatic tale about falling in love," dramatizing "the triumph of life, whose essence is love" (Barry Gradman 64, 79). The poem "is about one of the greatest commonplace experiences, the fusion of unreasoning desire, aching idealism, and overwhelming eroticism in youthful love" (John Barnard 85).

This might be called a naive reading (though the last critic quoted makes it clear that he is referring specifically to the version of the original draft). It ignores many details of the text and therefore appears uninfluenced by the methods of slow reading and minute analysis taught by several decades of New Criticism; it could as well be based on a simple plot summary, such as that given in the first paragraph of the section above headed "The Stories of the Poem." It is, however, a widespread response both in published writings about Keats and (at least initially) in college and high school literature classes and must be acknowledged as a standard reading. Rather than find fault with it, I prefer to consider it a legitimate response by a large group who perhaps do not read slowly or analytically. Its main characteristic is simplicity rather than distortion; indeed, it would be difficult to argue that the poem is *not* about romantic love, just as it would be difficult to argue that romantic love is its sole concern.

Interestingly, people who express this view are among the poem's greatest admirers and, therefore, among those helping to maintain its canonical status. As I shall suggest in the final section of chapter 6, such readers may in fact be responding to complexities that they cannot or prefer not to include in their descriptions of it. Their descriptions, in other words, may belie their actual experience in the reading.

2. *Keats's love life.*   The idea that the historical John Keats (1795–1821) is speaking for himself somewhere in the poem—through the narrator, through the character of Porphyro, even for that matter through the character of Madeline— is a narrowing and personalizing of the preceding more abstract thematic interest. It touches on the general question of autobiography in Romantic poetry, which arises whenever one asks *who* is speaking in, say, *Tintern Abbey* or the Intimations Ode; in *Childe Harold's Pilgrimage* or *Don Juan*; in the introductory note to *Kubla Khan* and the fifty-four lines of verse that follow the note. The range of possible answers in each case includes the historical author at one extreme of opinion, a completely fictional character at the other end of the scale, and various mixtures of the two in the middle. It has long been common critical practice, however, and especially with the Romantics, to identify first-person speakers and characters with the historical authors who created them; the characters say and feel what the authors wanted to express about themselves and therefore can be read as mouthpieces for the authors' "philosophy." Keats thought he saw Coleridge and Wordsworth expressing themselves in this way and registered disapproval, preferring, in theory at least, his own ideals of negative capability and the chameleonlike adaptability of the poet's sympathetic imagination (see *Letters* 1:193–94, 386–88). But it is almost impossible, in practical reading (and practical criticism), to believe that something in a text, no matter what the occasion or point of view, was created without passing through the writer's mind and being affected by what the writer thought and felt.

The Eve of St. Agnes has a narrator who gets increasingly excited as the action progresses ("Now prepare, / Young Porphyro, for gazing on that bed," lines 196–97) and who has an opinion of his own concerning the severity of the storm that comes up toward the end (lines 325, 327). But the critics who have studied

Keats's narrator—Marian Cusac, William Stephenson, Robert Kern, Neil Fraistat, and especially Michael Ragussis and Susan Wolfson—have been interested primarily in narrative technique and have not emphasized autobiographical interpretation.

It is, rather, the love interest and the character of Porphyro that critics have long identified with Keats, as manifested in offhand remarks about the poem as a reflection of Keats's feelings (as in this of Douglas Bush, *John Keats* 111: "The superstition connected with St. Agnes' Eve . . . invited all the emotional warmth now awakened in the relatively happy lover of Fanny Brawne"), in statements equating Keats and Fanny Brawne with the principal characters (see reading 3), and, more recently, in feminist readings of the poem as an expression of Keats's ambivalence toward women (see reading 57). A quite novel biographical reading that caused a stir in the mid-1950s was Robert Gittings's suggestion, in *John Keats: The Living Year*, that the poem was the immediate product of a sexual liaison between Keats and Isabella Jones, a woman whom he had first met at Hastings in May or June 1817, had seen again in October 1818, and had received "many presents of game" from about the time that he drafted *The Eve of St. Agnes* (*Letters* 2:65). The evidence for such an affair is next to nonexistent—and Gittings abandoned most of the case in his fine biography fourteen years later—but Isabella Jones is still permanently connected with the poem in Woodhouse's enigmatic note opposite the first stanza in his W^2 notebook: "St Agnes' day is the 21st of January. / The Poem was written on the suggestion of Mrs Jones."

3. *Keats's love specifically for Fanny Brawne.* This reading (a subdivision or special focusing of the preceding) was prevalent in the most influential works on Keats of the 1920s and 1930s. Amy Lowell in her biography of 1925 calls the poem "a great choral hymn written to celebrate [Keats's] love for Fanny Brawne" (2:169). On the British side of the Atlantic, John Middleton Murry writes in the same year, "If the crude equation be taken with enough imaginative margin, we may say that Madeline is Fanny and Keats Porphyro." Murry then continues, after quotation of lines 208–43, 316–22 (with the significant omission of lines 244–315 represented by three ellipsis dots), "That is essentially Keats' dream-consummation of his love for Fanny Brawne" (109–10). Claude Lee Finney echoes Lowell and Murry in his magisterial work of 1936: "*The Eve of St. Agnes* was the first poem in which Keats was inspired by his love for Fanny Brawne" (2:538). And the idea has regularly resurfaced since, as in Jean Hagstrum's statement of 1985 that "the sexual consummation of the poem was surely a dream of union with Fanny Brawne" (52).

This view is by no means unreasonable. Keats had met Fanny Brawne in the summer or early autumn of 1818, after he returned from his walking tour of the Lakes and Scotland, and had instantly fallen in love; as he told her in a letter of July 1819, using a word that Porphyro applies to himself in line 335, "the very first week I knew you I wrote myself your vassal" (*Letters* 2:132). A love poem written by a young man in love, it is supposed, must refer to the historical love object. Similarly, Murry translates *Lamia* into "imaginative autobiography, and of the most exact and faithful kind" in a later chapter of his work of 1925: "Keats

is Lycius, Fanny Brawne is the Lamia, and Apollonius is Charles Brown the realist, trying to break Fanny's spell over Keats by insisting upon her as the female
animal. The identification seems transparent" (157). It would be ridiculous to
suggest as one of the grounds for this kind of identification the fact that both
Apollonius (in the poem, 1.364, 2.245) and Brown (in real life) were bald. But
still, one may ask, why did Keats so pointedly insist on Apollonius's baldness? Even
if any such one-to-one autobiographical scheme seems a drastic oversimplifica-
tion, it need not rule out either real-life details in descriptions and expressions of
ideas and feelings or the reader's interest in the origin of such details.

4. *Celebration of sexual love.*   As I have mentioned, Woodhouse learned from the
revised version that Keats read him in September 1819, and from the "Keats-like
rhodomontade" that followed in response to his objections, that Porphyro and
Madeline are sexually united in the poem. Others—not counting readers who
already had their suspicions from the version in print—found out about it when
Woodhouse's letter to Taylor about the revisions was published in Amy Lowell's
1925 biography. One way or another, critics have had to deal with sex in the poem
ever since.[4] Many do so by explaining (just as Angela insists in lines 179–80 of
the poem) that the lovers are going to be married and that, indeed, Porphyro
already calls Madeline his bride even before they leave the castle. Some, however,
consider sex itself as a main theme. For example, Harold Bloom, early in his criticism, sets up a Keatsian opposition of real and ideal and then makes sex the lit-
eral embodiment of reality: "[Keats's] lovers are completely physical in a physical world. . . . *The Eve of St. Agnes* is a hymn in honor of the senses" (*Visionary
Company* 370–71). But the most enthusiastic of these critics, Jean Hagstrum, has
no interest in allegorical abstraction: "The poem is a masterpiece of the intensest
eroticism. . . . 'Love's fev'rous citadel' (line 84) is not unlike the creating mind
of the poet, as we shall see; the palpitatingly vivid description of the viands, the
casement, and the warm gules on Madeline's breast are all of a piece—the sensuous becoming the sensual, intensifying by degrees into full sexual realization.
Madeline . . . fully partakes, though in the different manner of a renewed dream,
in the sexual ecstasy" (52–53).

More cerebrally, Gary Farnell, in a recent essay much influenced by Theodor
Adorno and headed with a quotation from Woodhouse's judgment on the sexual
explicitness of Keats's revision ("Unfit for Ladies"), interprets the poem as an
ideological piece concerned with the power of fantasy to ease society's restric-
tions on sexual expression: "Things need not necessarily be as they are in the
future, or what they have been in the past, or indeed what they appear to be in
the present" (408).

5. *Celebration of Christian marriage.*   The poem repeatedly emphasizes Madeline's
(and St. Agnes') purity and, set as it is in medieval times, is full of Christian, and
especially Catholic, iconography: Mary, saints, priest, angels, lambs, prayers, pilgrimage, and a religious "miracle" (line 339). Why not, then, read the poem as
representation of a Christian marriage? This is Katharine Garvin's view in "The
Christianity of St. Agnes' Eve: Keats' Catholic Inspiration." "St. Agnes was one

of the earliest saints who claimed a mystical marriage as a reason for avoiding a human one. . . . She established the precedent for a girl to choose her own destiny, and to follow the lead of her heart in seeking a spouse. . . . This is the secret of 'The Eve of St. Agnes'" (358). "Madeline is a humanized Agnes, and the poem a portrayal of perfection and promise in an earthly union modelled upon the heavenly bridal of Agnes" (360). Garvin points out that Porphyro, Madeline, Angela, and the Beadsman were Catholic, even if Keats was not. This is the earliest criticism to analyze the poem in terms of Keats's religious knowledge; for another view using the same materials, see Gail Gibson's essay in reading 40.

6. *Erotic love versus religious purity.*   This reading is suggested, if not quite stated, in Jeffrey Baker's "Aphrodite and the Virgin," in effect, an unresolved opposition between readings 4 and 5. "Although the ostensible subject matter of the poem is a simple mediaeval tale with a simple romantic hero, its real substance is a delicate exploration of a complex erotic sensibility, and the conflicting idealisations created by that sensibility" (103). The "complex erotic sensibility" is Keats's own, expressed through Porphyro's feelings and behavior, and the "conflicting idealisations" are the two different ways in which Porphyro views Madeline, as Agnes or the Virgin Mary on the one hand—the essence of religious purity and devotion—and as Aphrodite on the other, with all the sexual implications associated with the goddess of love. Baker's is the first interpretation in this list (though not, of course, the earliest historically) that reads the poem in terms of a conflict of opposing ideas, values, or symbols; see readings 48 and 49 for a gathering of others.

7. *Sexual Politics I: Porphyro the peeping Tom/rapist, Madeline the victim.*   Porphyro's character, actions, and motivations occupy more pages of recent criticism than any other aspect of the poem. He is, to be sure, one of the two principals of the narrative, but the extraordinary attention has to be explained in terms of certain seeming contradictions: he enters the poem and Madeline's castle as a typical romance hero, then rescues Madeline from hostile surroundings, taking her home to be his bride, in similarly heroic style, at the end; but in a large part of the middle of the poem, he is more like a villain than a hero. He is linked with witches, elves, and evil magic (lines 120–22, 168–71). His plan for uniting with Madeline is a "stratagem"—artifice, deception—that involves hiding in a closet (a "covert") and spying on her "in close secrecy" while she undresses for bed (lines 139, 163–66, 188). His approach to her and the sexual consummation that follows, while Madeline is asleep or in a senseless stupor, are attended by images and echoes of the rape of Philomel (206), Satan approaching Eve in *Paradise Lost* (lines 224–26), the villainous Iachimo gazing on the sleeping Imogen in *Cymbeline* (lines 244–63), and other illicit happenings in literature and legend. Narrative events are related in language full of serious moral connotations, as in the verbs "Stol'n," "crept," and "peep'd" and the ominous Spenserian echo in "Noiseless as fear in a wide wilderness," all brought together in stanza 28, where Porphyro tiptoes out of the closet and hovers over the sleeping Madeline, checking her breathing to make sure she is sound asleep.

I think I was the first critic to connect these details interpretively, portraying Porphyro as peeping Tom and rapist in the first third of my 1961 essay "The Hoodwinking of Madeline," though, as I explained at the time, I did not think his stratagem was the main concern of the poem (I was mainly interested in separating Madeline and Porphyro into protagonist and antagonist, as introduction to a point about Keats's skepticism concerning the visionary imagination, an interpretation that figures as reading 20 later in this list). The complexities and contradictions of Porphyro's character are material for several different ways of looking at the poem. The view of reading 7, emphasizing Porphyro as cowardly stalker and seducer, has been intensified in subsequent criticism by, among others, Beverly Fields and John Kerrigan. Fields ("Keats and the Tongueless Nightingale") takes the myth of Philomel, symbolic of rape, mutilation, violent revenge, and metamorphosis, as the poem's "undersong": Porphyro is Tereus, Madeline the mutilated Philomel (suffering, in this case, mutilation "of the senses"), and the poem a "fantasy of eroticized destructiveness" (246, 248, 249). Kerrigan ("Keats and *Lucrece*"), working from Keats's reading and marking of an 1806 copy of Shakespeare's *Poetical Works* now at Keats House, Hampstead, finds many points of comparison between Porphyro's actions and the leering overtones and violence of *The Rape of Lucrece*. The "most significant echo," when the lovers come together in Keats's poem, "is Shakespearian and suggestive of deception, substitution, and sexual threat" (112).[5] For other readings specially focusing on Porphyro, see readings 11, 12, and 21.

8. *Sexual politics II: Madeline the seducer, Porphyro the victim (husband caught at last!).* This reversal of the protagonist and antagonist roles of reading 7 has so far arisen mainly in my graduate and undergraduate class discussions of the poem, as a reaction to the depiction of Porphyro as the exclusively active character, the one always in control, while Madeline remains the helpless, passive (indeed, even unconscious) victim. It is, in effect, a sort of "Let's-hear-it-for-Madeline" countermovement, based in part on the idea that Porphyro is *drawn* to the castle and to Madeline by a combination of love, sexual attraction, and her conjuring (line 124), and even "Into her dream" (320). The idea is just now getting into print as well. Heidi Thomson's piece on Madeline's "sensual ear" marshals evidence from the text—for example, the sexiness of the dream she yearns for, her reaction to Porphyro's music (when she utters a soft moan and thereby breaks her ritual's rule of silence), and her fears that he may be dead when she sees him in her room—to read the poem as a story of reciprocal seduction, in which the sexual consummation, like the marriage that accompanies it, is effected by mutual consent, with Madeline yielding to her own desire just as much as to Porphyro's.

   Mary Arseneau's "Madeline, Mermaids, and Medusas" further empowers Madeline, reading her as a precursor of La Belle Dame and Lamia, *femmes fatales* who lure men from mundane reality into otherworldly realms of imagination and artifice and, in the process, ruin their lives. And in a short piece subtitled "The Hoodwinking of Porphyro," Fleming McClelland makes an ingenious suggestion concerning the stage business of stanza 22, where Madeline meets and escorts Angela down the stairs, namely, that Angela here tells Madeline about

Porphyro's hidden presence in her bedroom and that the rest of Madeline's action (kneeling in her room, praying, undressing, and so on through the consummation) is conscious calculation for the purpose of winning Porphyro. There is no textual support for such a reading, but one has to explain, otherwise, why the presumably loyal Angela would *not* have mentioned Porphyro on the occasion.

THE NEXT NINE READINGS, 9–17, are grouped (in Appendix B) under the heading Magic, Fairy Tale, Myth. There are, intermixed with the pervasive religious language and imagery of the poem, many references to magic and fairy lore: "faery fancy," "witch's sieve," "Elves and Fays," "conjuror," "enchantments," "legends," "legion'd fairies," "pale enchantment," "Merlin" and "his demon," "charmed maid," "spirits of the air," "mermaid," "midnight charm," "stedfast spell," "woofed phantasies," "elfin-storm from faery land," "sleeping dragons," "phantoms," "witch, and demon." The readings of this group also take positions concerning the activities of Porphyro and Madeline, but the principal focus moves from human relationships to the poem's connection with myths, many of which emphasize unreality amid otherwise worldly detail.

9. *Romance, enthrallment, enchantment.*   Clifford Adelman studies enthrallment as a recurring situation in Keats's poems, a dreamlike condition in which, to use the language of Keats's "Mansion of Many Apartments" letter, a person is trapped in a single chamber with a fixed set of ideas and attitudes, unable to awaken. In *The Eve of St. Agnes*, which Adelman reads as Keats's most elaborate representation of the dangers of enthrallment, every character except the narrator is shown to be trapped in this way: the Beadsman in religious orthodoxy, Madeline in faery fancy, Porphyro in romance and his design on Madeline, Angela in mundane reality. The lovers alone break out of their dream by "actualiz[ing] the visionary experience" (113).

In a more scholarly work also taking enthrallment as the main theme, Karen Harvey approaches the poem by way of the Merlin allusion (for which there is no agreed-on explanation) in lines 170–71: "Never on such a night have lovers met, / Since Merlin paid his Demon all the monstrous debt." Her comprehensive survey of critics' opinions, Arthurian reference, and the state of knowledge concerning demons leads to the conclusion that Merlin's "monstrous debt" was "the debt of his entrapment and perpetual imprisonment paid, through the working of one of his own spells, to the demonic fay Vivien as a result of his enthrallment to her" (89). In the application that follows, Porphyro is the Merlin figure and Madeline the Vivien who enchants him. And since Madeline is herself already under the spell of faery fancy, both lovers represent the dangers of enthrallment, which continue to the end as they flee the castle into the further unreality of the "elfin-storm."

10. *Sleeping Beauty.*   As I suggested earlier in this chapter, an innocent version of the plot (in contrast to the "dangers of enthrallment" just preceding) tends to make *The Eve of St. Agnes* a fairy tale in itself. Brother Baldwin Peter's study of resemblances to the tale of Sleeping Beauty (in the late seventeenth-century

French version by Charles Perrault) can represent such a view in the present
list. Madeline is the princess put by curse into a hundred-year sleep, Angela
a type of fairy godmother, and Porphyro the prince who breaks into the castle
to awaken the princess with a kiss. Keats's drunken revelers are the counterpart of the rest of the dwellers in the princess's castle (who in the tale, however, are in a deathlike state at the beginning and are returned to normal life
at the end, rather than vice versa, in effect, as in Keats's poem). There are several significant details in common between the tale and the poem, and Brother
Baldwin's conclusion is reasonably modest: "the sleeping-beauty archetype is
part of the poem's structure" (6).

11. *Porphyro as liberator of Madeline.*   If we imagine Madeline and Porphyro to
be occupying separate "worlds" through much of the poem—Madeline in a
dream-world somewhere above Porphyro's world of actual experience (the
"aboveness" signified literally by the location of Madeline's bedchamber upstairs
in the castle)—does Madeline, at the end, bring Porphyro up to join her in her
dream, or, conversely, does Porphyro bring Madeline down to his reality? The
poem can be read either way, but the more common view is the latter. Karla
Alwes's discussion of the poem is a good example, starting with life and death as
the primary oppositions in the poem. Madeline is associated with death in the
form of religion, ritual, and sterility (all prefigured in the Beadsman in the opening stanzas), and Porphyro, whom Alwes connects with a series of mythical and
historical figures such as Eros (in Apuleius's tale of Cupid and Psyche) and the
Platonic philosopher Porphyry, is the contrasting embodiment of life, passion,
and imagination. In effect, Porphyro liberates Madeline from her world of death,
and the conclusion magically transports the lovers to the eternal life and warmth
of Porphyro's southern moors.

12. *Porphyro as vampire.*   A quite different view of Porphyro's mythical origins
is proposed by James Twitchell: "He is a destroyer, a villain of the first order, not
an imaginary Adam in Madeline's Edenic dream, but rather the poisoner of the
apple. He is, in short, the Satan of the piece . . . drawn from . . . the myth of the
vampire" (*Living Dead* 94). Twitchell's evidence includes a number of narrative
and descriptive details relatable to vampirism, as well as similarities between
Porphyro and the vampire-like Geraldine in Coleridge's *Christabel*, and a speculative connection of his name with porphyria, a disease marked by extreme sen-
sitivity to sunlight: "A person with porphyria can look terrifying, for his teeth
and nails take on a strange fluorescent glow. This disease became one of the major
nineteenth-century explanations of vampirism and quite possibly was known
to Keats as a young apothecary surgeon" (95). Twitchell admits that this is a
"grisly reading," but points to the "wormy circumstance" of the earlier *Isabella*
and later *La Belle Dame* and *Lamia* to show that Keats clearly could write in the
grisly vein when he wanted to (100).

   If all this work seems overly academic, based on special knowledge that "ordinary" readers do not usually have, imagine the poem through the eyes of an
undergraduate who has recently read Stoker's *Dracula* or seen one of the nu-

merous movies based on it. Porphyro and the narrator admire Madeline's "fair breast," bathed in a reddish light from the moon shining through the stained-glass casement (lines 217–18); Porphyro "grows faint" just three lines after a mention of Madeline's "silver cross," then revives when she removes the cross with the rest of her jewelry (lines 221, 224, 226–28); three separate times Keats places him close to her ear (lines 293, 308, and the revised manuscript text of 314–22). For this hypothetical undergraduate, it may be difficult *not* to see elements of vampirism in the poem.

13. *The triumph of Fairy over Christian religion.*   Judith Arcana views *The Eve of St. Agnes* as the enactment of a sacred ritual in what she calls the "old religion" of the Britons, also known as "the Craft, Witchcraft, or Faery," in the time of the early Celts, with ritual practices similar to those of contemporary cultures in Europe, Africa, Scandinavia, and the Middle East. "By weaving together two strands of imagery, Christian and Faery, Keats has presented the triumph of the old religion over Christianity as his theme." Arcana offers "a Faery reading" of the poem that explains the basic mythology, displays the intertwined sets of contrasting images, Faery and Christian, and relates Keats's characters to the ritual: Angela is the Crone (a type of guide or priestess); Madeline is the "maiden-to-be-mother" in the ritual (see reading 14); Porphyro is the young god who aids in the initiation; and the Beadsman is "the lone representative of the Christian church" (43).

14. *Initiation and transformation of maiden into mother.*   Another element of Judith Arcana's "Faery reading"—central to the ritual described in reading 13 but important and distinctive enough to be listed as a separate reading—is Madeline's "initiation into ripeness as a woman." "In the old religion, 'young virgins' would be trained by older women, taught to watch the phases of the moon, fast in silence, seek their visions and prepare for sexual initiation. . . . Madeline would know that she was to embody the moon goddess and that her lover would embody the young god, her partner in the metamorphosis from maiden to mother" (Arcana 48). Such analysis blames neither Porphyro nor Madeline; they are just doing what comes anthropologically: "It is Faery imagery which determines the character of the consummation scene in stanza thirty-six. If the lovers are Christian, Porphyro is a villain, Madeline a victim. . . . But if we continue to read these characters through the imagery of Faery, the young lovers are together in intent, enacting a timeless ritual and their union is blessed by the Great Mother" (51–52).

15. *A version of Joseph Campbell's monomyth.*   Joseph Campbell's *The Hero with a Thousand Faces*, establishing a "nuclear plot" common to thousands of myths, legends, and fairy tales throughout the world, was tremendously influential for a quarter of a century following its publication in 1949. The basic narrative, about a hero who ventures from the real world into a higher (or lower) realm to battle supernatural forces, wins a decisive victory, and returns home to do good for his people, is widely applicable and almost always helps in the analysis of a

poem's or story's structure; we translate a character's desire into a protagonist's "quest" and thereby clarify what the character wants, what stands in the way, who is on whose side, and the like.

Dorothy Van Ghent's *Keats: The Myth of the Hero*, posthumously published from a manuscript in progress when she died in 1967, is the most useful and comprehensive application of Campbell's monomyth to Keats's poems in general and this poem in particular. "In *The Eve of St. Agnes*, the hero enters a dangerous castle where the love-maiden is immured, finds his way by tortuous passages to the secret, inner chamber where she sleeps, and there consummates a mystic marriage with her under the enchantments of a holy night" (89). Not surprisingly, the season, the old people (the Beadsman and Angela), Madeline's self-induced enchantment, Porphyro's "passage through the castle-maze," the hostile kinsmen, the "sacramental act of food-magic" (the feast that Porphyro sets out), and much more are readily associated with the monomyth (90–98). As in reading 14, "What would be otherwise a mean and brutal trick, a ruthless defloration, is converted by the strength and authority of the mythical substrate and the sacramental approach of the lover, into a high religious act, the resurrection of life from its wintry sleep" (100).

Myth criticism of this sort may seem to ignore details that fail to fit the pattern. What Van Ghent calls "the strong unconscious intuition . . . that the ritual plot is traditional and inevitable" (90) could hinder individual reading and interpretation; the myths are already in place before the reading gets under way. Another approach based on the same mythic materials might read the down-to-earth, unheroic elements of Porphyro's and Madeline's actions and characters as Keats's conscious attempt to make his story conspicuously *different* from those that accord with the standard myth of the hero.

16. *The Fortunate Fall.*   Still another myth brought to bear on *The Eve of St. Agnes*, akin to the view of Porphyro as rescuer of Madeline in reading 11 and relatable to the religious concerns grouped together in readings 36–42, is the "fortunate fall," the Romantics' secularized version of the original Fall as a liberation from an ideal state of innocence and ignorance into a more fulfilling realm of experience, consciousness, and process. David Wiener has made a case for the presence of this "secondary tradition" in Keats's poem, emphasizing the sterility and joylessness of Madeline's Edenic dream-world and Porphyro's role as "a Satanic hero removing his heroine from pristine innocence out into a fallen, but superior, world of experience, a vale of soul-making" (122). "Madeline's world is a paradise freed from mortal taint that does not go anywhere, that ultimately negates the very joys it seeks to enshrine . . . an Eden whose only virtue lies in its rejection. Porphyro makes possible Madeline's fortunate fall, and, given the nature of her paradise, it is indeed a fortunate fall regardless of what she will experience in the future" (126).

17. *Masturbatory ritual.*   This is the item that well-intentioned friends and colleagues, wishing to help me pare down so large and ungainly a number as fifty-nine readings of just a single poem, have most frequently recommended remov-

ing from the list. But the linking of Keats's poems and masturbation, far from being a late twentieth-century critical invention, dates from the poet's own time, showing up repeatedly in hostile contemporary reviews and in several now-famous comments about Keats in Byron's letters—for example, "Jack Keats . . . the *Onanism* of Poetry," "miserable Self-polluter of the human Mind," "a sort of mental masturbation—he is always f—gg—g his *Imagination*" (*Byron's Letters and Journals* 7:217, 225).

The modern version of such a view, taking off from Byron and the reviewers, is Marjorie Levinson's interpretation of Keats in terms of a "dream of mastur-bation: the fantasy of 'the perpetual cockstand', that solution to castration anxi-ety" (*Keats's Life* 26). *The Eve of St. Agnes*, in the 95-page chapter that she devotes to it, is a "masturbatory ritual," with Madeline as "self-seduced: ravished by her own voluptuous, voluntary, and in short masturbatory dreaming," while Porphyro, "melting" into her dream of him, in effect has sex with himself (161, 111, 107). Although intentionally extravagant, these statements usefully call attention to certain elements of luxurious self-indulgence of both principal char-acters and to a type of adolescent voyeurism on everybody's part that is easily associated with masturbatory fantasy: "Voyeurs ourselves, we watch another voyeur (Keats), watching another (Porphyro), watching a woman who broods voluptuously upon herself" (122). These elements are indisputable and for some of us—perhaps a sizable proportion of readers, both male and female—they are inextricably linked to our own self-indulgent pleasure in the sensations of the poem.

THE NEXT HALF-DOZEN READINGS, 18–23, are grouped under the heading of Imagi-nation, a faculty seemingly exercised by everybody in the poem, including the narrator. The Beadsman's religious imagination is fixed on the Virgin and the hereafter. Madeline, brooding "all that wintry day, / On love, and wing'd St. Agnes' saintly care" (lines 43–44), practices a ritual that will produce a dream-vision of her future husband. Porphyro's imagination comes to life like a cartoon lightbulb above his head: "Sudden a thought came like a full-blown rose . . . then doth he propose / A stratagem" (lines 136–39). Angela, foreseeing—that is, imagining—the practical consequences of Porphyro's stratagem, says that he must make Madeline an honest woman: "Ah! thou must needs the lady wed" (line 179). The narrator, for the most part describing events as they happen, looks ahead excitedly to Madeline's undressing: "Now prepare, / Young Porphyro, for gazing on that bed" (lines 196–97). In the final stanza, the kinsmen and revelers are having dreams as well, in this case, nightmares "Of witch, and demon, and large coffin-worm" (line 374). Obviously, imagination is a reiterated preoccupa-tion, but just what kind (or kinds) of imagination the poem is thought to empha-size and its attitudes toward imagination vary considerably among the readings.

18. *Authenticity of dreams.*   Dreaming is one of the commonest images in Ro-mantic poetry, and the various forms of "dream" as noun, adjective, and verb occupy many columns in the standard concordances. The word denotes or im-plies aspiration, ardent feeling, transcendent experience, special appearance, and

much else on the positive side. It also, more often, conveys unreality, emptiness, misplaced reliance, muddy thinking. Phrases such as "fallacious as a dream," "idle dream," "no dream, but things oracular," "unsubstantial dreams," "empty dreams," "wild dream, or worse illusion," "only in a dream," "unstable as a dream" abound in the period. When Wordsworth wants to emphasize the unreality of his experience as a student at Cambridge, he writes "I was the Dreamer, they the Dream" (1850 *Prelude* 3.30); and when, after the shipwreck death of his brother John, he rejects his former trust in the beneficence of nature, he associates it with the double mistake of dreaming and separating oneself from humanity:

> Farewell, farewell the heart that lives alone,
> Housed in a dream, at distance from the Kind!
> Such happiness, wherever it be known,
> Is to be pitied; for 'tis surely blind.
> (*Elegiac Stanzas* lines 53–56)

The ambiguous character of dreaming, true and wonderful on the one hand, false and perhaps even ruinous on the other, figures prominently all through Keats's most important work. The plot of *Endymion* proceeds from the hero's dream of an unknown goddess; much of the first book of the poem debates whether the dream-goddess is a reality, and for a while, at least, in the fourth book, Endymion decides that the dream he is pursuing is false: "I have clung / To nothing, lov'd a nothing, nothing seen / Or felt but a great dream!" (4.636–38).[6] *La Belle Dame* recounts "The latest dream I ever dream'd / On the cold hill's side" (lines 35–36), an enchanting experience that has paralyzed the knight who is telling the story. *Ode to Psyche* begins, after an invocation, "Surely I dreamt today, or did I see / The winged Psyche with awaken'd eyes?" (lines 5–6). *Ode to a Nightingale* ends with questions: "Was it a vision, or a waking dream? . . . Do I wake or sleep?" (lines 79–80; in Keats's draft in the Fitzwilliam Museum, Cambridge, the wording is "vision real or waking dream"). *Lamia* includes, among the working hypotheses of the introductory lines, the statement that "Real are the dreams of Gods, and smoothly pass / Their pleasures in a long immortal dream" (1.127–28); the main story relates the downfall of the dreamer Lycius, captivated by the snake-woman Lamia, whom he banishes, just before he dies, with "Begone, foul dream!" (2.271). The long introduction to *The Fall of Hyperion*, debating the connection between poetry and dreaming, includes this significant-sounding generalization about their difference: "The poet and the dreamer are distinct, / Diverse, sheer opposite, antipodes. / The one pours out a balm upon the world, / The other vexes it" (1.199–202).

With so many references to dreaming in Keats's poems overall, it is not surprising that critics have seized on the numerous references to dreams, visions, and the countering state of wakening in *The Eve of St. Agnes*. Madeline sighs "for Agnes' dreams, the sweetest of the year" (line 63); a central element of the plot is her ritually produced dream of Porphyro; when Madeline and Porphyro come together sexually, he melts "Into her dream" (line 320); awakening her to a reality that, as he says, is "no dream," he calls her his "sweet dreamer! lovely bride!" (lines 324, 334); and the outcome of the story is just what, in a sense, Porphyro has dreamed of all along. At a very basic level, the poem is about dreams becoming reality. Wolf Hirst, in his Twayne study of Keats, provides a handy representative description: "Madeline's dream of Porphyro, like Adam's of Eve, comes true. . . . Now [with the consummation] the imagined scene has been translated into actuality: Porphyro's dream has also come true. When he takes up Madeline's challenge to restore her lost dream vision, they die together into the higher life of immortal passion" (107–8).

19. *The visionary imagination succeeding (celebration).*   Hirst's mention of Adam's dream of Eve leads to the next level of allegorical abstraction, the first of two readings in which dreaming symbolizes the visionary imagination. In his most frequently quoted letter, to Benjamin Bailey, 22 November 1817, first published in Milnes's *Life* of the poet in 1848, Keats invites this interpretation by affirming "the truth of Imagination," relating the faculty to Adam's dream and suggesting that it provides "a Shadow of reality to come":

> I wish I was as certain of the end of all your troubles as that of your momentary start about the authenticity of the Imagination. I am certain of nothing but of the holiness of the Heart's affections and the truth of Imagination—What the imagination seizes as Beauty must be truth—whether it existed before or not. . . . The Imagination may be compared to Adam's dream—he awoke and found it truth. . . . It is "a Vision in the form of Youth" a Shadow of reality to come—and this consideration . . . has come as auxiliary to another favorite Speculation of mine, that we shall enjoy ourselves here after by having what we called happiness on Earth repeated in a finer tone and so repeated. . . . Adam's dream will do here and seems to be a conviction that Imagination and its empyreal reflection is the same as human Life and its spiritual repetition. (*Letters* 1:184–85)[7]

Both Newell Ford and Earl Wasserman, writing in the early 1950s, discern a Keatsian theory of visionary—that is, prefigurative, transcendental—imagination in this letter, and Wasserman in particular uses it as the grounds of an elaborate metaphysical reading in which Madeline's dream of Porphyro prefigures authentic truth and the lovers, immortalized by their passion, enjoy spiritual repetition of their earthly happiness "in a finer tone."

To this letter on the imagination, Wasserman adds three other basic texts for his reading: Keats's simile of life as a "Mansion of Many Apartments" (*Letters* 1:280–81); the Hymn to Pan from the first book of *Endymion*, with its reference to "the very bourne of heaven" (1.232 ff.); and Endymion's speech on gradations of happiness (1.777 ff.), which Keats, when he sent Taylor some revised lines for it in January 1818, called "a kind of Pleasure Thermometer," "a regular stepping of the Imagination towards a Truth" (*Letters* 1:218). Wasserman aligns these with Porphyro's upward progress from room to room in the castle, making his way to heaven's bourne in Madeline's bedchamber. Porphyro transcends his mortal existence by joining Madeline in the heaven of her dream, which thus, by his apotheosis, is turned into a truth. As I remarked early on, some of Wasserman's ideas and phrasings imply that both Madeline and Porphyro have prior knowledge of *Endymion*, Keats's letters, and Wasserman's own explication of the poem (*Hoodwinking* 72). Nowadays, however, I prefer to encourage (rather than reject) such overreading; Keats, after all, had written *Endymion* and his letters. Such intertextual allusions may well be part of the poem's texture, and, for the last forty-five years, serious readers have had Wasserman in addition to *Endymion* and the letters to influence their responses.

20. *The visionary imagination failing miserably (skepticism).*   It is the nature of intertextual connections among passages in a complex author's writings to produce varied and contradictory tendencies. A quite different view of visionary imagination from that in the previous reading—a view proposed by me in the early 1960s, A. D. Nuttall in the later 1980s, and others in between—relates Madeline's dream-state, not to Adam's dream and spiritual repetition in a finer tone, but to the unfortunate, sometimes disastrous consequences of dreaming and imagination depicted in other Keats poems of around the same time. The truth of imagination that Keats so passionately affirmed in his letter to Bailey may have been appropriate for 1817 and the happy outcome of *Endymion*, but it seems conspicuously absent in the work of 1819, or rather, seems to have turned into the opposite idea of *falsity* of imagination.[8]

Hints of a later skepticism toward the visionary imagination are already present in Endymion's (momentary) renunciation of dreams in book 4: his "great dream," he says, is "a nothing," consisting of "cloudy phantasms," "air of visions," "monstrous swell of visionary seas," and "airy voices" that "cheat" (4.637–38, 651–54). The distrustful attitude implied in such phrases accelerates during the winter of 1817–1818, when Keats was hard at work revising *Endymion* and at the same time becoming increasingly dissatisfied with his involvement in "poetic romance" (the subtitle of *Endymion*). Romance is a "barren dream" in his January 1818 sonnet *On Sitting Down to Read "King Lear" Once Again*. His verse epistle to John Hamilton Reynolds two months later sets forth the insufficiencies of dreaming; a crucial question about imagination is followed by the declaration that "It is a flaw / In happiness to see beyond our bourn" (*Dear Reynolds* lines 82–83). *Isabella*, the longest new work of the spring of 1818, starts out as courtly-love romance but turns into a story of murder, madness, and death, a grisly modernization, and implicit rejection, of "the gentleness of old Romance" (387), Boccaccio's tale that served as Keats's main source.

It could be argued that from this time forward in his career, Keats's most interesting protagonists, including the speakers in several of the odes, are characters who invest in some kind of imaginary attraction or ideal—a saint's life, a fairy enchantress, the timelessness of life painted on an ancient urn, the immortal conditions of a nightingale's forest, an impossible marriage with a snake-woman—but then learn (some of them too late) that their otherworldly investment, just like Endymion's in the renunciation passage of book 4, is "a nothing." Bertha in *The Eve of St. Mark*, ignoring the warm human life in the village outside her darkening room, is a "poor cheated soul" (line 69). The knight's love match with la Belle Dame ends in nightmare and paralysis. The "happy" life on the Grecian urn turns out to be death, cold, motionless, desolate, and the speaker's experience has been a "teas[ing] . . . out of thought" (line 44). Imagination in the Nightingale ode becomes "fancy," a "deceiving elf" famed for cheating (lines 73–74). The dreaming hero of *Lamia*, awakening to reality too late, falls dead at the end of the poem.[9]

In a skeptical reading of *The Eve of St. Agnes*, Madeline is another of these Keatsian overinvesters in visionary imagination who, like the Beadsman at the beginning of the poem, is engrossed in an ascetic practice that separates her from reality. Her ritual is an old wives' tale (line 45)—in the narrator's opinion, a "whim" (line 53)—and she is "Hoodwink'd with faery fancy," dead ("all amort") to the world around her (line 70). The unfeeling, unnatural character of her dreaming condition is conveyed in the paired images of lines 240–43: she is "Blissfully haven'd both from joy and pain" (a good situation if one wishes to escape pain, a bad situation if one desires joy), "Blinded alike from sunshine and from rain, / As though a rose should shut, and be a bud again." Angela uses "deceive" to describe Madeline's self-delusion (line 125); Madeline herself, awakening to learn that "This is no dream," calls herself "a deceived thing" (lines 326, 332). In fact, she may be triply deceived: by Angela (presumably the "traitor" of line 330), by Porphyro, and especially by her own trust in the superstitious ritual. In this reading, the poem exhibits the possibly dangerous unreliability of visionary thinking. Madeline's dream turns into some truths that she was not looking for: a Porphyro who is "pallid, chill, and drear" (line 311), the loss of her virginity, and the ambiguous conclusion of flight from the castle into an icy storm.

21. *Porphyro's creative (seizing, adaptive) imagination.* A quite different view of imagination in the poem focuses on Porphyro's rather than Madeline's mental activity. Leon Waldoff, in a 1977 essay revised as chapter 3 of his influential *Keats and the Silent Work of Imagination* (1985), is the most clearheaded and comprehensive of the arguers for Porphyro's centrality in the poem: "Porphyro is the hero . . . and, more important, the protagonist of a significant aspect of Keats's imagination" (*Keats* 64). Emphasizing the references to Porphyro's eyes (as in line 132, "But soon his eyes grew brilliant") and the related activities of seeing, gazing, feasting, and possessing, Waldoff reads Porphyro's quest as "a psychological allegory in which he represents the seizing and adaptive imagination" (79), a blend of the seizing imagination of Keats's 22 November 1817 letter to Bailey ("What the imagination seizes as Beauty . . .") and the creative, transforming faculty that Wordsworth celebrated in *Lyrical Ballads* and *The Excursion*. Porphyro, for Waldoff, "represents the romantic realist in Keats . . . the passionate, aspiring, and even heroic intensity of an imagination that will fly at desire, or win a peerless bride, or is forever winning near the goal" (81)—the exemplar, that is, of Keats's "position" concerning reality that pervades the poems of 1819 more generally.

Lyndel Colglazier reaches a similar conclusion about Porphyro's creative imagination, without reference to Waldoff, in a simpler essay of 1992. "Keats uses the context of romance in 'The Eve of St. Agnes' to explore the seductive mystery of imagination and its power to shape and alter perception, its capacity to envision the impossible as possible, to stretch reality's limits" (2). "As fanciful and wondrous as Madeline's visions may be, it is Porphyro who gives the better example of the imaginative heart working its way through reality, not excluding but including the tangible world of sense, with all its potential for perversion and evil" (8).

22. *Contrast (or conflict) of two kinds of imagination.* This reading takes the next logical step, in effect combining 20 and 21 in a "both/and" rather than "either/or" relationship: Madeline's is one kind of imagination, Porphyro's another, and the poem considers the particular efficacies and values of the two kinds. Leon Waldoff and Jean Hall pursue this line in their recent contributions to Evert and Rhodes's *Approaches to Teaching Keats's Poetry*. Waldoff's piece, "The Question of Porphyro's Stratagem," shorter but more complex than his essay of 1977 (reading 21), poses a practical question for classroom discussion to focus the poem's attitudes toward imagination: whether Porphyro's "stratagem" includes, from the start, the sexual consummation. The different lines of argument (as the students debate now one side, now another) lead to an interesting situation. If Porphyro all along intended to seduce Madeline, then the poem is "an expression of a skeptical, ironic, and antiromantic view of dreams, dreamers, and imagination." If he did not, however, then "he seems to make Madeline's dream come true . . . and the poem affirms romance and the power of imagination to bring desire to fulfillment" (41). There is plentiful evidence to support both views, as the students come to appreciate, and the classroom discussion mirrors the accumulated criticism more generally: "there is no definitive interpretation" (43).

   Hall, whose contribution is subtitled "Love's Dream and the Conflicted Imagination," reads (or has her students read) the poem as a rivalry of fantasies between Madeline's ritualism and Porphyro's activism, with, again, no clear-cut solution. The hero's action is manipulative and invasive, yet if he had not carried out his stratagem, "the lovers would have remained confined in their separate dreams," and Madeline's virginity would have been preserved "at the expense of her fulfillment" (126–27). "Students realize that the poem presents a dilemma: if Madeline's dreamworld is deceptive insofar as it avoids actualizing love, Porphyro's imagination actualizes love through a deception both immoral and dangerous." Neither side is approvable; yet both are essential for the "temporary harmony" achieved at the end (127).

23. *The hoodwinking of everyone (Beadsman, Angela, Madeline, Porphyro, the kinsmen and revelers).* The idea that all the characters are tricked in one way or another—the Beadsman by religious imagination, Angela by Porphyro's protestations, Madeline by her superstitious ritual, Porphyro by his devotion to Madeline, the kinsmen by the lovers as they tiptoe out of the castle—is not the richest possible reading of the poem. But it does suggest that there are more hoodwinked dreamers than just Madeline. Judy Little makes the point incidentally in *Keats as a Narrative Poet*, ending a list of the various deceptions with the

observation that "Keats does not supply, in this poem, a context by which we can direct skepticism [solely] at Madeline and Porphyro" (92).

THE NEXT THREE READINGS, grouped in Appendix B as a subdivision of the preceding concern with imagination, see some form of Wish-fulfillment as a (or the) major theme of the poem. Stuart Sperry (in reading 26) is the most comprehensive, and the most frequently cited, of the critics taking this approach, but it is a widespread view, bound up with the notions of desire, fantasy, and romance (as a cast of mind rather than a literary mode) all at once. The discriminations that follow are purely a matter of convenience; the numbered list could be expanded indefinitely on this topic, and, conversely, the complexities of the various types of wish-fulfillment could as well be generalized into a single reading.

24. *Narrative of desire.* "Narrative of desire" is Martin Aske's phrase (198), in a primarily phenomenological reading of the function of doors and chambers in the poem. "In effect the mansion becomes for Porphyro a series of thresholds, each one to be mastered and crossed before he can proceed to his desired object. . . . The geography of the home is integral to Porphyro's tracing of magical spaces and contours prior to discovering the ultimate space of Madeline's chamber" (201). The climax involves "transformations, displacements, magical traffickings between self and object, the caressing and intermingling of dream-spaces" (205). Keats's images and syntax alike work to dispel our worries about Porphyro's motives and Madeline's foolishness. "The poem externalizes the lovers' dream-desires in a veritable erotics of space" (208).

25. *Fantasy of wish-fulfillment.* Miriam Allott, in an early essay on Keats's principal narratives of 1818–1819, describes a pattern common to the group (and, in part, to the major odes as well) in which a lover falls into a swoon or sleep, passes into some kind of enchantment or love-trance, experiences intense indulgence of the senses culminating in lovemaking, then awakens to a repellent and hostile reality ("'Isabella'" 47). Allott's special focus is the narratives' "romantic dissatisfaction with the actual" (45), represented in the final awakening that exposes the wish-fulfillment as mere fantasy. *The Eve of St. Agnes* fits the description if we take the "lover" to be Porphyro and Madeline jointly, acting out between them selected elements of the pattern. Allott grants that "the experience of love is a happy one" in the poem (47); yet "our main interest ought . . . to be in the remarkable change of tone within the story at the awakening from enchantment to reality" (55).

26. *Successful merging of romance and reality, or of beauty and truth.* It is the *merging* of the two sides of a fundamental Keatsian antithesis, rather than the (inevitable) canceling of one side or the other, that has always been the chief desideratum, the very pinnacle of everybody's wish list, starting with Keats himself. Romance and reality are standard opposites, in both logic and human experience, and the impossibility of ultimately bringing them together is represented everywhere in Keats's plots, characters, and numerous details of

imagery. For a single epitomizing example, consider the implications of line 243 of *The Eve of St. Agnes*: the rose *cannot* "shut, and be a bud again"; there is no other way to read this particular image. These stern facts of logic and life have not, however, prevented readers of *The Eve of St. Agnes* from believing that such a union of romance and reality is possible, or at least that Keats, by his brilliant rhetorical art, had the skill to make it seem so for the duration of the poem.

Stuart Sperry's seminal reading of the poem as a drama of wish-fulfillment is a case in point. "*St. Agnes* is a poem about the etherealizing power of human desire and passion . . . an exceptionally subtle study of the psychology of the imagination and its processes, a further testing . . . of the quality and limits of poetic belief. More than anything else, perhaps, the element most central to the poem is its concern with wish-fulfillment" (*Keats the Poet* 202). This concern is "equally primitive and fundamental to the nature of romance, as well as to 'romanticism,' in all its various forms: the power of wishing, willing, and the kind of fulfillment it can bring in fiction, love, and art" (218). Sperry's careful exegesis finds it in Porphyro's action, in Madeline's accommodation between imagination and reality, and in Keats's overall meaning. The success of the union, and of the poem, lies in Keats's skillful manipulation of tones, conventions, genres, and psychological devices. The poem is simultaneously serious and playful (Madeline is "a little child put to bed early with visions of sugar plums," Porphyro comes onstage "like a big Italian tenor" [201]). It combines domestic realism with religious ritual, Gothicism, courtly love, opera, folk legend, and fairy tale, both using and parodying their conventions at the same time; and it invokes, along with the high romance, the countering tendencies of repression, anxiety, disguise, censorship, and sublimation (205). For Sperry, so much is happening in the poem, and happening so artfully, that the "stern facts of logic and life" get no chance to register.

Practically all subsequent critics owe something to Sperry's interpretation. Constance Rooke, for example, in a simpler essay of 1978, likewise reads the poem as a dramatic contest between romance and reality, arguing "that reality is not restricted to the frame, that romance is characteristic of more than the internal picture, and that there is very considerable interaction between contrasting elements" (27). By the end of the action, "Porphyro, the worldly pursuer of stratagems, has been successful equally with Madeline, the dreamer. The beauty of imagination has joined with truth; the lovers on the Grecian Urn have come together" (37). Robert Kern, in an essay of 1979, develops the importance of the narrator as "a practiced and self-conscious manipulator of romantic conventions" who provides the irony, distance, and perspective necessary to keep the reader aware of the fictionality of the poem's high romance (de Almeida, *Critical Essays* especially 78–84). Charles Rzepka, whose section on the poem in *The Self as Mind* (1986) is headed "Miraculous Stratagems" (thus bringing together the contrary notions of Porphyro's success as both a stratagem and a religious miracle), similarly emphasizes the poem's theatricality and the impingement of waking dreams and reality (193–204).

THE NEXT NINE READINGS, 27–35, form a group under the heading Poetry, Art, Creativity, a group in which literary art is not just the product of Keats's efforts but a principal thematic preoccupation as well.

27. *Parable (allegory) of literary creativity.*   Though everyone in the 1950s was reading poems as being primarily about poetry, C. F. Burgess in an essay of 1965 appears to have been the first to locate this kind of self-reflexivity in *The Eve of St. Agnes.* "Porphyro's plight parallels that of the poet himself. Keats made this same journey into the imaginative world on a number of occasions only to find that return is inevitable. The world of the castle and especially Madeline's charmed bower is the world of the nightingale which the poet can reach for one transcendent moment only; it is the world of the Grecian urn, 'forever warm' and 'forever young,' realized for an instant and then lost again." Unlike the odes, however, the narrative "represents a triumph of imagination," because Porphyro, returning to his real world outside the castle, brings Madeline with him. Thus, "Porphyro's invasion of the enchanted castle may be read as a parable of the poetic process"; "the journey into the regions of the fancy is not without purpose if, like Porphyro, the poet can bring back a token, that is, the poem itself" (394).

James Wilson finds a more elaborate set of allegorical equivalences two decades later. The poem "is about the process of its own composition, a self-reflexive narrative that traces . . . the evolution of a poem from the artist's initial inspiration to create, through the necessary union of unfocused imagination and purposeful direction, to culmination in transcendent artistic achievement." Madeline represents "unstructured, holy imagination" in Wilson's scheme, while Porphyro is the embodiment of "reasoned, calculated or measured thought." The Beadsman and Angela, "lesser though necessary functionaries, represent the poet and poetic structure respectively" (46).

28. *Antiromance; illustration of the limitations of romance.*   It has been common practice since the 1960s (as in my "Keats and Romance: The Reality of *Isabella,*" *Hoodwinking* 31–45) to make something of the antiromantic tendencies of Keats's romantic poems. Keats himself offers a basis for this in several passages of his letters—for example, his remarks to Bailey about the ineffectualness of "skyey Knight errantry" on 23 January 1818 (*Letters* 1:209). An impressive list of seemingly antiromantic sentiments can be gathered from the poems, as in *The Eve of St. Agnes* lines 40–41, where mention of "triumphs gay / Of old romance" is followed by the abruptly dismissive "These let us wish away." "Romance" has many different overlapping meanings, of course, but in so literary a poem as *The Eve of St. Agnes,* it is difficult not to take "romance" as a reference to, among other topics, romance literature.

Beth Lau, in "Madeline at Northanger Abbey: Keats's Anti-Romances and Gothic Satire," connects Keats's narratives with contemporary satires such as Eaton Stannard Barrett's *The Heroine* (1813) and Jane Austen's *Northanger Abbey* (1818) directed against Gothic and sentimental literature of the time. "What

Keats's anti-romances share with [these] Gothic parodies . . . is a warning of the ills that befall young women whose heads have been turned by too much romance reading and who can no longer distinguish the land of fiction from reality" (30). Madeline is not a reader of early nineteenth-century romances, obviously, but her belief in the fantasy world of old wives' tales about St. Agnes' Eve is a medieval counterpart. Keats does not, in Lau's view, "reject outright the Gothic and larger romance tradition. . . . What he did wish to do in *St. Agnes* was to expose the worst abuses and greatest dangers of romance and, chiefly by means of a self-conscious manipulation of stock conventions that is at times playful, at times ironic, to invest the genre with greater sophistication and authority" (47).

Antiromance also figures in Neil Fraistat's discussion of the poem in the context of Keats's 1820 volume overall. "Ultimately, 'The Eve of St. Agnes' is a romance whose concern is the limitations of romance" (115), and in this presentation it is Keats's narrator, even more than Madeline, who suffers a rough return to the actual world. "The consequence of enchantment is invariably disenchantment"; the narrator at the end is "trapped between a paradisal vision of fulfilled desire and a hellish reality" (118).

29. *Remake of* Romeo and Juliet I: *imitation.*   Each of Keats's long narratives has significant connections to a specific precursor. *Endymion*, besides being an elaborate expansion of the legend of the eponymous shepherd prince in Lemprière's *Classical Dictionary*, is a reworking of the plot and the themes of Percy Shelley's *Alastor*. *Isabella* is a retelling of one of Boccaccio's tales in the *Decameron*, with lengthy self-conscious apologies to both the original author and the modern reader. *Lamia* expands, versifies, and thematizes a story in Burton's *Anatomy of Melancholy*, and Keats again, as he had in *Isabella*, calls attention to his principal source, this time by actually printing it in a note to the last line of the poetic text.

The precursor of *The Eve of St. Agnes* in this scheme is *Romeo and Juliet*, which has counterparts for Porphyro, Madeline, Angela, and the Beadsman, narrative similarities in the feuding families and details of the lovers' wooing and elopement, and numerous likenesses with Keats's poem in wording and imagery. C. L. Finney is one of several early scholars to discuss the relationship between the play and the poem (2:543–54 passim); Jonathan Bate is prominent among the more recent (*Shakespeare* especially 186–87). In her annotated *Poems of John Keats*, Miriam Allott points out echoes of the play in more than twenty notes to the poem. R. S. White adds information from Keats's marking of the play in his 1808 reprint of the First Folio (now at Keats House, Hampstead) and suggests that Keats's view of Shakespeare's lovers was influenced by William Hazlitt's *Characters of Shakespear's Plays* (159–68).

One way of viewing the poem in relation to the play is illustrated by Roger Sharrock's "Keats and the Young Lovers," arguing that Keats is "not just the supreme poet for adolescents, but supremely the adolescent poet" whose main theme—in *Isabella*, *The Eve of St. Agnes*, and *Lamia* in particular—is "a pair of young lovers . . . set down in the middle of a cold and hostile adult world" (79–80). The repeated question of these narratives ("as the adolescent mind guesses and gropes its way into the world of love") is "how can romantic love be possible in a harsh grown-ups' world?" (81). One provisional answer—certainly more upbeat than the heart-wrenching outcome of *Romeo and Juliet*—is to get the lovers quietly out of the castle before the Baron and his warrior-guests recover from their drunken nightmares.

30. *Remake of* Romeo and Juliet *II: modernization (*"tough-minded 'modern' recasting" as in* Isabella*).*   In another possible view of the relationship with Shakespeare's play, Keats is, in effect, on the side of the adults rather than the adolescents. The parenthetical phrase in the heading just above, quoted from a 1968 essay that I reprinted in *The Hoodwinking of Madeline*, refers to the narrator's stance in *Isabella* as reteller of an old story that, in Boccaccio's original, is too sentimental and naive for the narrator's more sophisticated, more practical modern perspective. Boccaccio's tale is "the gentleness of old Romance, / The simple plaining of a minstrel's song" (*Isabella* lines 387–88); Keats's modernization, emphasizing with medical-school precision the "wormy circumstance" of the murder, the exhumation, the decapitation of the corpse, and the rotting of the severed head, turns courtly-love romance into a tale of betrayal, isolation, madness, and death.

The contrast between modern version and the precursor original is not so striking in *The Eve of St. Agnes*. But the antiromantic elements mentioned so far in this chapter—the details of Porphyro's stratagem, the questionableness of his motives, the peeping-Tom/rapist aspects of his behavior, the silliness of Madeline's self-delusion, the self-denial of the Beadsman, the weakness of Angela, the drunkenness of the revelers, the potential deadliness of the storm—are all on the side of realism, skepticism, and practicality. Perhaps Keats was contrasting them with the "gentleness of old Romance"—in this instance, a type of romantic love story where moral problems and dangers are played down rather than emphasized—in order to expose the sentimentality that a stock response like reading 29 necessarily involves. All through his career, in poems and letters alike, Keats was acutely aware of differences between his own situation as a modern and that of poets of an earlier, simpler age; the realistic elements of *The Eve of St. Agnes* may be another product of this awareness.

31. *Exercise in Gothicism.*   Keats is one of the two best-known Gothic writers in British poetry (Coleridge is the other), and *The Eve of St. Agnes* is his most sustained production in the Gothic mode. We are given the requisite setting in a medieval castle, an innocent maiden, a seducer-antagonist, hostile kinsmen, a beadsman, an ineffectively protective female, religious images, prayers, curses, superstition, witchcraft, candlelight, moonlight, the tolling of bells, dream-visions, a midnight visit, spying from a closet, sex, and corpses. By the time the lovers escape the castle, the "sleeping dragons" that Madeline thinks she sees "all around" (line 353) are just part of the Gothic furniture.

The most comprehensive expounder of Gothic elements in the poem is Rosemarie Maier, who, in an essay titled "The Bitch and the Bloodhound," sets forth the "generic similarity" between Keats's poem and Coleridge's *Christabel*. There are several ways to view the Gothicism in both these works. In reading 31, Keats can be thought of as taking up a challenge, just as he says he did in writing *Endymion*, to create a narrative poem out of "one bare circumstance" (in this case, the popular superstition connected with St. Agnes' Eve) as "a test, a trial of my Powers of Imagination and chiefly of my invention" (*Letters* 1:169–70). Prose Gothic romances were the thing to write at the time; Keats met the challenge in poetry.

Anne Williams, giving a detailed account of similarities and differences between Keats's poem and Matthew Gregory Lewis's *The Monk*, reads the poem as a Gothic rescue fantasy in which, however, the generic signals are never stabilized: it is neither traditional male Gothic (as in, for example, Horace Walpole's *The Castle of Otranto*) nor traditional female Gothic (as in Ann Radcliffe's novels) but a mixture of the two modes (*Art of Darkness* 226–38).

32. *Satire on (parody of) Gothicism.* This reading, the next step up from the preceding, acknowledges Gothic elements but detects a satiric or parodic intention behind them, again (as in readings 28 and 30) primarily because of the intercalation of realistic details and sentiments. Maier comments on Keats's strong irony and earthiness in the poem (69, 75). Lau views the poem as a warning to young women against too much reading of Gothic romances. John Collick is another critic who reads the poem as parody, but this time with a specific point concerning the depiction of desire and sexual activity in poetry. In Collick's view, Keats means to show that desire and sex cannot be adequately expressed in the Gothic mode because in passage after passage the principals, especially Madeline, are displaced by details of architecture, art, or decoration (the shielded scutcheon in the famous triple-arched window, for example). The eleven stanzas leading up to Madeline's awakening (lines 199–297) are "a futile attempt to embody passion and sex in poetic language. . . . Porphyro and Madeline are incapable of actually uniting fully within the poem because they are manifestations of that poem itself . . . set in an oppressive and authoritarian quasi-Gothic world" (42). Collick emphasizes the frequency with which Keats's (or his narrator's) warm-blooded human characters turn into pictures or statues.

33. *Completion of Coleridge's* Christabel. After *Romeo and Juliet*, the next most influential precursor for *The Eve of St. Agnes* is the fragmentary *Christabel*, written in 1798–1800 but not published until May 1816 and therefore a fairly recent work (and much in the public eye) when Keats drafted *St. Agnes* two and a half years later. The numerous similarities between *Christabel* and Keats's poems— especially *St. Agnes* and *Lamia*—have been discussed in detail by Rosemarie Maier and James Twitchell and listed in tabular form by Beth Lau (*Keats's Reading* 95– 101). Twitchell, citing Maier, even suggests that in *St. Agnes* Keats was "consciously retelling" Coleridge's poem (*Living Dead* 94). The relationship is important. Porphyro and Geraldine are not exact counterparts in their roles as demonic seducer-antagonists, and Coleridge appears to have had abstract metaphysical and theological concerns in his work that Keats, focusing more practically on human-centered problems, probably did not share. But the two works mutually illuminate one another in many particulars of theme, image, and narrative detail. *Christabel* was published as a fragment (Coleridge makes a point of this in

his 1816 preface, saying that he hopes to supply "the three parts yet to come, in the course of the present year"); Keats, for purposes of an interesting reading, can be thought of as carrying the work to completion.

34. *Rich Romantic tapestry.* This is an older view of the poem, starting with Keats's contemporaries (see note 2 to this chapter) and continuing at least into the 1960s. Hugh Miller in the middle of the nineteenth century called it "a gorgeous gallery of poetic pictures" (quoted in Wasserman 99); William Michael Rossetti characterized it as "a monody of dreamy richness, a pictured and scenic presentment," in which Keats was "making pictures out of words, or turning words into pictures" (182–83); Douglas Bush uses the terms "opulent romantic tapestry" and "gorgeous tapestry" (*Selected Poems and Letters* 339; *John Keats* 111). Certainly the poem fits these enthusiastic descriptions. And tapestry and carpets are mentioned in lines 251, 285, 358–60, while the predominant colors (various shades and combinations of red and blue) and the incidental presence of animals and birds all through the poem can be seen as further connections with medieval tapestry. The critics who support this view, however, point to the pictorial and tapestry effects as a way of saying that the poem lacks both narrative interest and moral or philosophical meaning, that is, to quote Bush a third time, "*no more than* a romantic tapestry" (*Selected Poems* xvi).

35. *Pure aestheticism: art is the only thing that matters.* A more reflexive reading in the same vein deems the poem a serious statement about the nature and importance of art. Many of Keats's closest friends were artists, musicians, and writers. He spent much of his time, when he was not creating art of his own, relishing other people's art in performances, exhibitions, musical evenings, and in lengthy discussions of such topics as the supreme importance of beauty over everything else. His poems are full of artworks, not just striking verbal descriptions that constitute "art" in themselves but real or imaginary paintings, sculptures, "marbles," urns, weavings, illuminated manuscripts, and architectural and household decorations of every sort. His incorporation of artworks into his poetry, frequently noticed by critics, has been studied at length by Ian Jack and Grant Scott, among others.

His poems have provided inspiration and subjects for hundreds of paintings and other graphic illustrations since his death, with a special concentration of activity among the Pre-Raphaelite Brotherhood, a group of artists and writers formed in the same year that R. M. Milnes issued his *Life* of Keats (see Julie Codell's "Painting Keats" and the references there).[10] In now-famous letters made public for the first time in 1848, Keats tells his brothers that "with a great poet the sense of Beauty overcomes every other consideration, or rather obliterates all consideration"; he mentions to Woodhouse "the mere yearning and fondness I have for the Beautiful" and to his brother and sister-in-law in America "the mighty abstract Idea I have of Beauty in all things," and says (again to George and Georgiana), "I never can feel certain of any truth but from a clear perception of its Beauty" (*Letters* 1:194, 388, 403; 2:19). Such utterances, richly backed by his mature poetry, made Keats an instant hero to the Pre-Raphaelites, and along with further memorable statements in letters that surfaced later in the century—for example, his remark to Fanny Brawne, "I have lov'd the principle of beauty in all things" (2:263)—established him as a chief representative of British aestheticism for a span of decades well into the 1920s.

All these facts and quotations can serve as background to any reading of *The Eve of St. Agnes* that emphasizes Keats's consciousness of art as a principal subject of the poem. An interesting recent example is Wendy Steiner's, in *Pictures of Romance*, which views the work as an amalgam of images and motifs from the life of St. Agnes and the story of Cupid and Psyche in which Keats is directly concerned with the relationship of narrative to visual art. "The poem . . . sets up a consistent meaning for the visual arts by merging the experience of visual aesthetic perception with that of passive enthrallment. It establishes an implicit hierarchy within the arts, with painting at the very bottom, then frieze and sculpture, then stained-glass window with its blending of material artifact and spiritual light, and then tapestry with its connection to weaving, text, and process art. . . . Whatever transcendence is possible in life is antithetical to the closed, eternal beauty of these arts" (73).

IN THE NEXT GROUP, readings 36–42, we turn from art to interpretations that focus on religion. Keats was brought up as a Christian, and his letters show him to have been well versed in the Bible and theological matters (Robert Ryan's *Keats: The Religious Sense* is still the best authority). *The Eve of St. Agnes* invokes the life and attributes of a saint and uses religious language and symbols throughout. How seriously should we read these religious elements? Many poets before Keats, including Shakespeare in *Romeo and Juliet*, have routinely employed religious terms in hyperbolic love language, writing about saints, pilgrims, shrines, angels, heaven, paradise, and hell as a way of describing human lovers' hopes, passions, and despair. Even so, and with full awareness of the religious aspects of courtly-love and romance traditions, some readers think that Keats's religious language in the poem was meant to convey religious or antireligious ideas.

36. *Religion of experience.* A 1973 essay by Douglas Atkins, "*The Eve of St. Agnes* Reconsidered," can exemplify the very general notion that Keats (or the poem) makes a religion out of the richness of human experience. The Beadsman's stereotypical Christian asceticism is rejected, in Atkins's view, for "a vibrant, joyous, and efficacious alternative"—namely, Madeline and Porphyro's love for one another, which, although described in the same kind of religious terms used in the passages about the Beadsman, is grounded in reality rather than fantasy or delusion (119). "The poem never leaves us in any doubt as to where religious meaning lies. Here, as elsewhere in Keats, it is squarely in and through, but not beyond, the physical" (123). In asserting this value, the poem serves the same function as traditional religion. It "graphically illustrates that some human fulfillment is possible, and in thus showing this possibility for consolation it acts as balm" (130).

37. *Religion of beauty.* Another secular alternative to the Beadsman's Christianity is the humanistic scheme set forth by Ronald Sharp in *Keats, Skepticism, and the Religion of Beauty* (1979). Sharp takes his cue from passages in Keats's letters—for example, remarks to Bailey in November 1817 that "the Beautiful . . . the poetical in all things" could be a better consolation than traditional religion for wrongs in the world, and that love and the rest of our passions are "creative of essential Beauty" (*Letters* 1:179, 184)—and reads *The Eve of St. Agnes* as a "version of that fully humanized religion of beauty which emerges not as an escape from reality but as a conscious choice to find consolation in a world of transience and suffering" (38). Porphyro is "the messenger of the new religion"; Madeline's "conversion to Porphyro's humanized religion represents an embracing of life . . . [which includes] pain as well as pleasure, sorrow as well as joy" (42, 45). The saving "miracle" that Porphyro refers to in line 339 is "the beauty of love, which, like all beauty, is mysteriously sacred," the more so because, in the life-affirming terms of *Endymion* 1.7, it "binds us to the earth" (46–47).

38. *Love as a religious sacrament.* James Boulger, in an essay on Keats's symbolism, offers a specific set of correspondences between details in the poem and the Christian ritual of the Eucharist. "Madeline's room is the scene for the performance of the mysteries and the miracle . . . a fit repository for such a sacred action." She approaches it "like a mission'd spirit," kneels, prays, and prepares her body for a love sacrifice. Her bed is the altar; Porphyro acts the part of the adoring congregation; and there are the ritualistic food offering, a sacrifice table, and an altar cloth. The climax is Porphyro's "consummation with his *Agnus Dei*," Madeline in her role as the Lamb of God (256–58). "Keats has subsumed the conventional religious symbolism of Christian ritual for a very special purpose in this poem. . . . Love has replaced the Eucharist as the sacrament in his system. . . . By borrowing and reworking for his own purpose the central mystery of the Christian ritual, clearly removed from its original sacred context, he was able to use the Beadsman as a foil to develop successfully, in this poem at least, the *mysterium fidei* of his own sacramental universe" (258–59).

39. *Keats's attack on religion.* For Robin Mayhead, in a short introductory volume written for students and general readers, each of the four characters fills an allegorical role: the Beadsman "represents orthodox Christianity at its most austere"; Angela is another Christian figure at a "more ordinary" level; "Madeline's position is midway between Christianity and paganism"; Porphyro "stands very much for the human and unsanctified" (50–52). Because the Beadsman and Angela are dead at the end, and the lovers, escaping the castle, leave "the spiritual aspect behind with the dead bodies" of the two old people, Mayhead suggests that the poem is "an attack upon institutional Christianity, a celebration of earthly joys at the expense of religious orthodoxy"—though not an entirely one-sided attack, since "the storm into which the lovers fly is pregnant with ominous possibilities" (54–55).

40. *Ironic version of the Annunciation.*   This reading is developed in detail by Gail Gibson, reacting to the iconographical assemblage by Katherine Garvin (see reading 5) and arguing that the religious language and imagery of the poem are "neither consistently articulated Catholic theology (nor Anglican nor any other kind) nor merely gratuitous atmospheric effects, but part of a recurrent and ironic use . . . of a Christian myth—the Annunciation by Gabriel to the Virgin Mary" as represented in thousands of paintings and other graphic forms from the Middle Ages and the Renaissance (41). The references to Mary begin with the Beadsman's rosary and "the sweet Virgin's picture" in lines 6 and 9 and continue in what Gibson calls "a small but continuous thread" all through the narrative: the atmosphere of waiting and penance; mentions of lily, violet, rose, dove wings, halo, and weaving; the extinguishing of candlelight; the position of Porphyro close to Madeline's ear, which in the paintings signifies God's speaking through Gabriel's mouth into Mary's ear, resulting in the miraculous *conceptio per aurem* (43–48). For Gibson, the important implication of the Annunciation story is "its resolution of the otherwise irresolvable contraries of immortal and mortal experience" (42). Keats's version is ironic, even parodic, but not primarily for purposes of satire. "The parodied Annunciation . . . emphasizes the inadequate nature of Madeline's and Porphyro's heaven in each other . . . [and] man's necessarily ephemeral realization of love and beauty" (50).

41. *Parody of a saint's life.*   Still another interesting set of correspondences has been pointed out—by Tom Stillinger in an unpublished paper of 1973 and Wendy Steiner in her book of 1988 (*Pictures* 60–66)—between Keats's poem and the legend of St. Agnes as recounted in one of the standard lives of the saints. Agnes and Madeline reject the advances of worldly lovers to remain faithful to their envisioned future husbands (Christ and Porphyro, respectively); the bridegrooms offer them feasts and other favors; there is major emphasis on their chastity; both women figure in a brothel or brothel-like situation, and both are the objects of lewd viewing; Madeline's disrobing and letting down her hair are counterparts of Agnes' preparing for her execution; both women suffer a form of martyrdom (in Madeline's case, the loss of her virginity). A conspicuous difference, as with the details of the Eucharist (reading 38) and the Annunciation (reading 40), is the outcome, which for these critics makes Keats's version an ironic or parodic refashioning rather than a more straightforward modern retelling. In Tom Stillinger's account, "a vision of eternity is debased into a preview of domestic happiness" at best. Steiner comments summarily, "Whereas Agnes becomes an immortal saint singing eternally with the angels and appearing with her lamb before the faithful, Porphyro and Madeline fade into shadows, fleeing into the snow of the distant romance past" (65–66).

42. *Paganism versus religion; the triumph of old religion over Christianity.*   This is another version of reading 13, but here the main focus is the poem's attitude toward Christianity rather than the machinery of competing myth systems. Marcia Gilbreath, investigating the etymology of Porphyro's name, proposes connections with the giant Porphyrion, one of the fallen Titans who waged war

against Jupiter and the Olympians. In Joseph Spence's mid-eighteenth-century *Polymetis*, a book that Keats read at Clarke's school, Porphyrion is among the "strange monsters in the antient mythology" who "seem to have been pretty exact emblems of the disbelievers so much in fashion in our times." In Burton's *Anatomy*, the rebel giants "are commonly professed Atheists," exhibit "monstrous melancholie," and "scoffe at all Religion," caring only "to satisfie their lust and appetite." In Abbé Banier's *Mythology and Fables of the Ancients*, a work of about the same time as Spence's, Porphyrion is in a class with robbers, ruffians, and rapists. Gilbreath offers these references as background for a reading in which Porphyro's paganism triumphs over the contrasting Christian values established in the poem. "Just as Madeline in one sense is St. Agnes, so Porphyro is a young pagan ravisher with no regard for the religious taboo he is breaking. In short, Porphyro represents eros, the pagan life force, reasserting its claim as a legitimate suitor to the poetic imagination from which it had been too long estranged by the barren religious ideal of sexual purity" (25).

THE NEXT THREE READINGS, 43–45, make a more general point about human experience in the poem. Jacqueline Banerjee, in a recent essay on the treatment of Keats by several kinds of historicist criticism, remarks in passing that *The Eve of St. Agnes* "can be seen as a moving allegory of the human condition, with Keats himself yearning over the splendor of romance but poignantly recognizing its limitations" (533). The chief limitation of romance is of course its inability to accommodate the human realities of time and death.

43. *Mortality and Madeline's fall from innocence.*   The most original and comprehensive work on the poem's concern with mortality is Michael Ragussis's 1975 essay, "Narrative Structure and the Problem of the Divided Reader in *The Eve of St. Agnes*," revised as chapter 4 in *The Subterfuge of Art* (1978). Ragussis begins with Woodhouse's report on the ending of the poem after he heard Keats read the revised version in September 1819: "[Keats] has altered the last 3 lines to leave on the reader a sense of pettish disgust. . . . He says he likes that the poem should leave off with this Change of Sentiment—it was what he aimed at, and was glad to find from my objections that he had succeeded." Ragussis thinks Keats meant to "divide" the reader (as he clearly divided Woodhouse) between the "happy romance" aspects of the story and "the poem's dark conclusion"—the storm, the drunken revelers, the nightmares of witch, demon, and coffin-worm, the deaths of Angela and the Beadsman. This divisive "Change of Sentiment," which has always been a problem in reading and interpreting, is for Ragussis basically a problem of narrative structure. The key to resolving it lies in the character of Keats's narrator, whose changes of perspective on the story parallel those of Madeline herself: she, the narrator, *and* the reader—all three—unexpectedly awaken to reality at the end. The awakening is a fall from innocence into the world of experience, the world of natural process with its inescapable entailment of mortality.

In support of this reading, Ragussis quotes two passages from Keats's spring 1819 journal letter to George and Georgiana, written in the next several weeks after he drafted the poem. In one of them, under the date of 21 April, leading into the famous treatise on the world as a "vale of Soul-making," Keats considers the vulnerability of the rose: "Suppose a rose to have sensation, it blooms on a beautiful morning it enjoys itself—but there comes a cold wind, a hot sun—it can not escape it, it cannot destroy its annoyances—they are as native to the world as itself" (*Letters* 2:101). Ragussis connects this with the poem's comparison of Madeline to a rose. " 'The Eve of St. Agnes' is organized around the basic analogy of this letter: all men, like the creatures of nature, are ultimately subject to time and the worldly elements" (*Subterfuge* 78). The other letter passage, written on 19 March, is similar in tendency: "This is the world. . . . Circumstances are like Clouds continually gathering and bursting—While we are laughing the seed of some trouble is put into the wide arable land of events" (2:79). For Ragussis, this passage "explicitly describes what the poem enacts at several levels. The encounter with reality is seen essentially as an unexpected encounter with time, with natural process" (*Subterfuge* 81). Ultimately the poem illustrates Keats's "sense of uncompromising truthfulness"; "even as we temporarily enter the distant past that art revives, and even within the apparent framework of the regressive dream, we find to our surprise an enactment of the inevitable passage out of innocence" (84).

44. *Tragedy.* More than fifty years ago, Herbert Wright asked a provocative question in the title of a short article in *Modern Language Review*: "Has Keats's 'Eve of St. Agnes' a Tragic Ending?" Critics have been pondering the question ever since, citing Wright and responding with their own opinions (see reading 59 for a representative sampling). On the basis of a long list of dark, foreboding details of atmosphere and description in the poem, along with consideration of the pessimistic outcomes of other poems written by Keats at about the same time and parallels with the conclusion of *Romeo and Juliet*, Wright's own answer is that the lovers die at the end. "They escape from the inmates of the castle, but only to be engulfed in the storm. The climax is reached, and we know that Porphyro and Madeline are gone for ever. . . . The tragedy of Porphyro and Madeline, so dramatic in its suspense, is over, and an austere calm descends. Death the omnipotent has come to young and old" (93–94).

45. *The inconsequentiality of human life (death takes all).*   An even gloomier view, in accord with the ideas of natural process and "Death the omnipotent" in readings 43 and 44, is the realization that, whatever the immediate outcome (the subject of Wright's query), the lovers and everyone else in the poem have been dead for centuries and that, somehow in keeping with this somber Macbethian note at the end ("they should have died hereafter"), human life does not much matter in the long run. This may be one implication of the pointed distancing of events in line 370: "And they are gone: ay, ages long ago." Some readers have even imagined the lovers growing old together, becoming increasingly feeble and dying in old age. Jeffrey Baker, for example, at the conclusion of his essay on Aphrodite and the Virgin, thinks we should "suppose the best for them. At the end of it all they will be like the Beadsman and Angela. Porphyro who spurred

across the moors with heart on fire will shuffle, meagre, barefoot wan; Madeline, who danced along with vague, regardless eyes will hobble off, beset with busy fears, and agues in her brain" (108). This is not exactly a reading of the poem as such, but it responds to some prominent lines at the beginning of the final stanza.

SIX MORE READINGS, 46–51, are grouped (in Appendix B) under the heading Epistemology, Ambiguity. These emphasize several kinds of uncertainty, distortion, and contradiction, arguing that the disjunctions are more important than either the overall story or the closure.

46. *Uncertainty of the phenomenal world.*   The most alert reader of the architectural details, Alan Boehm, in "Madeline's Castle: Setting and Visual Discrepancy," makes a case for two contradictory kinds of description of physical reality in the poem. On one hand, the tangible, concrete particulars have always been admired as part of the famous "opulent romantic tapestry." On the other hand, coexisting with the tangible and the certain are "disturbing effects of fragmentation, spatial and architectural distortions, a grotesque confusion of sculptured and human forms, and other optical uncertainties that undermine or complicate the beauty and concreteness of the castle setting" (21). Boehm finds examples of "visual discrepancy" all through the text. The castle itself, which at first seems so solid, unified, and interconnected, consists of "disjointed pieces of architecture . . . an unorganized jumble" of chambers, passages, hallways, windows, and doors (22). Except for the main characters, people are synecdoches rather than human figures: the partygoers are "argent revelry . . . Numerous as shadows"; the musicians are "silver, snarling trumpets"; passersby are "many a sweeping train"; Porphyro's enemies are "a hundred swords." Spatial relationships in the castle are unfixed and fluid; the rooms expand and contract at random, giving the structure the character of a living organism. Lifeless statuary and living beings exchange roles; people are repeatedly described as statues, while real stone sculptures come to life as if they were human.

Boehm connects this "doubleness" of intelligibility and mystification with Keats's 3 May 1818 letter to Reynolds on life as a "Mansion of Many Apartments," where in the "Chamber of Maiden Thought" the doors are "all dark—all leading to dark passages—We see not the ballance of good and evil. We are in a Mist. . . . We feel the 'burden of the Mystery'" (*Letters* 1:281). Boehm thinks the castle represents Keats's idea of an ambivalent "reality." The poem is "concerned with complex perspectives and implications of the phenomenal world, which can at times appear substantial and enchanting, or insubstantial and strange—but always problematic" (25–26).

47. *The semiotics of vision (looking, gazing): scopophilia.*   "Semiotics of vision" is Andrew Bennett's phrase, at the beginning of a 1992 essay (and then a 1994 chapter) reading the poem in terms of the several kinds of looking, or "ocular fixation," that take place. We have Porphyro "implor[ing] / All saints to give him sight of Madeline, / But for one moment" (lines 77–79), and then proposing a stratagem to "see her beauty unespied" while she undresses for bed (line 166).

We have Madeline, in a state of blindness, decidedly *not* looking at either the amorous cavaliers who approach her or the real Porphyro when he crosses the room to her bed but, at the same time, obsessed with an imagined sight of Porphyro in her dream. The narrator, or the text representing the narrator, watches both Porphyro and Madeline in their ocular and visionary activities. And the reader sees all the preceding in the act of "watching" the text. "The significance . . . of sight-lines," says Bennett, "is not primarily thematic: what is important is the way that this internal tale of seeing infects and affects both the narratorial strategies and the reader's relation with the tale." Thus, the poem is above all about Keats's manipulation of the reader's looking at a story about looking. "The characters' looks provide potential models, embedded within the text, of the reader's gaze" (*Keats* 100–101).

Laura Mulvey's now-classical "Visual Pleasure and Narrative Cinema" (1975) does not mention *The Eve of St. Agnes*. She writes about movies made a century or more after Keats's death. But her ideas of the centrality of the "male gaze" and the relegation of women in films to roles in which their main purpose is to be looked at are usefully applicable to Porphyro's and the narrator's (and, again, the reader's) activities in Keats's poem. Christopher Ricks, in *Keats and Embarrassment*, slightly earlier than Mulvey's essay, finds "a purified and liberated scopophilia" in the poem, especially in stanzas 25–26, "as we hidden watch this hidden man watching this woman undress" (89–90). Marjorie Levinson also writes about voyeurism in the poem (see reading 17), and Wendy Steiner adds the concept of "sleepwatching" from her examination of connections with the legend of Cupid and Psyche (67–75).

48. *Ambiguity of idealism and reality.*   Many critics have discerned an opposition of "reality" and some kind of ideal in *The Eve of St. Agnes* and the poems of 1819 more generally. In one view of the matter, it functions as both the main theme and the main structure of many of Keats's mature works. What is interesting these days, as the commentary grows in range and complexity, is critics' awareness of how the real and the ideal overlap, producing situations of internal conflict and ambiguity ultimately unresolved except by the individual reader's imposition of ad hoc solutions and closures.

Greg Kucich has been studying this kind of ambiguity as a form of modern Spenserianism, Keats's "revision," as it were, of the writer who first (in Charles Brown's words) "awakened his genius" and was the inspiration of his earliest known poem, *Imitation of Spenser*. Kucich's preliminary report, "Spenserian Versification in Keats's *The Eve of St. Agnes*" (1983), has Keats adopting, along with Spenser's own stanza, two conflicting ways of writing: one the mode of romance and imaginative vision, based on "Spenser the artificer of sensuous delights," the other the mode of psychological realism, based on "Spenser the dramatist of human psychology." In the amalgam that results, "Porphyro is both a romantic hero and a treacherous seducer. Madeline is an angelic lover and a foolish dreamer. Keats's original manipulation of the Spenserian stanza reinforces this modern view of an ambiguous universe" (107–8).

In the full study that followed eight years later, *Keats, Shelley, and Romantic Spenserianism*, Kucich clarifies and expands on the differences that make Keats a modern revisionist rather than merely an imitator: rhetorical compression, narrative ellipsis, intensification of contrasts, absence of closure, an allegorical machinery that turns out to have no clear allegorical meanings, and a much reduced role for the authorial voice in the poem (Keats's narrator is much less conclusive than Spenser's and offers nothing in the way of moral interpretation). At the end, the lovers "glide" into what is simultaneously "an elfin-storm from faery land" and a real world of coldness, suffering, and death. "Spenser's continuous and conclusive allegory thus reemerges [in Keats's poem] as a fragmentary picture, or a compressed tapestry of antiallegorical allegory made up of calculated glimpses into the 'mist' of the human heart" (*Keats* 207).

49. *Poem of disjunctions, equivocation—open-endedness in the extreme.* Deconstruction as a critical approach inspired by Jacques Derrida and his immediate followers, originating in the late 1960s, ran an impressive and influential course through the 1970s and much of the 1980s. In the larger view, however, deconstruction is at least two centuries old, because major poems of the British Romantic period—from *Tintern Abbey* and *The Ancient Mariner* in the late 1790s to Keats's odes and Byron's romantic satires two decades later (and this is to speak only of Romantic works)—have all along been deconstructing themselves, without benefit of critical assistance. The contradictions, inconsistencies, lapses, miswritings, aporias, and other flaws that we now acknowledge in the works have been there from the beginning, written into the texts as a result of the contradictory character—and also the clever artistry—of the poets who authored them. I shall develop this topic in my last two chapters. For now, such disjunctions are the focus of reading 49, which, instead of constituting yet another interpretation of Keats's narrative, in effect proposes that the narrative cannot be interpreted.

Tilottama Rajan, in her much-cited *Dark Interpreter* (1980), speaks of the poem's "emotional indeterminacy," describing the reader's puzzlement in not knowing whether to take it as sentimental or ironic, because it is sentimental and ironic at the same time (101). It is a poem "concerned not simply with the deconstruction of illusion"—were it that simple, we could determine the meanings with confidence—"but also with the radical homelessness of a poetic voice that is unable to make habitable the empty space that follows the expulsion of illusions" (102). The work lives "in the space of a discontinuity between the real and the ideal, between the empty verbal sign and the thing it evokes but does not possess" (107). Rajan examines the poem in detail, using phrases such as "ambiguities at the heart of dreams," "radical ambivalence of the incarnate . . . aesthetic sign," "mutually irreconcilable alternatives" (109–14). Everything is hedged with questions about what is actually happening.

A similar view is available in plainer language in Anne Mellor's *English Romantic Irony* (also 1980). "Everything in the poem is qualified: Keats undercuts his romance with cynicism, his cynicism with romance, his seriousness with comedy, his comedy with seriousness. Ambiguity pervades the poem: nearly every character, every action, can be—and has been—interpreted in opposing ways, and both ways are equally valid" (89). Single-meaning interpretations (Wasserman and my "Hoodwinking" are the examples) "fail to allow for the open-endedness, for the ability to hold two opposed ideas in mind at the same time, that is at the core of 'The Eve of St. Agnes' and of Keats's romantic irony" (90).

For Susan Wolfson, whose *The Questioning Presence* appeared six years after Rajan's and Mellor's books, *The Eve of St. Agnes* is "a narrative in the interrogative mode," raising questions rather than providing answers, dislocating rather than satisfying our expectations. The range of characters and events "produces questions about Porphyro (traitor or true?) and Madeline (betrayed or betrothed?), for the interrogative character of this romance derives less from sentences punctuated with question marks than from the way Keats's narrator entertains a pro and a con about almost every character, desire, event, motivation, and consequence and keeps the play of possibilities in perpetual motion. . . . Even the familiar conventions . . . are being put into devious operation" (290–91). The "genius" of the narrative lies in "deft equivocation" and "conflicting interpretive clues" (293).

50. *Poem about speech, language, communication (and their unreliability).*   About a fourth of the lines in *The Eve of St. Agnes* (24.1%) are quoted speech—dialogue between Angela and Porphyro when he enters the castle and again when he reveals his stratagem and enlists her help, and between Porphyro and Madeline in her bedroom when he awakens her and soothes her fears. There are numerous references to speech without actual quotation: the Beadsman's prayers; the fact that the "joys of all his life were said and sung," meaning finished (line 23); the "sculptur'd dead . . . praying in dumb orat'ries" (lines 14–16); the old dames telling Madeline about the ritual of St. Agnes' Eve; Porphyro imploring all saints to give him sight of Madeline; and various hushings, mutterings, and whisperings. Marjorie Levinson makes a point about the amount of whispering in the poem (*Keats's Life* 150–51), and indeed forms of "whisper" occur in lines 68, 82, 147, 183, and 280. Perhaps some, at least, of this hushing and muting of utterances has to do with their unreliability. The Beadsman's prayers seem to go unanswered (as do those of the dead in the chapel); the old wives' tale, characterized as a whim, leads in some readings to Madeline's downfall; Porphyro lies to Angela and may lie to Madeline as well. Some of this is necessary to the drama of the poem, but there is enough falsity and deception of spoken language to suggest that it may be a thematic concern as well.

51. *Poem about the weather, the seasons, day and night, and so on (phenomenological reading).*   My heading here is meant to stand for various possible phenomenological readings in the manner of Gaston Bachelard and Georges Poulet, whose approaches, Jungian and Freudian, respectively, had considerable influence on criticism in the 1960s and 1970s. In these readings, what we would ordinarily consider elements of background and atmosphere are promoted to the status of main subject, so that the poem, quite apart from the interests of story and characters, is really about perceptions of time, space, the weather, the change of sea-

sons, and so on. Essays on architectural design and space in *The Eve of St. Agnes* by W. S. Ward, Arthur Bell ("Madeline's House" and "Keats and Human Space"), Martin Aske, and Alan Boehm (see reading 46) fall into this category. So would any piece arguing that Keats's principal purpose was to explain the January storm, in the same way that Milton explained the origin of the seasons in *Paradise Lost* or Wordsworth the memorable appearance of a stunted hawthorn in *The Thorn*.

Keats's poem contains a great deal about weather, and sooner or later (perhaps before this book is published) somebody will do a "green reading" of it on the model of Jonathan Bate's recent explanation of *To Autumn*, making an important point about weather as the primary sign of the inextricability of culture and nature ("Living with the Weather").

THE LAST EIGHT OF MY TOKEN "FIFTY-NINE WAYS," readings 52–59, are collected under the heading of Politics, which includes family relationships, class conflicts, the "woman question," and much else. Two contrasting interpretations labeled "sexual politics" have been described earlier, in another section, as readings 7 and 8.

52. *Family politics* (*the* Romeo and Juliet *situation, with emphasis on social conflict*). This is a variant of reading 29 (imitation of *Romeo and Juliet*) in which the focus is more on the enmity between Porphyro and Madeline's kinsmen than, as in the earlier entry, on the youthfulness, innocence, and ardor of the lovers. Stanzas 10 and 12, along with scattered lines elsewhere, are devoted to the narrator's and Angela's assessment of the danger that Porphyro faces in entering the enemy's castle. Madeline's relatives (and their "warrior-guests") are "barbarian hordes," "Hyena foemen," "hot-blooded lords," a "blood-thirsty race"; even their dogs hate Porphyro's "lineage." "Dwarfish Hildebrand" and "old Lord Maurice," the only two who are named, clearly would kill Porphyro on the spot if they encountered him in the castle and presumably would do harm to both the lovers if they discovered them in the act of eloping. Ultimately they do not seem much of a threat, first because Porphyro himself seems so unperturbed by the supposed danger (as in his response to Angela in lines 105–6, "Ah, Gossip dear, / We're safe enough"), and later because the lovers make their escape from the castle so effortlessly (in stanza 41 "They glide . . . they glide . . . the bolts full easy slide"). But the hostility between families is emphasized at certain points and deserves inclusion as one of the several political components of the poem.

53. *The rottenness of aristocratic society* (Hamlet *theme*). A certain tone toward the aristocratic inhabitants of Madeline's castle is established as early as the first two stanzas, where a lowly beadsman is shown at his routine task of praying for the household and some representative ancestors—the knights and ladies figured as the "sculptur'd dead" in the chapel—are imagined experiencing a torturous afterlife, aching with cold and imprisoned in "black, purgatorial rails." At the other end of the poem, we see Madeline's kinsmen and their guests in a drunken stupor, suffering nightmares of witch, demon, and coffin-worm. Casual refer-

ences in between point to lavishness of display ("thousand guests," "argent revelry," "plume, tiara, and all rich array," lines 33, 37–38), noisy partying ("snarling trumpets," "timbrels," "boisterous, midnight, festive clarion," "kettle-drum,"
"clarionet," lines 31, 67, 258–59), and especially shortness of temper ("whisperers
in anger," "looks of . . . defiance, hate, and scorn," lines 68–69). The menacing
heads of the family (see reading 52) are dwarfish and old. The heraldic scutcheon
in Madeline's bedroom window "blush'd with blood of queens and kings" (line
216), suggesting royal connection in the first place but also scandalous wrong-
doing. The nobility in this poem, from the middle-class view of the writer and
most readers, is not an admirable group.

Descriptive phrases such as "bloated wassaillers" and "Drown'd all in
Rhenish" (lines 346, 349), along with the trumpets and kettledrum, are more
than vaguely reminiscent of Hamlet's account of the "heavy-headed revel" at
the Danish court: "The King doth wake to-night and takes his rouse, / Keeps
wassail . . . And as he drains his draughts of Rhenish down, / The kettle-drum
and trumpet thus bray out / The triumph of his pledge" (*Hamlet* 1.4.8–12). This
is the scene that ends with Marcellus's now-famous "Something is rotten in
the state of Denmark," and at this early point in the play, even before the Ghost
has explained Claudius's crime, at least some of that rottenness has to be associated with characteristic bad behavior of the people who have the power and
money.

54. *The crisis of feudalism (feudal decay, mercantile ascendancy, disruption of the class
system).*   The most elaborate political reading, much more detailed than anything in readings 52 and 53, is by Daniel Watkins, who in *Keats's Poetry and the
Politics of the Imagination* treats the poem as "an allegory of the inner workings
of feudalism at the moment of its collapse," an allegory that applies to Keats's
present as well because it is written "in terms of the modern bourgeois poet's
vision of that collapse" (65). The castle, the Beadsman, Angela, Hildebrand,
Maurice, and Madeline herself are the feudal components, whereas Porphyro,
though he too has "lineage" of some sort, represents "the forces that are invad-
ing and disrupting feudal order" (75): he enters a castle whose "chambers, ready
with their pride, / Were glowing" (lines 32–33), and leaves it in a state of total
disarray.

Watkins makes pertinent connections with Keats's letters of the time, as well
as with passages from the poet's reading (for example, William Robertson's *History of the Reign of Charles the Fifth* and Hazlitt's ideas about feudalism that later
appeared in his *Life of Napoleon Buonaparte*). Especially in stanza 30, Watkins
finds internal support in the feast that Porphyro sets out, where "Fez," "silken
Samarcand," and "cedar'd Lebanon" are read as references to the mercantile
forces that overturned aristocratic feudal rule. The linking of Porphyro's name
as "purple" with the precious dye produced by the ancient Lebanese "purple
industry" is just one of several elements in a speculative network that also includes allusion to the neo-Platonist Porphyry, well known as a staunch enemy
of Christianity: "Porphyro's name, in short, combines both commercial and religious elements that directly challenge the structures of authority controlling

Madeline's world" (76–77). The storm at the end "is the objective correlative of history itself. Porphyro . . . destroys [the castle] and everything it represents" (83).

55. *Dynastic oppression (Madeline the victim).*   This and the next two readings are a sampling of feminist perspectives on the plight of Madeline and Keats's representations of women more generally. This one takes its heading from an offhand remark by John Collick (cited earlier in reading 32): "In broader terms, the theme of dynastic oppression is symbolised both by the barbaric revels of the castle's inhabitants and the imagery of cold statues, shields and ancient legends. The heroine, Madeline, is especially singled out as a victim of this. 'Asleep in lap of legends old' . . . her existence is determined by her position within a society that uses women as commodities to be bargained for and exchanged" (39).

Ultimately, Collick is more interested in the politics of language: in his reading, Madeline is, in effect, prisoner of the symbols and Gothic expressions of the poem. A simpler view of Madeline's "oppression" might make comparisons with a couple of Isabellas—the heroines of Horace Walpole's *The Castle of Otranto* and Keats's own *Isabella*, both of whom, like Madeline, are powerless to combat cruel relatives in situations involving their part in dynastic succession. Madeline seems trapped less by language than by the fact that she has no status independent of her family, no livelihood, and not even anything very interesting to do to pass the time. From lines 174–75 we know that she embroiders and plays the lute. The rest of her observable activity is the superstitious ritual of praying, sleeping, and dreaming.

56. *Patriarchal domination of women (Madeline again the victim).*   This one could be joined with the preceding as a single theme, but it seems useful to make a distinction between domination of Madeline by her hateful kinsmen and (what in a traditional romance plot ought to be something quite different) domination by her lover, if only to emphasize that the two kinds proceed from the same set of cultural and biological assumptions. Watkins (cited in reading 54) can again serve as spokesperson.[11] In her relations with Porphyro, Watkins says, Madeline represents "woman as the Other, as the silent and passive object of masculine power that makes the masculine transcendental ego possible; she is the site whereon masculine identity is stamped; she is, in short, without identity except insofar as she receives identity from that which controls her" (79).

Watkins sees this aspect of the poem as dramatizing "a very real and specific type of domination that arises alongside the emergence of commercial culture" (78), the very commercialism that was so destructive to aristocratic feudal rule in reading 54. Whether or not he is right about the historical development of patriarchy, it seems clear in the poem that Madeline's passing from one form of male control or ownership (by her family) to another (by Porphyro)—representing the situation of women in real life for centuries—is not exactly, from a feminist point of view, a liberation.

57. *Keats's disparagement of women (characters and readers alike).*   In this reading, Keats supplants Madeline's kinsmen and Porphyro and becomes himself,

authorially, the principal patriarch and oppressor. The human women of the poem (as opposed to the Virgin Mary and St. Agnes) are a silly and ineffective lot, consisting of a superstition-prone heroine, the "old dames" who feed her fantasies, and the feeble, palsy-stricken Angela, who does nothing to protect her. The plot can be read as involving rape (see reading 7) or at least a kind of "male gaze" lewd viewing on the part of Porphyro and the narrator (reading 47); *all* the males in the poem, and the male author as well, seem to be ganging up on Madeline. In a different but related type of deprecating situation, Madeline herself can be thought to be of questionable character, leading Porphyro on, if not actually seducing and destroying him (reading 8). Women may seem to be presented unfavorably in several ways in the poem, and Keats (with the cooperation of his readers) has to be considered responsible.

And then there is, hovering just outside the text, the problem of Keats's conflicting attitudes toward women in general, toward the women he knew personally, and toward women readers of his poetry. Margaret Homans's magisterial study, "Keats Reading Women, Women Reading Keats," does not offer an interpretation of *The Eve of St. Agnes* but provides plenty of background commentary and close analysis of the disagreement between Woodhouse and Keats in September 1819 (detailed above in the first section of chapter 2). Woodhouse remarked that the greater sexual explicitness of the revised manuscript version would "render the poem unfit for ladies" and Keats responded that "he does not want ladies to read his poetry: that he writes for men—& that if in the former poem [i.e., the original draft] there was an opening for doubt what took place, it was his fault for not writing clearly & comprehensibly—that he sh[d] despise a man who would be such an eunuch in sentiment as to leave a maid, with that Character about her, in such a situation" (*Letters* 2:163). Women were the principal readers and, more important, the principal purchasers of poetry at the time, and Keats badly wanted both current popularity and immortal fame, with some financial return along the way, if that were at all possible. It is an immensely complicated topic, which Homans treats complexly. For purposes of this skimming survey, reading 57 treats the poem primarily as a site for controversy over Keats's attitudes toward women and his women readers.

58. *Poem about escape—from the castle, from family and/or society, from reality.* The basic notion of Romantic escapism, which drew heavy(-handed) censure from New Humanist critics such as Irving Babbitt in the early decades of this century, is too familiar to require documentation. Wordsworth seems to be constantly retreating from the world, either to some favorite nook in nature or, even further from the world, to some internal preserve not even a part of nature. Coleridge has his lime-tree bowers and inner imaginings as well, and also the fantasy worlds of the Mariner's voyage, Kubla Khan's Xanadu, and Christabel's medieval castle. Percy Shelley writes about excursions into the remotest reaches of the Caucasus in his early work and "the abode where the Eternal are" generally thereafter. The events of Keats's major poems almost always take place in medieval, ancient, or purely mythological settings, and his characters direct their visionary aspirations toward places that do not exist in reality.

In *The Eve of St. Agnes*, both the Beadsman and Madeline reject the noisy activities of the revelers in order to concentrate on fantasy worlds of their own creation. Porphyro and Madeline literally escape the castle—and the family and social oppression that it represents—in the final stanzas. And Keats, setting his poem in medieval times, "ages long ago," has seemingly produced yet another work *not* about England in 1819. Elizabeth Barrett Browning could have had Keats and *St. Agnes* in mind when she wrote, in the fifth book of *Aurora Leigh*, "I do distrust the poet who discerns / No character or glory in his times, / And trundles back his soul five hundred years, / Past moat and drawbridge, into a castle-court . . ." (lines 189–92).

Even though *The Eve of St. Agnes* does not loom large in Nicholas Roe's gathering of mainly historical materialist essays in *Keats and History* (1995) and is barely mentioned in the collection on Keats and politics that Susan Wolfson edited for *Studies in Romanticism* in 1986, these different manifestations of escapism do in fact have political implications for both the world of the poem and the world in which Keats was writing. The politics of the world that Madeline and Porphyro wish to escape have already been touched on in readings 54–56. The poem's connections with England of 1819, and the politics of Keats's setting his story so far back in time, remain to be worked out, though Daniel Watkins has made a start in a paragraph observing how Keats's "view of international politics, and of the militarization of the modern world" in the years immediately following Waterloo "helps to explain why (as the characterizations of Hildebrand, Maurice, and even Porphyro emphatically demonstrate) in the poem diplomacy does not exist and military power and physical violence are the rule rather than the exception" (64–65).

59. *Politics of interpretation: who gets to say what things mean (Madeline? Porphyro? the narrator? the critic? the teacher? the reader?).*   This last topic is essentially the crux of my book. Interpretation here is political not in the manner of Marxism or feminism, say, but in the more general sense of having to do with power—in this case, the power of assessing what is going on in the poem. From the very first stanza, countless questions can be answered only interpretively: the role of the Beadsman; the character of the revelers; the seriousness of the St. Agnes' Eve ritual; Madeline's behavior at the party; Porphyro's intentions on entering the castle; the nature of Angela's complicity; and so on and on. Just how are these questions to be decided? Possibly this, too, is one of the themes of the poem.

Take, as an example, the storm that comes up just after Madeline loses her virginity (lines 322 ff.). Madeline seems afraid of the storm, connecting it with the prospect of abandonment by Porphyro. Porphyro assures her that it is an "elfin-storm from faery land" and therefore nothing to worry about (he calls it "a boon," because it will help hide their escape from the castle). The narrator insists that it is a real storm, directing attention to the wind, the sleet, and the icy cold. Then Madeline and Porphyro go out into the storm—and have not been heard from since.

At this point, the critics take over. One group, headed by Herbert Wright (see reading 44), think that the lovers perish in the storm. A second group, influenced by Earl Wasserman, suggest, on the contrary, that they transcend mortality, entering an otherworld of eternal felicity, while Angela, the Beadsman, and the warriors remain to die or writhe benightmared. Another group believe that they live happily ever after in Porphyro's home across the moors (one of the later nineteenth-century illustrations printed with a text of the poem shows Madeline and Porphyro with two children and a dog, the perfect nuclear family).[12] Some argue that Madeline and Porphyro enter Dante's second circle of hell (the subject of Keats's sonnet *As Hermes once took to his feathers light*, written in April 1819) and are perpetually orbiting the world with other famous lovers who sinned carnally. Still other critics say that the question is beside the point: the lovers would be dead now in any case, because this all happened "ages long ago."

In general, the critics express strong opinions on the matter. Here, for example, is Charles Patterson, in *The Daemonic in the Poetry of John Keats*, taking his stand in favor of a concluding "happy life in the human world" for Madeline and Porphyro: "The preponderance of evidence and suggestion in the poem surely supports this . . . view" (117 n.). One might respond that there is no textual evidence concerning the fate of the lovers; the sum of what we know is given in lines 370–71, "And they are gone . . . These lovers fled away into the storm." But actually the text is overloaded with evidence, with literally thousands of separate details, starting with the Beadsman and the "sculptur'd dead" in the opening stanzas, that contribute to a reader's impressions about how this story will, or did, or *should* end. Taken all together, they are a mass of contradictions that each individual reader has to sort out. As I shall suggest in the next chapter, no single reader's "preponderance of evidence and suggestion" is exactly the same as any other reader's. This leaves questions of interpretation, and of who gets to do the interpreting, quite up in the air.

THIS OVERVIEW OF READINGS, which in spite of its length is hardly more than a collection of sound bites, marshals a great many different interpretations of the poem. But this is just a token array of possibilities. Colleagues to whom I have shown the list on which it is based (Appendix B) have proposed still others, and so have people in my lecture audiences. One freshman came up at the end of a lecture in El Paso to say that he had always thought Angela and the Beadsman were having a sexual affair. I saw nothing in the text to support such an idea, but I told him, because I felt bound to practice what I was preaching about no-fault reading, that it could be number 60 in my list. Later I thought of some reasons why it is not a totally worthless suggestion.

My "fifty-nine ways" are mostly opinions about the meaning of the poem overall: what *The Eve of St. Agnes* is "really" about, the principal theme or notion or structure that explains the parts and connects them (for the occasion of a reading, at least) into a critical unity. The list does not begin to suggest the additional complications that arise when we consider possibilities for variation in the interpretation of individual lines, words, and images—the things that a reader *could* imagine from such phrases as (to select examples almost at random) "a little moonlight room, / Pale, lattic'd, chill, and silent as a tomb" (lines 112–13), or "legion'd fairies pac[ing] the coverlet" (line 168), or "ring-dove fray'd and fled" (line 198), or "the tiger-moth's deep-damask'd wings" (line 213). I shall examine these further complications in the next chapter, the first of two undertaking to explain why there have been (and will continue to be) so many different readings of Keats's poem.

FOUR

WHY THERE ARE SO MANY MEANINGS (I)

Complex Readership

T HE PRECEDING CHAPTER emphasized the variety of interpretations that readers of *The Eve of St. Agnes* have constructed. My materials were mostly the published criticism, but the array was guided by a sense of the plausible, hence intended to illustrate responses of any reader, professional or amateur (the "general reader"). Some of the interpretations there will no doubt seem more plausible than others to my readers. But individual ideas of plausibility are the same as individual readings in the first place: everybody's idea is different from everybody else's. We could attempt to simplify by eliminating ten or twenty of the least plausible among the initial fifty-nine, producing a shorter list of forty-nine or thirty-nine. But I do not think even the most sophisticated interpretive community among the professionals could agree on which ten or twenty to eliminate. And even if we could shorten the list in this way, still the remaining thirty-nine or forty-nine interpretations would be an impressive display of differences among readers of the poem.

In this chapter and the next I shall try to explain why there has been such diversity of response. In general, the explanation lies in the nature of the transaction between a complex work and a complex readership. On one hand, we have *The Eve of St. Agnes*, sending out many thousands of impulses of meaning in all directions, so many that the reader cannot possibly absorb all of them and therefore has to make a selection. On the other hand, we have a complex readership that consists, first, of any individual reader (already a complex system of personal knowledge and experience at the time of reading) and, second, the combination of all the readers who have ever read the poem taken together simultaneously. Each of these individual readers will be creative (rather than passive) while engaged in the activity of reading and will be creative in some different ways from all the other readers. Each individual reader, that is, will separately put together a unique combination of selected and emphasized meanings, adding and suppressing according to his or her own creative activity in the process.

This chapter considers the constitution of this complex readership and the reading process. Chapter 5 then elaborates on the character of the complex work—at the other end of the reader-work transaction—by analyzing the complex authorship that produced the work, accomplishing the essential first step toward making the literary transaction possible.

Multiple Readers

Obviously the most numerous agent in the Author-Text-Reader scheme would be the readers. For multiple authorship we have Keats and his associates (principally Woodhouse and the publishers, who "helped" Keats clean up the poem by insisting on a more innocent version than the revision that he presented them with), plus a handful of other, mostly anonymous contributors in the printing, editing, and illustrating of the work over the years. For multiple texts there are the three main versions described in the middle section of chapter 2—the original draft that Keats wrote in January and February 1819, the revised manuscript version that he produced eight months later, and the printed text of 1820—plus whatever later printings one cares to single out for their distinctive editorial emendations and/or printer's errors. The number of multiple readers is, by comparison, almost unimaginable. I mentioned "many hundreds of thousands" in the second sentence of Chapter 3. But I wrote that sentence at the end of the fall semester, and the number has grown by several more thousands, because I am now writing in the middle of the spring semester, and surveys of the second half of English literature like the one I teach each spring have finished studying the Romantics (and *The Eve of St. Agnes* among the Keats assignments) and have progressed well into the Victorians. The students in these surveys and others here and abroad taking introductions to poetry, major authors courses, advanced courses in the Romantics, honors seminars, and so on can now be added to the number.[1]

So who are these "many hundreds of thousands" of readers? Actually we have almost no information about individual readers of the poem over the past 180 years. We can construct categories of readers, starting with a meager record of responses from Keats's contemporaries—first Woodhouse and the publishers, when they fussed over the manuscripts, and then a relative handful of friends, associates, and reviewers who we know read the first printed text: Charles Lamb, Leigh Hunt, William Hazlitt, John Scott, and John Clare, among others.[2] One finds scattered comments on the poem in periodicals and books mostly after the middle of the nineteenth century, as Keats's reputation began to be established, and there was major interest in it (along with *Isabella*) on the part of the Pre-Raphaelites. Then come the professional readers, the serious critics and explicators of the poem from the 1880s right up to the latest issue of the *Keats-Shelley Review*, many of whom are named and quoted in chapter 3.

The readers whom I know best (apart from my own experience with the poem) are in yet another category: the students in my classes at the University of Illinois. I have already mentioned my spring survey of the second half of English literature (Blake to the 1950s). This course is required for our English majors, but in the most recent offering more than half the students (out of a total of 197 on the initial roster) are concentrating in some other subject. They represent all four undergraduate years (with sophomores and juniors outnumbering the freshmen and seniors), come from all seven of our undergraduate colleges, and are pursuing, in the aggregate, forty-four different curricula: English, rhetoric, and teacher education in English, certainly, but also animal science, aviation, finance, marketing, broadcast journalism, architecture, biochemistry, computer science, psychology, pre-medicine, and a great many others that *The Eve of St. Agnes* would seem to have very little to do with.

I lecture to the whole group on Mondays and Wednesdays, and the students get to express themselves in discussion sections led by teaching assistants— twenty students per section—on Fridays. I visit the Friday sections on a rotating basis and keep in touch with the students in other ways. One of the most useful of these is the written responses that I get from the students (via the TAs) every Friday, commenting on the week's lectures and reading. These amount to a page or two of scrawl or printout per student, and I spend a couple of hours each week going through them. Here is a small sample of excerpts from their recent remarks specifically on *The Eve of St. Agnes*:[3]

> The lovers, surrounded by darkness and decay, by false music and false joy, their very motives hedged by the poet's near ironies, can only escape into myth and legend. They free themselves of this dark environment only by becoming "phantoms" of "ages long ago." . . . All in all, *The Eve of St. Agnes* was a powerful poem. The images were striking and the tone very sensual. This is my first experience dealing with Keats, and I'm happy to say I was actually interested in his writing.

> Keats's poem paints a three-dimensional work of art laden with incredible, dense, beautiful, pure and impure images. After reading a stanza of *The Eve of St. Agnes*, I would catch myself falling into an enchanted, wonderful dream-world, characterized by Disney animation. I was a bystander, unseen by the characters of the poem, lurking in the shadows of Madeline's household. I was incapable of affecting the outcome of the story that unfolded before my eyes. . . .

> The third time I read the poem, I began to think that Porphyro was almost completely innocent. . . . Though not wholly blameless for the act of spying upon Madeline, he cannot recognize Madeline's half-dream state, and naturally assumes she is in full possession of her faculties. The narrator seems unable to discern whether or not she is awake, or half asleep, or hallucinating with visions of Porphyro. Porphyro, who is sexually aroused with his vision of the naked Madeline, cannot help himself when Madeline awakens, also sexually aroused, and pleads with him to "melt" with her, so that she may regain the delusions she experienced in the dream. "Oh

leave me not in this eternal woe," she says, the woe being the sadness of the loss of her dream, as she seeks to substitute the real Porphyro for the one lost in her deluded visions.

Shades of purple and violet are mentioned many times in the poem. . . . One particular passage is when Porphyro slips into bed with Madeline. In lines 320–21, "Into her dream he melted, as the rose / Blendeth its odour with the violet." When you mix red with blue, you get violet, a color very symbolic of their joining.

Why is it that although Angela and the Beadsman represent two opposite forces, they die together, thus giving them some kind of connection? . . . Could it be that both of these forces are necessary to maintain the balance of the universe?

I think the story is beautiful, and the language very rich, but Keats leaves the final tone ambiguous. Are we supposed to feel happy for the lovers? Sad or displeased with the "tainting" of Madeline? Porphyro breaks the dream-like state of Madeline. If her dreaming is representative of beauty and the romantic notion of a supernatural ideal, why does Keats have Madeline awaken? I see this as a conflict in the romantic theory of beauty in dreams. Does Porphyro serve as the counterreaction to the romantic ideal?

There seem to be two protagonists with both a separate and a similar goal. Madeline wants to dream of her husband, and at the same time Porphyro is waiting to seduce her. The ending has the lovers going out into the storm together, leaving it ambiguous whether they escape the life of the castle to begin their own together, or are lost forever in the storm as a type of supernatural punishment.

My question this week is what would Keats say about the fifty-nine interpretations of *The Eve of St. Agnes?*

Such comments do not pretend to be as polished as those of the professional critics quoted in chapter 3, but they are no less serious and thoughtful. These student readers, just like the professionals, have reconstituted the poem in their imaginations, and that is where, for each individual reader, the "meaning" of the poem ultimately resides. The account of the reading process in the next section applies to readers at all levels of competence and sophistication.

The Reading Process

Every reader's construction of a complex work such as *The Eve of St. Agnes* is an imposition of order on a chaos of information.[4] This is true whether the reader proceeds linearly, a word at a time through one sentence of the text after another, or by scanning a whole stanza or a whole page at once, mentally assembling pieces of image and meaning as they happen to come to notice. It is true whether one reads by sight alone, or by a combination of sight and sound (adding the unheard melodies, as it were), or exclusively by sound, as when one hears the poem read aloud in a performance or on a tape. It is true whether one is reading the poem for the first time or for the fortieth or the hundredth time. And it is true as well whether the reader is a newcomer to the English language, a high school student, a college English major, a graduate student, a tenured professor specializing in Romantic poetry, or, apart from all these categories, just someone who likes to read poetry. Each reader's knowledge of English vocabulary, of literary genres, of poetic forms and conventions, of biblical and classical myths, of ancient and modern history, of human psychology (and so on and on) will affect that reader's responses to stimuli radiating from the text. But all alike, from Earl Wasserman and Stuart Sperry to the freshest of naive readers—are in the same business of imposing order in the process of reading. No individual reader can take it all in at once.

To illustrate the text's excess of potential meaning and how I think individual readers cope with it, let me use the opening stanza, a passage that seemingly has nothing to do with plot as such but initiates the atmosphere and the frame within which the plot takes place.

> St. Agnes' Eve—Ah, bitter chill it was!
> The owl, for all his feathers, was a-cold;
> The hare limp'd trembling through the frozen grass,
> And silent was the flock in woolly fold:
> Numb were the Beadsman's fingers, while he told
> His rosary, and while his frosted breath,
> Like pious incense·from a censer old,
> Seem'd taking flight for heaven, without a death,
> Past the sweet Virgin's picture, while his prayer he saith.

This stanza has twenty or more ideas and images in just the first four lines. "St. Agnes" by itself, the first two words of the poem, carries at least the ideas of saintliness, martyrdom, and (for readers who know the saint's legend) virginity. There is "eve" in the sense of evening and nighttime, as well as the more specific sense of the night before a saint's day; and then come bitterness, chill, owl, feathers, cold, hare, limping, trembling, frozenness, grass, silence, flock, woolliness, and fold (this last both a farm structure and a social concept). The next four lines of the stanza contain fourteen more images: numbness, beadsman, fingers, telling (or counting), rosary, frostedness, breath, piety, incense, censer, oldness, flight, heaven, and death. The last line of the stanza has at least three more: Virgin, picture, and praying. Altogether, I count thirty-seven images in just these first nine lines of the poem.

An individual reader cannot possibly absorb and respond to all thirty-seven of these separate stimuli. So the reader selects some; overlooks, ignores, or suppresses others; and creates his or her own peculiar version of the content of the nine lines. Readers cannot help selecting and creating in this way; it is the main way that people read.

But, to continue this illustration, there is more at issue than just a question of different combinations among thirty-seven or so items. Each of these ideas and images has the potential of conveying many separate shades of meaning and therefore can produce considerable variation of response according to the individual reader's interpretation. For example, I extracted five items in my list—hare, limping, trembling, frozenness, and grass—from the third line of the stanza, "The hare limp'd trembling through the frozen grass." But what does this hare actually look like to the reader? None of the dozen students in my most recent graduate seminar had ever seen a hare. Among a much larger number of my most recent undergraduates, two students on summer trips out West had spotted a jackrabbit and a snowshoe rabbit; but these North American species of hare, which are brown in the summer, turn white in the winter. Should we imagine Keats's hare, in the late-January winter of St. Agnes' eve, as brown or white? In Keats's mind, the animal (*Lepus europaeus*) would have been reddish-brown, but here we are talking about readers, not about the author, and so the question remains unresolved. There is the further question of how much color (whatever it is) the reader should expect to be visible in this night scene, illuminated, as we learn eight stanzas later, by moonlight. And then everybody's idea of the animal's limping will differ from everybody else's, as will the notion of trembling while limping. Is this trembling primarily a visual image, which we take in from a spectator's point of view, or is it an internal body image, felt from within? How tall, how stiff, how sharp (and so on) is the frozen grass? Is the grass primarily surrounding the hare (or its legs), or primarily underneath the hare's feet? Are we supposed somehow to imagine the *grass's* feelings as well the hare's in this line?[5]

One could go on indefinitely posing questions like this about specific words in the text. And when the words conveying the images and ideas are seen as crucial to plot, character, and theme—the meanings of "whim" and "thoughtful," for example (line 55), "faery fancy" and "amort" (line 70), "stratagem" (line 139), "Merlin" and "his Demon" (line 171), "tongueless nightingale" (line 206), "heaven" and "eremite" (line 277), "melted" (line 320), and "they are gone" (line 370), to list just a handful almost at random—the different possibilities for response will obviously result in different views of plot, character, and theme, and thus different readings of the poem overall.

I. A. Richards once voiced the opinion that simple stimuli in a text produce more varied responses among readers than modified or interconnected ones:

> Even so unambiguous an object as a plain colour . . . can arouse in different persons and in the same person at different times extremely different states of mind. . . . There seems to be good reason to suppose that the more simple the object contemplated the more varied the responses will be which can be expected from it. For it is difficult, perhaps impossible, to contemplate a comparatively simple object by itself. . . . A single word by itself, let us say "night," will raise almost as many different thoughts and feelings as there are persons who hear it. (*Principles* 9–10)[6]

Richards goes on to say that responses to such stimuli are much reduced when the simple object or word is placed in an elaborate context—the whole line, or stanza, or poem. I would argue, on the contrary, that the range of responses is increased rather than lessened by contextual impingements. The third line of the poem, "The hare limp'd trembling through the frozen grass," is made up of five separate "simple" stimuli. The fact that they are in a straightforward sentence, with subject, verb, and prepositional phrase, in a stanza establishing the atmosphere of some opening scenes, ought not to reduce the variety of possible responses to each image taken separately. The same will be true of every multi-image line bearing more directly on plot, character, and theme.

Each reader will put his or her "spin" on whatever images are singled out in the selection process I have described. With so many images and so many possibilities for variation, as in *The Eve of St. Agnes*, each reader-constructed version will necessarily differ in some or many particulars from every other reader-constructed version. In a poem of 378 lines, the mathematical possibilities for variation are astronomical.[7] This is one reason why we have significant differences in the readings of the poem overall and, if the readers write them up, a considerable accumulation of different readings in the critical literature.

With Keats's poems, there is still another cause of multiple meanings in addition to large numbers of readers and the text's excess of information: a characteristic frequency of ambiguous and contradictory details in the texts.[8] The opening description of the Beadsman can serve as an example. Certain details in the first two stanzas emphasize the Beadsman's piety, patience, and sympathy for the dead who lie about the chapel where he is praying; from these a reader might think that he is to be admired. Other details tend to make the Beadsman pitiable rather than admirable, as in his joyless self-denial and harsh penance; the fact that he is barefoot is an especially painful detail, given the emphasis on bitter cold in the opening stanzas. The different kinds of detail produce conflicting perceptions of the Beadsman, and these in turn have a bearing on the reader's view of important matters that occur later in the poem if the ritualistic, self-denying Beadsman is interpreted to prefigure the ritualistic, self-denying Madeline in the main narrative. What one thinks of the Beadsman to an extent affects what one thinks of Madeline.

For larger, more complicated examples of contradictory detail in the poem, consider these statements about the two main characters:

Porphyro is Prince Charming, on a mission to rescue an imprisoned maiden.
He is a confederate of sorcerers, a worker of evil magic.
He is a peeping Tom.
He is an ardent lover.
He is a rapist.
He is Madeline's future husband.

Madeline is beautiful and desirable, the belle of the ball.
She is hoodwinked with faery fancy, shutting herself off from the real world.
She is a pious Christian.
She is a victim of self-deception.

She is a victim of Porphyro's stratagem.
She is Porphyro's happy bride.

About half of these statements do not "fit" (are not congruent with) the other half, yet each statement is true in the sense that there is support for it in the text and agreement among some of the readers and critics. Oppositions of this sort are central to the plot, characterizations, speeches, and descriptions. No wonder different readers have different ideas of what is happening in the poem.

The most common principle by which individual readers select meanings and choose among oppositions is *unity* of some sort, the very kind of unity that Coleridge extolled and theorized throughout his writings, both in poetry and prose, and (as a result of Coleridge's influence, by way of I. A. Richards and other early New Critics) the kind of unity that constituted the main goal of critical activity for at least the middle half of the twentieth century, from the 1920s through the 1970s and on into the 1980s.[9] Coleridgean unity has lately been attacked by several categories of theorist, in particular, for different reasons, by deconstructionists, new historicists, Marxists, and feminists. But classroom experience, empirical research on reading, and the most cursory familiarity with the critical literature on one's favorite canonical work constitute good evidence of a continuing urge toward unity and closure. Formalism may be dead just now among many theorists in English departments, but it is very much alive in the real-life situations of classroom and personal reading, as well as in much practical criticism published in the journals.

Readers cannot help constructing Coleridgean unities. It seems to be basic to human mental activity, perhaps as a part of some innate structuring mechanism. European structuralism of the 1950s and 1960s, led by Claude Lévi-Strauss, Roman Jakobson, and Roland Barthes, among others, ran its influential course without ever proving the existence of the "deep" structures on which the method and theory were founded. But the human ability to compose structures out of virtually any given materials, no matter how disorganized in themselves, is everywhere observable.

In summary form (an orderly structure of my own making!), the reading process described in this section can be theorized in the following five statements:

1. Textual meaning is an interpretive construct created (that is, imagined) by a reader.
2. Each interpretive construct is based on a selection of details from the text.
3. The most common principle of selection is unity of some sort.
4. In a complex work, each reader's selection will differ from every other reader's selection.
5. Each such difference in selection will be, in effect, the difference of one kind of reader-constructed unity from another.

For practical demonstration to accompany this theorizing, I offer the variousness of the fifty-nine ways surveyed in the preceding chapter. In one way or another, all fifty-nine impose order on the chaos of details in the text, and at least most of them argue for closure, even if (as with reading 49) the closure takes the form of a bold assertion of indeterminacy.

Keats's "Innumerable Compositions"

At the same time that Coleridge was theorizing about reader-constructed unity, Keats also understood the importance of the individual reader's creativity in the reading process. According to the first of the famous "axioms" that he set down in a letter to Taylor of 27 February 1818, "Poetry . . . should strike the Reader as a wording of his own highest thoughts, and appear almost a Remembrance" (*Letters* 1:238). This could not possibly come about if the reader did not bring his or her individual thoughts and recollections to bear on the reading process. Six weeks later, in a letter to Benjamin Robert Haydon of 8 April, Keats mentions the "innumerable compositions and decompositions which take place between the intellect and its thousand materials before it arrives at that trembling delicate and snail-horn perception of Beauty" (1:265). In such an expression, Keats again seems to be on the side of multiple interpretation, which should be an inevitable outcome any time the reader's part of the transaction involves "innumerable compositions and decompositions" in the process of perception. Keats's own best odes can be read as illustrations of the theory: the *text* in each instance—the urn, or the nightingale, or the fields and the sky in autumn—stays always the same; it is the speaker in the poem, becoming reader of the text at hand, who keeps changing the interpretation, first seeing (for example) life on the urn, then seeing death, and finally seeing both life and death at the same time.

It is not at all far-fetched to consider Keats an early advocate of some fundamental ideas of twentieth-century reception theorists. Here, for instance, is Keats's clear understanding of a text's excess of meaning: "Do not the Lovers of Poetry like to have a little Region to wander in where they may pick and choose, and in which the images are so numerous that many are forgotten and found new in a second Reading" (1:170). Keats is explaining—to his brother George, in the spring of 1817, about the time that he was writing the first book of *Endymion*—why he is "endeavour[ing] after a long Poem"; the reader's picking and choosing among the numerous images is the selection process, pretty much as I described it in plainer terms in the preceding section of this chapter, and the notion that "many [images] are forgotten and found new in a second Reading" hints at the idea of a complex text's inexhaustibility. Some ten or eleven months later, writing to John Hamilton Reynolds on 19 February 1818, Keats expanded on this notion of the reader's wandering: "I have an idea that a Man might pass a very pleasant life in this manner—let him on any certain day read a certain Page of full Poesy or distilled Prose and let him wander with it, and muse upon it, and reflect from it, and bring home to it, and prophesy upon it, and dream upon it." The emphasis is again on the reader's (rather than the writer's) creative activity in the transaction: the page of poetry provides materials for not just a day but part of "a very pleasant life," and the reading process is simultaneously a "voyage of conception" and a "delicious diligent Indolence" (1:231).[10]

Both the well-known "Negative Capability" and Keats's related idea of the chameleonlike "poetical Character," in letters to George and Tom Keats, late December 1817, and Woodhouse, 27 October 1818, are on the side of openness and multiplicity, and therefore have a bearing on the concept of multiple readings. The first, the quality forming "a Man of Achievement especially in Literature & which Shakespeare posessed so enormously," is primarily a philosophical and moral position (or, more accurately, as Keats defines and illustrates it, nonposition): "*Negative Capability* . . . when man is capable of being in uncertainties, Mysteries, doubts, without any irritable reaching after fact & reason—Coleridge, for instance, would let go by a fine isolated verisimilitude caught from the Penetralium of mystery, from being incapable of remaining content with half knowledge" (1:193–94). It is the *not* having to resolve the contraries of ideas, emotions, and human experiences that constitutes greatness. The "Man of Achievement especially in Literature"—Shakespeare is the successful example, Coleridge (here the author of *Biographia Literaria* rather than of *The Ancient Mariner*, *Kubla Khan*, and *Christabel*) the contrasting failure—is the one who writes without having to dictate what everything means; it is left to the readers, one at a time on an individual basis, to compose "uncertainties, Mysteries, doubts . . . half knowledge" into their unified systems of philosophy and morality or, where fiction is at hand, their unified views of plot, character, subject, and theme.

Keats's letter on "the poetical Character," ten months later, again refers to Shakespeare as the prime exemplar of the self-annihilating sympathetic imagination:

> As to the poetical Character itself, (I mean that sort of which, if I am any thing, I am a Member; that sort distinguished from the wordsworthian or egotistical sublime; which is a thing per se and stands alone) it is not it-self—it has no self—it is every thing and nothing—It has no character—it enjoys light and shade; it lives in gusto, be it foul or fair, high or low, rich or poor, mean or elevated—It has as much delight in conceiving an Iago as an Imogen. What shocks the virtuous philosop[h]er, delights the camelion Poet. It does no harm from its relish of the dark side of things any more than from its taste for the bright one; because they both end in speculation. A Poet is the most unpoetical of any thing in existence; because he has no Identity—he is continually . . . filling some other Body. (1:386–87)

Here Keats thoroughly admires Shakespeare's multiplicity of sympathies and perceptions,[11] this time in contrast to Wordsworth's authorial imposition of his own "egotistical sublime" on the reader, with whole (rather than half) knowledge as the main content. And he is pondering Shakespeare, Wordsworth, and "the poetical Character" in this way less than three months before the start of his famous "living year"—January–September 1819—during which he turned out one major poem after another, practically all of which, in effect, end in "uncertainties, Mysteries, doubts" that the picking-and-choosing reader must assume responsibility for resolving.

The nonconclusion of *The Eve of St. Agnes* ("they are gone") is the first instance of this new level of ambiguity. *The Eve of St. Mark*, abandoned before the plot gets under way, is the next, coming to us wide open to interpretation. *La Belle Dame* never explains what "ails" the knight-at-arms, even though three-fourths of the stanzas purport to be explanation ("And this is why . . ."). *Ode to Psyche* concludes with nameless stars, feigning, and a strange notion of "warm Love" produced by "shadowy thought." In *Ode on Melancholy*, the heroic burster of Joy's grape winds up ignominiously "hung" among Melancholy's "cloudy trophies." The final lines of the Nightingale ode pose questions that are not followed by answers. The last two lines of the Grecian urn ode are impressive but empirically ununderstandable (there has never been a satisfactory explanation of their meaning). At the end of *Lamia*, the heroine vanishes, the hero drops dead, and we are directed immediately, without a recognizable conclusion, to the source-passage in Burton's *Anatomy*. The celebration of life in the last stanza of *To Autumn* is wrapped up with mourning, sinking, and dying. Keats created all these works; but in his relative egolessness (relative, that is, to Coleridge and Wordsworth in the letters quoted just above), he seems to be positioned on the reader's side, outside the works rather than within, sharing the reader's interested view of what is going on in them and wondering, just like the reader, how to deal with the ambiguities they pose.

A Practical Theory of Multiple Interpretation

Despite broad hints like those just cited from Keats's letters and poems, as well as teachers' cumulative experience of multiple readings in their classes, single-meaning interpretation remains the principal goal of critical articles and pedagogical practice. Many of the fifty-nine readings in chapter 3, taken one at a time, are cases in point. And most of the essays in the Modern Language Association's recent "approaches to teaching" series explain strategies for inculcating interpretations upon the class. The focus is not how to get the students to do their own creative selecting and constructing of unities but how to get them to learn and accept the teacher's way of reading instead.

> Initially, I approach Keats by discussing . . .
> The story I tell is . . .
> I then try to convince . . .
> At this stage I point out . . .
> And most members of the class begin to see . . .
> What I want my students to see is that . . .
> The first step in getting the students to see . . .
> Students begin to realize that . . .
> I try to persuade students . . .
> (Evert and Rhodes 72, 107, 111, 121, 123, 130, 135).[12]

One encounters single-meaning interpretation again and again in other teachers' literature classes (for example, when I visit my TAs in their Friday discussion sections early in the semester or observe classes of younger colleagues being considered for promotion). The main way of teaching over the years has been to ask the class a question about something in a text, and then keep asking the question until a student comes up with the "right" answer, in effect, the reading in the teacher's mind. This method is almost impossible to avoid in the classroom. I find that I cannot help doing it myself, even though I am constantly proclaiming against it, and I notice that writers in recent books on the day-to-day practice of reader-response methods in teaching cannot help doing it either.

An epitomizing example (all the more interesting because it clearly was meant to illustrate just the opposite) occurs in Robert Small's "Connecting Students and Literature," the opening essay in Nicholas Karolides's collection titled *Reader Response in the Classroom*. Small creates transcripts of two quite different seventh-grade classes devoted to Emily Dickinson's *A Bird came down the Walk*. The first, taught by "Helen Johnson," employs the traditional method of lecture followed by a "discussion" consisting of Ms. Johnson's questions and the students' attempts to come up with the predetermined correct answers. "We had a really good discussion of the poem," Ms. Johnson comments afterward; "It took them awhile, but they finally saw . . ." (9). The second class, taught by "Jane Graham," uses a more open method in which the students are encouraged to think and say whatever they wish. Remarkably, the response-oriented class arrives at the same interpretation as the more traditional class, and in almost exactly the same words: Dickinson's poem is really about the poet watching herself. "Ah," Ms. Graham says to the class. "And the bell rings" (15). What has happened is that Small, the researcher, has unwittingly made his own interpretation the desired outcome of both classes that he purports to transcribe. The tradition of single-meaning interpretation is indeed hard to overcome.[13]

Clearly this traditional practice of single meanings laid on by authority is at odds with the reality of the way people read, as I have described it earlier in this chapter, in which everybody's reading is necessarily different from everybody else's. No doubt the conflict will continue as long as teachers feel a threat to their authority when they encounter readings that differ from their own. But there is no real reason why teachers should feel threatened in this way. There are many other things to teach about literature besides the meanings.

I wish to resolve this conflict in favor of the legitimacy of multiple meanings and toward that end shall offer a practical theory of multiple interpretation allowing for an openness in reading and teaching that much better accords with the way people actually read. My 1991 book on multiple authorship implied a practical theory of authorship—the idea that, in addition to the nominal author, a great many other individuals participate in the authorship and production of a literary work and therefore have a hand in expanding the range of possible meanings in the work. The final chapter of my *Coleridge and Textual Instability* (1994), titled "A Practical Theory of Versions," argued that each individual version of a work is a distinct text in its own right, with unique aesthetic character and unique authorial intention. My practical theory of multiple interpretation here likewise emphasizes the existence and legitimacy of diversity—in this case, the multiple and even contradictory meanings of a complex work.

Here is a statement of the theory consisting of four extremely simple points:

1. Multiple meanings do exist, and we should acknowledge their existence.
2. Multiple meanings are an essential component of competent reading.
3. Multiple meanings are an important feature—I think a defining feature —of canonical works.
4. There is no substance to theoretical or practical arguments against the legitimacy of multiple meanings.

The first of these principles is the reiterated burden of my book from the beginning. The second and third are expanded further in the final section of this chapter and in chapter 6, respectively. I shall take up the last of the four points here.

The chief problem with multiple readings is the question of validity. Any time we allow that the meaning of a work—or some part of it—is lodged, not with the author or in the text, but in an individual reader's response, we face the problem of the validity, or truth, of an interpretation. On what grounds does one decide what is correct and what is not correct? On what grounds does a teacher tell a student that the student's interpretation is wrong? How can literature be a field of knowledge when anybody and everybody can be a player?[14]

The idea that each interpretation is as good—as valid, or true, or correct—as any other sometimes makes students uncomfortable (how will they know the "right" answers for the final exam?), and it regularly horrifies certain types among English faculty. Consider these remarks by Alvin Kernan, in his 1990 jeremiad titled *The Death of Literature*:

> Interpretation, a very subjective activity, has replaced reading and understanding. The extreme democratic view, in which anyone's reading of a text is as true as any other, is legitimated by hermeneutics, a general theory of interpretation that posits that meaning is never in the text but always in the theory of interpretation applied to it. . . . We can sum up this reader-centered criticism by saying that the concept of the *book*—ordered, controlled, teleological, referential, and autonomously meaningful—to be *read* by literate readers has been replaced by the *text*, fragmented, contradictory, incomplete, relativistic, arbitrary, and indeterminate, to be *interpreted* by people who have a great deal of difficulty piecing out the broken signs on the printed page. (144)

> The insistence that literature has no meaning, or has any meaning the reader cares to give it, wears away the positive authority and even the reality of the subject. . . . (201)[15]

Several easy points could be raised against such a lament, and I shall say something briefly about three of them. The first involves a standard of *factuality*. Almost always we can make, or at least attempt, a distinction between information, on one hand, and opinion, on the other; and then it is possible to say that some kinds of statement, those in the category of information, can be considered right or wrong in a way that some other kinds, those in the category of opinion, cannot. Opponents of reader response like Kernan usually do not make the distinction, but it is valid at some level and should be made nevertheless. It would be wrong to say that Percy Shelley wrote *The Eve of St. Agnes* or that the heroine's name is Samantha. But in matters of opinion—for example, when a reader is interpreting Madeline's or Porphyro's action or a speech or a motive— it seems much more sensible to judge the reading on a scale, not of right or wrong, but of interesting as opposed to boring or linguistically plausible as opposed to obfuscating. In practice, there will of course be large gray areas where fact and opinion are intermingled: the color, motion, and sensations of Keats's hare in line 3 are all open to interpretation, but the animal is still a hare and not, for example, a hippopotamus. The relative degrees of fact and opinion are themselves describable and negotiable.

The second point against opponents of reader-centered criticism involves a standard of *comprehensiveness*, meaning the extent of the correspondence between an interpretation and the particulars of the text being interpreted. There are various ways of formulating this: for example, that the interpretation ought to include as many events, descriptive details, and implications of language as possible, and that there should not be major events or details in the work that flatly contradict the interpretation.[16] The degree of comprehensiveness is related to what Jonathan Culler in *The Pursuit of Signs* describes as narrative power; the large meanings and telling effects of a work are ultimately achieved by the interrelatedness of the most important particulars. Some theorists add to this the criterion of *coherence*: the interpretation should produce a coherent account of what goes on in the work or what the work is "about" (though this might be considered an obstacle standing in the way of recognition that an incoherent work is in fact incoherent). One can test both comprehensiveness and coherence and still have room for a variety of differing interpretations.

The third point against opponents of reader response involves a process of *consensus*. Interpretive opinions do tend to sort themselves out in the same way that literary works enter and drop out of the canon. The less interesting interpretations, the less illuminating, fade from view, while the more interesting stay around for a while. The process just seems to happen of itself.

Instead of worrying about the rightness or wrongness of interpretations, I should like to see developed a concept of no-fault reading. No-fault reading is the acknowledgment that, where imaginative literature is concerned (as opposed, for example, to religious or political or legal documents), so-called "wrong" readings do not really do any serious harm or damage. It is better to allow people the freedom to make mistakes in thinking and speaking—the freedom, that is, to think or utter *mis*interpretations. Even the freshman in El Paso whom I mentioned at the end of chapter 3—the one who thought that Angela and the Beadsman were having a sexual affair—could, if the class discussion were focusing too narrowly on Madeline and Porphyro, be making a contribution by shifting the focus to these minor characters and raising questions about what they are doing in the poem.

Multiple Meanings and the Improvement of Reading

It seems clear that, for *The Eve of St. Agnes*, there is no single "correct" meaning. Some accounts of the poem are richer, more encompassing, more complex than others, but in the absence of authorial intention—which in this case is demonstrably unrecoverable—there is no common standard for assessing right and wrong in any large matter of interpretation. We can, though, have opinions about what constitutes richer, more encompassing, and more complex; and I think we can teach students (and any others who want to go along) to heighten their individual experiences of the poem by enlarging the range and complexity of their responses. No-fault reading does not eliminate the teacher's role so much as redefine it.

Multiple interpretation enhances understanding, appreciation, and complexity of response—all three—by speeding up the reading process. For years I have been advocating the redefinition of interpretation as *improvement of reading* on the grounds that, if interpretation (and here I am talking about critical interpretation in the classroom or in a journal article or a book) has any practical use at all, it lies in how it makes available increasing numbers of possible meanings and therefore enlarges a person's openness to what *could* be happening in a work.

A single interpretation constructed on one's own—the result, say, of a reader's first run-through of a text—produces an experience of the text of a certain size and import; a second reading enlarges the size and import, and then a third and a fourth and a fifth increase these complexities accordingly. If the reader is open to multiple meanings, and more so if the reader plugs into a multiplicity of already existing interpretations—the fifty-nine ways in chapter 3 are an example close at hand—the reading process is considerably accelerated. The relative beginner goes from something like a third reading to something like a thirty-third or a sixty-third reading in much less time than it would take to actually read the work thirty-three or sixty-three times. The multiple meanings, instead of competing in a sort of king-of-the-mountain elimination contest, in fact bolster, reinforce, and enrich one another.

One sees this in teaching any time one has a free-ranging discussion of a complex work like *The Eve of St. Agnes*. Consider what a student understands about the poem at the beginning of the discussion and then what he or she understands about the poem at the end of the discussion, fifteen or thirty minutes or two hours later, after many single-reading interpretations have been shared and combined interactively. The difference between the beginning and ending understandings is tremendous. This will usually include even the understanding of the teacher who is facilitating the discussion. I have never yet had a discussion session on a complex poem without hearing some new interpretive idea never before seen in print or (in my own experience) even voiced.

Let me illustrate this process with Keats's image of the tongueless nightingale at the end of stanza 23. Having helped old Angela down the stairs, Madeline resumes her progress upward to her bedchamber, and then:

> Out went the taper as she hurried in;
> Its little smoke, in pallid moonshine, died:
> She clos'd the door, she panted, all akin
> To spirits of the air, and visions wide:
> No uttered syllable, or, woe betide!
> But to her heart, her heart was voluble,
> Paining with eloquence her balmy side;
> As though a tongueless nightingale should swell
> Her throat in vain, and die, heart-stifled, in her dell.
>
> (lines 199–207)

As part of the ritual she is practicing, Madeline cannot speak aloud, even when she is alone (as she thinks) in her bedroom. The last four lines of the stanza describe an internal eloquence in her breast (literally, her heart is talking to itself) that is strong enough to be physically painful, almost as if she were going to burst and die.

"The nightingale!" exclaimed Leigh Hunt in his *London Journal*, 21 January 1835; "how touching the simile! the heart a 'tongueless nightingale,' dying in that dell of the bosom. What thorough sweetness, and perfection of lovely imagery! How one delicacy is heaped upon another!" (Matthews, *Keats: The Critical Heritage* 278). Although there is more to the image than mere "sweetness" and "perfection," Hunt is certainly right about delicacies being "heaped upon" one another. It is this multiple heaping that I wish to focus on for a moment.

At least four clusters of images are brought together in these lines—that is, four types of image, with the possibility of various shades of meaning (and therefore reader response) for each type. The first is the nightingale as actual bird, the species *Luscinia megarhynchos*, common all over Europe as far north as the top of Germany and in the southernmost third of England and Wales. Except for those who have been abroad, American readers will not have seen or heard a nightingale firsthand, though pictures and descriptions of the bird are available in field guides, and there are many recordings of its famous singing. (The U.S. northern mockingbird is similarly loud, melodious, and inventive in its night-singing, and could serve, though crudely, for illustrative comparison.) A remarkable oddity about the nightingale is the discrepancy between its rather featureless appearance, on one hand—it is a drab-looking small brown bird with a reddish or chestnut tail—and the arresting, large-toned musicality of its complex song, on the other. Somewhere within it, the bird unquestionably has a considerable vocal mechanism: it sings "full-throated," as Keats describes it in *Ode to a Nightingale*; it "pours forth [its] soul" in the act of singing (lines 10, 57). In this instance, the image "cluster" consists of the various degrees of familiarity that different readers of the poem will have with the species, ranging from a mass of encyclopedic details at one extreme to near total ignorance at the other: "it's some kind of bird."

The second cluster of images depends on the reader's familiarity with the nightingale in literature. This is not just an actual bird, but the most written-about species in English poetry, with well-known examples in Chaucer, Spenser,

Shakespeare, Milton, and practically anyone else worth mentioning. Instances in Keats's own time, when it was an especially popular topic, include poems and passages by William Cowper, Charlotte Smith, Mary Robinson, Coleridge, Wordsworth, and John Clare—to which one should add Keats's own famous ode, written four or five months after the first draft of *The Eve of St. Agnes* but nevertheless available to the original readers of the longer poem in Keats's volume of 1820 (and, as it happens, to all readers of Keats's poems ever since). The principal characteristics of the nightingale are summed up in Milton's *Il Penseroso* line 62: "Most musical, most melancholy!" But the main point for this image cluster is the bird's literariness. *The Eve of St. Agnes* is a consciously and conspicuously literary poem, bristling with allusions to earlier and contemporary poetry, drama, and fiction. The nightingale of lines 206–7 may be considered part of the literary machinery—again, though, depending on the reader's ability to make the connections.

The third cluster, evoked specifically by the *tonguelessness* of the nightingale in Keats's description, involves the story of Philomela, a daughter of Pandion, king of Athens. Philomela (to condense several hundred grisly lines of Ovid's *Metamorphoses* into three relatively tame sentences) was raped by her brother-in-law, Tereus, who cut out her tongue so that she could not tell what had happened. She conveyed to her sister Procne, Tereus's wife, an account of Tereus's brutality by weaving it into a tapestry, and the two women then punished Tereus by feeding his son's flesh to him at a banquet. When Tereus is about to retaliate by killing the women, the three are mercifully transformed into birds: Tereus into a hoopoe, Procne into a swallow, and Philomela into a nightingale. Keats's mention of "tongueless nightingale" thus encapsulates the entire story of the rape of Philomel and is one of several images of rape and seduction in the poem. The working of this cluster (where the shades of possible meaning range from random classical embellishment to serious suggestion of impending evil) depends on the reader's familiarity with the better-known stories of Greek and Latin mythology.

The fourth cluster takes shape from the medical-school physicality of the details surrounding the tongueless nightingale: painful side, swollen throat, and stifled (suffocated) heart. These images, variously suggesting constriction, blockage of respiration, choking, and finally strangling on material that cannot be got out of the way—it is in fact the *backing up* of unutterable eloquence that stifles the nightingale's heart—must have a basis in the lectures and laboratory experiences of Keats's yearlong course of medical training at Guy's Hospital in 1815–1816 (for an idea of the topics and the language of the lectures, see Hermione de Almeida's chapters on blood and the circulatory system in *Romantic Medicine* 87–110 and Keats's *Anatomical and Physiological Note Book* especially 4–13). In their poetic context, the images may be read as one more infusion of "wormy circumstance" working against the high romance of Madeline's expectations from her ritual.

I have been suggesting, in the preceding four paragraphs, a series of situations in which some readers know about real nightingales while others do not; some readers are more familiar than others with the nightingale in literary tradition; some, but not others, know the story of the rape and mutilation of Philomel; and some readers are more sensitive than the rest to the vascular and visceral effects of imagined swelling and suffocating (a sufferer from asthma, for example, might have a heightened response to the representation of these conditions). Imagine, then, a class of students in which *all* these various possible responses are brought up, considered, debated, and evaluated. The basic materials are unquestionably there in the text, some of them (the dark and grisly elements) seemingly in opposition to others (Milton's "musical . . . melancholy," Hunt's "sweetness . . . perfection"). It has to be a help in one's reading to be exposed to these multiple significances and resonances. One cannot remain content with "sweetness" and "perfection" (for example) when rape, mutilation, and stifling are present in the very same lines.[17]

So how, one may ask, does any or all of the above relate to authorial—that is, to John Keats's—intention in the lines? The answer is that we simply have no way of knowing, except by reading the lines themselves. But Keats was familiar with nightingales (they nested in his back garden). He had read at least most of the poems about nightingales among the English poets. He knew Ovid probably in the original and certainly in translation and had the story of Philomel in his favorite Lemprière's *Classical Dictionary* as well. And he was a conscientious observer and notetaker when he was a student at Guy's Hospital. He must, then, have had the materials of these clusters of images in his experience and memory, regardless of the effects he may have wished to achieve when he put them together in stanza 23 of *The Eve of St. Agnes*. No-fault interpretation is not disrespectful of the author. Let us consider this further as we turn to the complexity of the person who wrote the poem.

FIVE

WHY THERE ARE SO MANY MEANINGS (II)

Complex Authorship

I BEGAN THIS STUDY BY ARGUING (in the first two sections of chapter 1) that authorial intention is for all practical purposes unrecoverable, that texts have no meaning in themselves, and that therefore the readership end of the transaction—representing each individual reader and, at the same time, all the readers collectively—becomes the only possible locus of meaning. This sequence of thinking is partly theoretical, but for Keats is empirically demonstrable as well, and is supported by the poet's statements about intentionless spontaneity in composition, "Negative Capability" and other qualities of the ideally selfless author, and the picking-and-choosing process of ordinary reading, as well as by Keats's own relative egolessness in both his life and his poetry (see the third section of chapter 4).

I would not, however, carry this still-fashionable "death-of-the-author" tendency so far as to propose that Keats did not write *The Eve of St. Agnes* and the other poems attributed to him. On the contrary, I wish in this chapter to complete a circle by suggesting that the materials from which each reader's interpretive constructions take shape are, to some large degree, already in the text waiting for the reader to come along and, further, that it is the author of the text who put them there. It may seem regressive to return to the text and the author after making so much of the reader in the preceding four chapters, but I think it is entirely possible to have a reader-response-based theory of multiple interpretation that includes the text and the author as significant elements.

Let me refer back to my use (at the beginning of the second section of chapter 4) of the opening stanza of *The Eve of St. Agnes* to illustrate the text's excess of potential meaning. There are so many stimuli of idea and image in the stanza—I listed thirty-seven for a start, most of them readable in several different ways—that the reader cannot possibly absorb and respond to all of them and therefore has to construct the meaning of the stanza (or of the individual lines or words) from a selection of details. I am interested now in emphasizing that it was Keats who wrote these lines, imagining and setting down all those details at the beginning of the poem, as well as the several thousand others in the rest of the stanzas that follow. Keats need not have intended any of the particular meanings that we construct on the basis of his text. But he did create the text, and we would have no meanings at all without his authorship.

The Idea of Incongruity

My principal argument concerning Keatsian authorial complexity involves a notion of comic misfittingness, and I shall begin with three epitomizing examples in the form of a joke, a poem about Byron, Shelley, and Keats as the Three Stooges, and a typically zany passage from one of Keats's letters.

Here is the joke:

> Two fishermen are out in the middle of a reservoir in a rented boat, catching fish hand over fist, pulling them in as fast as they can get their lines back in the water.
> *First fisherman*: "This is a great place to fish. Don't you think we should mark the exact spot?"
> *Second fisherman*: "Sure, I'll put an X right here on the side of the boat." (*Marks an X on the side of the boat.*)
> *First fisherman*: "That's a stupid thing to do, that's dumb. [*Pause.*] What if we don't get the same boat?"

This will sound like something from a stand-up comedian on television. In fact I have appropriated it from a piece by my colleague Mike Madonick that appeared a few years ago in *Cimarron Review*. In Madonick's telling, the fishermen are literary theorists named Jacques and Harold. As their dialogue continues, the two decide that the fish they have caught are not real fish at all, merely linguistic constructs.

I use the joke to introduce the basic idea of incongruity. Everything funny has a central element of incongruity: something does not fit with something else. In Madonick's joke, the first incongruity is the idea of marking the spot with an X on the side of the boat. There is a second incongruity when the other fisherman thinks putting an X on the boat is stupid for the wrong reason: they might not get the same boat next time. When we add the implied identities of the fishermen—two of the most famous literary theorists of our time—the result is a still more complicated set of incongruities. Why would these two be out fishing together? Why would they say such dumb things?

The poem about Byron, Shelley, and Keats as the Three Stooges is by Charles Webb, who teaches writing at California State University at Long Beach. This was the final poem read at the concluding session of a Keats conference held at the Clark Library in Los Angeles in April 1995. It begins as follows:[1]

Decide to temper Romantic *Sturm und Drang* with comedy.
   Keats shaves his head;
      Shelley frizzes out his hair;
Byron submits to a bowl-cut.

   My heart aches, and a drowsy numbness pains
      My sense, as though of hemlock I had drunk,
Keats sighs, his head stuck in a cannon.

   Eternal Spirit of the chainless Mind!
      Brightest in dungeons, Liberty!
Byron shouts, and lights the fuse.

O wild West Wind, thou breath of Autumn's being,
   Thou, from whose unseen presence the leaves dead
      Are driven, like ghosts from an enchanter fleeing,
Shelley booms, and drops a cannonball on Byron's toe.

The poem continues with further slapstick intermingled with famous lines from the three poets, until—Webb says—

Until they die, too young, careening
   Into immortality covered with flour, squealing,
      Drainpipes on their heads—which explains why
For many years, the greatest poems

   In English have all ended *Nyuk, nyuk, nyuk,*
      And why, reading *She walks in beauty like the night;*
We are as clouds that veil the midnight moon;

   Season of mists and mellow fruitfulness,
      You may feel ghostly pliers tweak your nose,
And ghostly fingers poke the tear ducts in your eyes.

When Webb showed this poem to Beth Lau, his colleague at Long Beach, she referred him to a similarly ludicrous passage about "T wang dillo dee" from the last of Keats's journal letters to his brother and sister-in-law in America. Here is the passage, written on 17 January 1820. Keats is describing his social life and the people he has seen lately:

I know three people of no wit at all, each distinct in his excellence. A, B, and C. A is the soolishest, B the sulkiest, C is a negative—A makes you yawn, B makes you hate, as for C you never see him though he is six feet high. I bear the first, I forbear the second, I am not certain that the third is. The first is gruel, the Second Ditch water, the third is spilt—he ought to be wip'd up. . . . T wang dillo dee. This you must know is the Amen to nonsense. I know many places where Amen should be scratched out . . . and in its place "T wang-dillo-dee," written. This is the word I shall henceforth be tempted to write at the end of most modern Poems—Every American Book ought to have it. It would be a good distinction in Saiety. My Lords Wellington, Castlereagh and Canning and many more would do well to wear T wang-dillo-dee written on their Backs instead of wearing ribbands in their Button holes—How many people would go sideways along walls and quickset hedges to keep their T wang dillo dee out of sight, or wear large pigtails to hide it. . . . Thieves and Murderers would gain rank in the world—for would any one of them have the poorness of Spirit to conde-scend to be a T wang dillo dee—"I have robb'd in many a dwelling house, I have kill'd many a fowl many a goose and many a Man," (would such a gentleman say) but thank heaven I was never yet a T wang dillo dee"— Some philosophers in the Moon who spy at our Globe as we do at theirs say that T wang dillo dee is written in large Letters on our Globe of Earth— They say the beginning of the T is just on the spot where London stands. London being built within the Flourish—*wan* reach[es] downward and slant[s] as far a[s] Tumbutoo in africa, the tail of the G. goes slap across the Atlantic into the Rio della Plata—the remainder of the Letters wrap round new holland and the last e terminates on land we have not yet discoverd. However I must be silent, these are dangerous times to libel a man in, much more a world. (*Letters* 2:245–47)

At the conference in Los Angeles, Webb read this passage from Keats's letter first, then recited his poem about the Three Stooges, adding "T wang dillo dee" at the end:

> You may feel ghostly pliers tweak your nose,
> And ghostly fingers poke the tear ducts in your eyes.
> T wang dillo dee.

Thus, the celebration of Keats in Los Angeles concluded with a tweaking of the nose, tears in the eyes, and "T wang dillo dee." Everyone was delighted.

I wish to focus for a moment on why everyone was delighted. Why do such fundamental incongruities as the young Romantics as the Three Stooges and Keats's ridiculous excursus on "T wang dillo dee" give people so much pleasure? At the same Los Angeles conference the day before, I had delivered a paper on multiple interpretations of *The Eve of St. Agnes* (the origin of parts of chapters 3 and 4 in this book). When I heard Webb's poem in connection with the passage from Keats's letter, I thought I understood better than I had before why there are so many different and contradictory meanings in Keats's poems and why these differences and contradictions are received as attractive rather than disturbing or displeasing. Just as with the joke about the fishermen, the poem about the Three Stooges, and "T wang dillo dee," we seem to enjoy situations in which things do not fit together.

I wish to relate this comic misfittingness to some of the incongruities in Keats's best-liked poems. There are many general names for the phenomenon: *difference, division, disjunction, disharmony, contrariness,* and so on. Whatever name we give it, it is the extreme opposite of the concept of unity formerly so central in our critical activity. And it is initially the authorship rather than the reception that is thus disunified. In *The Eve of St. Agnes*, in effect, the authorship side of the trans-action—successively, as described in the next section, the multiple authorship of Keats and his collaborators, a conglomerate of multiple Keats*es* (plural), and finally, and most important, the complex character of "multiple Keats" (singu-lar)—creates incongruities that the readership side, by the ordinary processes of selection and unification, then partially puts together in whatever various ways it can. These "various ways," amounting to a different one for each indi-vidual reader, are the multiple readings of chapters 3 and 4; the materials on which they are based are the products of the complex authorship described in this chapter.

Multiple Keats

Now that we know the principal facts of composition and publication, the most readily understandable source of internal opposition creatively implanted in the text of *The Eve of St. Agnes* may be the conflict between Keats and his helpers, his friend Richard Woodhouse and his publishers (who were also his friends, of course) John Taylor and J. A. Hessey. All had the same long-range goal—to help get Keats permanently established "among the English Poets"—but they did not agree on the best practical means of attaining that goal. What can be recovered of the details of their collaboration has already been set forth in chapter 2. In essence, Keats in his revised manuscript text added elements of realism, irony, and skepticism, especially in the more explicitly physical account of Porphyro and Madeline's lovemaking in lines 314–22 and the earlier details that wryly prefigure this in the stanza inserted at 54/55. Then Woodhouse and the publish-ers rejected some but not all of the revisions, producing for the first printed text a composite of original and revised versions and, to an extent, a conflict of origi-nal and revised intentions.

To progress to the next source of opposition and focus more exclusively on the nominal author of the poem, we have to consider Keats's chameleonlike changeability as a "poetical Character." Everybody is familiar with the poet's variety and versatility and therefore with the idea of multiple Keats*es*. Several Keatses were on view in 1995 at the Houghton Library, the Grolier Club in New York, the Dove Cottage Museum in Grasmere, and elsewhere: the Keats of the poetry drafts, produced, as he told Woodhouse, as if by magic; the Keats of the boldly inscribed fair copies; the Keats first known to the public in the magazines and the three original volumes; posthumous Keats, in his character as creator of the one hundred poems first published after his death; the personal Keats seen in the privacy of his surviving letters; Keats as beloved friend at the center of what we now call the Keats Circle; the Keats of the various portraits; and Keats the artistic collaborator, providing materials for subsequent nineteenth- and twentieth-century book designers, printers, and binders who created so many beautiful printings of his poems.[2]

These are just the most obvious types represented by the manuscripts, books, and memorabilia in the bicentennial exhibitions. We can add many more Keatses both from traditional criticism and scholarship over the years and from poststructuralist theory more recently: Aesthetic Keats, the champion of art for art's sake; Sensuous Keats, the burster of Joy's grape, with or without cayenne pepper on his tongue, and the creator of some of the most palpable imagery in all of English poetry; Philosophic Keats, the describer of the vale of soul-making, for example, and life as a mansion of many apartments; Theoretical Keats, the formulator of negative capability and chameleon poetry; Topographical Keats, the well-traveled tourist who wrote a sonnet while dangling his legs from a precipice at the top of Ben Nevis; Theatrical Keats, the theatre reviewer and unproduced playwright; Intertextual Keats, including Spenserian Keats, Leigh Huntian Keats, Shakespearean Keats, Miltonic Keats, and Dantesque Keats (this is a sublisting that could be extended almost indefinitely). There are also Political Keats, especially in his early poems and letters, but through the rest of his career as well; Radical Keats, which is a sharper focusing of Political Keats; Vulgar Keats, the only canonical male Romantic poet besides Blake who did not attend a university and the one with the lowliest upbringing; Cockney Keats, a more specific tag deriving from this same lowly upbringing, plus the Cockney School articles in *Blackwood's* and, 180 years later, Nicholas Roe's latest investigations (see especially Roe's *John Keats and the Culture of Dissent*); Suburban Keats, a variant of the preceding produced by the research of Elizabeth Jones ("The Suburban School," "Keats in the Suburbs"); Effeminate Keats, first in the contemporary reviews of his own time and now in the criticism of Susan Wolfson, Marjorie Levinson, and others;[3] Masculine (even macho) Keats; Consumptive Keats, the one who dies so movingly and heroically every time we read a biography or make our way to the end of the letters.

The list could go on and on. But these multiple Keats*es* remain a random sampling of single Keatses—now one, now another, according to the approach, the method, the occasion, and the texts at hand. Here I am interested in something still more complicated.

"Multiple Keats" (singular) in the heading of this section stands for an internal complexity in our poet constituted primarily by self-division—a sort of unresolved imaginative dividedness between the serious and the humorous, the straight and the ironic, the fanciful and the real, the high-flying and the down-to-earth, the sentimental and the satiric, the puffed up and the deflated. It manifests itself in many places, both in biographical anecdote and in Keats's writings—and in the poetry, both in the frivolous pieces tossed off for immediate amusement and in the most serious efforts that Keats hoped would earn him a place among the English poets. One way of representing this self-division is by referring to various kinds of comedy: the antic, the zany, the farcical, the ridiculous—for example, the illustrations of comic incongruity with which I began this chapter.

Somebody in the North American Society for the Study of Romanticism (NASSR) user group recently raised the question of whether Keats had a sense of humor, and responses poured in to such an extent that one got the idea there were hardly any letters and poems in which Keats was *not* in some way being funny. Think of the hundreds of passages in the letters involving puns, practical jokes, self-mockery, and comic description. Everyone has his or her favorite examples. One of mine occurs in the last of the letters that Keats wrote during his walking tour in the summer of 1818 to Georgiana Keats's mother, Mrs. James Wylie, on the 6th of August (*Letters* 1:358–59):

> Tom tells me that you called on Mr Haslam with a Newspaper giving an account of a Gentleman in a Fur cap, falling over a precipice in Kirkudbrightshire. . . . I do not remember [any fur cap] beside my own, except at Carlisle—this was a very good Fur cap, I met in the High Street, & I daresay was the unfortunate one.

At this point, Keats invokes a bit of classical mythology to explain the newspaper account he has invented. The Three Fates, seeing two fur caps in the North, threw dice to eliminate one of them, and so the other fur cap, the one at Carlisle, went over the precipice and was drowned. But then Keats imagines that it would not have been so bad if he himself had been the loser, provided he had been only half drowned:

> Stop! let me see!—being half drowned by falling from a precipice is a very romantic affair. . . . How glorious to be introduced in a drawing room to a Lady who reads Novels, with—"M^r so & so—Miss so & so—Miss so & so. this is M^r so & so. who fell off a precipice, & was half drowned[."] Now I refer it to you whether I should loose so fine an opportunity of making my fortune—No romance lady could resist me—None—Being run under a Waggon; side lamed at a playhouse; Apoplectic, through Brandy; & a thousand other tolerably decent things for badness would be nothing; but being tumbled over a precipice into the sea—Oh it would make my fortune—especially if you could continue to hint . . . that I was not upset on my own account, but that I dashed into the waves after Jessy of Dumblane—& pulled her out by the hair. . . .

Just six weeks before Keats wrote this, Georgiana had left London to settle in America with her new husband, Keats's brother George. Emigration in those days was a serious disruption of family relationships; in most cases, the family members who stayed behind never again saw the ones who departed. Keats in this letter offers condolences to Georgiana's mother as if her daughter had died: "I should like to have remained near you, were it but for an atom of consolation, after parting with so dear a daughter. . . . I wish above all things, to say a word of Comfort to you, but I know not how. It is impossible to prove that black is white, It is impossible to make out, that sorrow is joy or joy is sorrow." It is at this point in the letter that, without any transition whatsoever, Keats launches into his account of the gentleman in the fur cap falling over a precipice in Kirkcudbrightshire.

This kind of oscillation, between seriousness and hilarity, pervades the letters and is indeed one of their chief attractions to readers. Even in his last known letter, written from Rome two and a half months before he died, when he was already leading what he called a "posthumous existence," Keats mentions punning: "I ride the little horse,—and, at my worst, even in Quarantine, summoned up more puns, in a sort of desperation, in one week than in any year of my life." He ends this letter with a poignantly comic gesture: "I can scarcely bid you good bye even in a letter. I always made an awkward bow" (2:359–60).

Many poems and passages are openly funny: the early lines about Keats's trinity of women, wine, and snuff; the sonnet celebrating the grand climacteric of Mrs. Reynolds's cat; the whimsical self-description beginning "There was a naughty boy"; the lines about the cursed gadfly; the lines about the cursed bagpipe; the silly dialogue between Mrs. Cameron and Ben Nevis; the Spenserian stanzas making fun of his friend Charles Brown; the extended self-parody in *The Jealousies*. The comedy in these pieces regularly depends on incongruous juxtaposition, as in the overthrow of expectation with a punch line. It is characteristically Keatsian to put together things that do not, themselves, go together.[4]

Keats wrote about this juxtaposing of contraries in the well-known lines that begin "Welcome joy, and welcome sorrow" and are sometimes printed under the heading "A Song of Opposites":

> Welcome joy, and welcome sorrow,
>   Lethe's weed, and Hermes' feather,
> Come to-day, and come to-morrow,
>   I do love you both together!
>   I love to mark sad faces in fair weather,
> And hear a merry laugh amid the thunder;
>   Fair and foul I love together. . . .

Keats often juxtaposes the comic and the serious in poems that are not primarily funny. The opening of the fragmentary *Calidore*—"Young Calidore is paddling o'er the lake"—could be an early (as Keats would say) smokable example, if we remember that the poet almost always took an ironic view of chivalric trappings. At the time of the early poetry-writing contests, it is easy to imagine Keats challenged to write a length of rhymed couplets following from the opening, "Young Calidore is paddling o'er the lake." In fact, he wrote 162 lines before coming, still plotless, to a halt.

Take the phrase "O bliss! / A naked waist" toward the end of the second book of *Endymion*, sometimes cited to illustrate Keats's bad taste or judgment. Endymion has been wandering from cave to cave underground until he arrives at a bower and finds

> The smoothest mossy bed and deepest, where
> He threw himself, and just into the air
> Stretching his indolent arms, he took, O bliss!
> A naked waist: "Fair Cupid, whence is this?" [Endymion asks]
> A well-known voice sigh'd, "Sweetest, here am I!"
> At which soft ravishment, with doating cry
> They trembled to each other.   (2.710–16)

That "Sweetest, here am I!" is pure Chaucer, like something lifted from *Troilus and Criseyde*.[5] Keats is recounting a passionate episode in the poem, with detailed physical description; but even though the narrator gets extremely worked up over the proceedings—he has to stop to invoke Helicon and the Muses—there is no question about the intentionally comic mixture of irony and literary allusion in "O bliss! / A naked waist. . . . 'Sweetest, here am I!'"

Another comic example from the same poem comes in the middle of book 4, when Endymion is in bed with his newly beloved Indian maiden and his heavenly love Phoebe rises and glares down on the couple:

> O state perplexing! On the pinion bed,
> Too well awake, he feels the panting side
> Of his delicious lady. He who died
> For soaring too audacious in the sun,
> When that same treacherous wax began to run,
> Felt not more tongue-tied than Endymion. . . .
> Ah, what perplexity! . . .   (4.439–47)

There are the grotesque images of the dream or nightmare at the beginning of the verse epistle to John Hamilton Reynolds:

> Things all disjointed come from north and south,
> Two witch's eyes above a cherub's mouth,
> Voltaire with casque and shield and habergeon,
> And Alexander with his night-cap on—
> Old Socrates a tying his cravat;
> And Hazlitt playing with Miss Edgeworth's cat. . . .

This ridiculous set of allusions leads into one of Keats's most serious considerations of the dangers of overinvesting in visionary imagination. In *The Eve of St. Mark*, another serious poem exploring the pros and cons of imaginative investment, similarly grotesque images adorn both the ancient volume that Bertha reads and the fire screen across the room. The earlier description ends anticlimactically with angels and mice; the latter passage has, among its "many monsters," not only mice again but several kinds of bird and, at the end of the list, the traditional enemy of both mice and birds, a fat cat.[6]

Shorter passages of incongruous images and wording, probably there for the value of the incongruity, include Porphyro's Pink Panther-like tiptoeing across Madeline's bedroom to check whether she is asleep and the redness of Hermes's blushing ears when, in the first paragraph of *Lamia*, he thinks of the beautiful nymph he is pursuing. An early writer on the humor in *Lamia* remarks, "There are many other parts of the body which can be described as turning red when the tone is serious—the cheeks, the forehead, the throat, all these can burn with dignity. But not the ears. Red ears are funny" (Dunbar 19). In *The Fall of Hyperion*, Keats depicts himself and the goddess Moneta, standing side by side, as "a stunt bramble by a solemn pine" (1.293).

It does not require a major critical leap to go from local incongruities to more serious mismatches central to our experience of the most important poems. Chapters 3 and 4 have highlighted some of the more obvious ones pervading *The Eve of St. Agnes*: Porphyro is the hero of the poem, an ardent lover, a Prince Charming to the rescue, Madeline's future husband, and at the same time is associated with images of sorcery, voyeurism, cruel seduction, and rape; Madeline is the beautiful heroine, the belle of the ball, Sleeping Beauty, a pious Christian, Porphyro's bride, and at the same time is a foolish victim of both Porphyro's stratagem and her own self-deception.

There are statements and situations of doubtful compatibility everywhere in Keats's good poems. Consider the speaker's musing about death in the sixth stanza of *Ode to a Nightingale*:

> Now more than ever seems it rich to die,
> To cease upon the midnight with no pain,
> While thou art pouring forth thy soul abroad
> In such an ecstasy!

The richness of this thought is immediately nullified by the realism of mortal extinction: "Still wouldst thou sing, and I have ears in vain— / To thy high requiem become a sod." Consider the fourth stanza of *Ode on a Grecian Urn*: a lovingly described procession of townspeople move toward some green altar— so far, so good—but then one realizes that these people will never reach their destination, they will never go back to the place where they came from, and their "little town" will be desolate "for evermore." Or take the lines about the happy/ frustrated lovers two stanzas earlier in the same poem:

> Bold lover, never, never canst thou kiss,
> Though winning near the goal—yet, do not grieve;
> She cannot fade, though thou hast not thy bliss,
> For ever wilt thou love, and she be fair!

(On one hand . . . on the other. . . . These lines do not need to be paraphrased.) In the ode *To Autumn* we read, first, a series of statements about how beautiful the season is; then we realize that all this beauty is dying; and finally (perhaps), if we put these two contrary notions together, we understand that death is somehow beautiful.

At this point it might seem that I am approaching dangerously close to the old New Criticism of forty and fifty years ago—the "mystic oxymoron" of Kenneth Burke, for example, and "oxymoronic fusion" of Earl Wasserman. Well, why not? We learned to read from the New Critics, and we constantly use New Critical methods in the privacy of our classrooms and personal reading. Maybe "mystic oxymoron" and "oxymoronic fusion" are not such bad terms for the authorial and textual complexity that I am trying to describe.

The Keats Map

One effective illustration of Keatsian authorial complexity is a sort of Keats map that starts with a horizontal line separating two realms in opposition: an actual world below the line and a contrasting ideal world above the line (see the precursor diagram included below on page 109). I have explained this (in the introduction to *John Keats: Complete Poems* xvi–xvii, among other places) as a "simplified cosmography" of the poems, where the two realms can stand for many related pairs of oppositions: earth and heaven, for example, mortality and immortality, time and timelessness, materiality and spirituality, the known and the unknown, the finite and the infinite, waking and dreaming, realism and romance, the natural and the supernatural—all prominent in the poems by Keats that readers and critics continue to find the most interesting.[7]

Endymion provides an archetype of the basic structure. For much of its four thousand lines, the hero is torn between his passion for the literally otherworldly goddess of the moon and his human responsibilities—to his sister, to the people whom he is supposed to be governing, and (in book 4) to the Indian maiden whom he falls madly in love with—in the sublunary world of Latmian reality. The division between ideal and real realms is hinted at in the opening lines of book 1 ("bind us to the earth" in line 7 and the image of the lamb straying beyond familiar surroundings to join "the herds of Pan" in lines 68–79), becomes more prominent in the Hymn to Pan (lines 232 ff., especially 293–302) and the depiction of the old shepherds' "fond imaginations" about heaven (lines 360–93), and is central to the narrative thereafter. Endymion is introduced as in a "fixed trance . . . Like one who on the earth had never stept" (lines 403–4). The events that follow are regularly plottable above and below (and occasionally on) the line separating the two worlds. Endymion's fervent renunciation of dreams in book 4 (lines 636 ff.), a last desperate attempt to resolve his internal conflict, is a rejection of the ideal realm. And then he is rewarded with eternal bliss in the upper region after all, as the supposedly human Indian maiden reveals that she is his moon goddess in disguise.

Each of the other major poems participates to some degree in this structural scheme. In *The Eve of St. Agnes*, Madeline's dream world is easily alignable with the values, tendencies, and images of the ideal realm, while Porphyro, Angela, Madeline's kinsmen, and the storm are a basic contrasting reality. In *The Eve of St. Mark*, the ideal is represented by the centuries-old life of St. Mark that Bertha is engrossed in and the reality by her situation in the darkening room and the images of the town and its inhabitants outside her window. In *La Belle Dame*, there is the fairy world to which the knight is attracted and then the real world that he has returned to upon awakening on "the cold hill's side." The supernatural world of the nightingale is played off against a kind of reality that the speaker says the nightingale has never known: "The weariness, the fever, and the fret / Here, where men sit and hear each other groan" (and so on through the whole of stanza 3 of the ode). The timelessness of life imagined on the Grecian urn repeatedly implies a contrasting world of process where trees shed their leaves,

MATERIALS OF THE KEATS MAP

IDEAL (world)—above the line	REAL (world)—below the line
Cynthia, Elysium	Endymion, Latmos
Madeline and her dream (ideal love)	Porphyro, the storm (physical love)
The legend of St. Mark	Bertha and the town
La Belle Dame's grot	The cold hill's side
Nightingale's forest	"Here, where . . ." (world of hungry generations)
Tempe, Arcady, urnly life	Process, passion, death
Lamia's palace	Lycius, the streets of Corinth
Songs of spring	Cottage farm, surroundings, in autumn

pipers get tired and stop piping, and lovers grow old but do, after all, become lovers. The unreality of Lamia's "purple-lined palace of sweet sin" and the reality of "the noisy world" of Lycius's native city, which he cannot quite forswear (2.27–33), are another pair of the same sort of opposites. In *To Autumn*, the focus is almost consistently on the here and now, but the opening of the third stanza—"Where are the songs of spring?"—is a significant reminder of what, in philosophical terms, the here and now is being contrasted with.

These are just a handful of examples. Other Keats poems can be related to the same basic structure: the poet's glimpse of otherworldly glories in the epistle *To My Brother George*; the upward flight of the charioteer in *Sleep and Poetry*; the bursting of mortal bars and soaring of the wandering spirit in *I stood tip-toe*; dissatisfaction with "see[ing] beyond our bourn" in the epistle to Reynolds; the murdered Lorenzo's separation from humanity in *Isabella*; the fear of being trapped "Beyond the sweet and bitter world" in *There is a joy in footing slow*; the "terrible division . . . when the soul is fled / Too high above our head" in *God of the meridian*; the bright star "in lone splendor hung aloft" in sharp contrast to "earth's human shores" down below; and so on.

Clearly Keats thought in such spatial terms, and so, of course, have numerous other writers. Wordsworth in *The Prelude* makes such a division in emphasizing the real-world interests of the youthful proponents of the French Revolution:

> Not in Utopia,—subterranean fields,—
> Or some secreted island, Heaven knows where!
> But in the very world, which is the world
> Of all of us,—the place where, in the end,
> We find our happiness, or not at all!   (11.140–44)

In many shorter works, he plays things remote, exotic, invisible, otherworldly, against "the common growth of mother-earth" (*Peter Bell*, with its high-flying/down-to-earth prologue, is an especially good example). Tennyson's *The Lady of Shalott* can be put on the Keats map—Shalott is both physically and symbolically above the line, Camelot below—and so can Yeats's *Sailing to Byzantium*: the realm of sensual music that is "no country for old men," the poet's Ireland of the 1920s, is the here and now below the line, while Byzantium, two thousand miles to the east and fourteen centuries into the past, is the ambiguous ideal above. Wallace Stevens's *Sunday Morning* repeatedly plays an upper realm ("Jove in the clouds," "paradise," "imperishable bliss," "isolation of the sky") against the reality of "our perishing earth." These are just four among hundreds of possible examples.

In Keats's poems there is frequent shuttling between the lower and upper regions, as his human characters—Endymion, Madeline, Bertha, the knight at arms, the speakers in the odes, Lycius in *Lamia*—attempt imaginatively to transcend their mortal world of mutability, natural process, and death, seeking another realm, most often of gods or fairies, where the condition of timelessness, they hope, will solve all those human problems. But except perhaps in *Endymion*, the attempt to escape mortality in these poems never succeeds. Something is wanting in the ideal, or the would-be escapist, being a native of the real world, learns that it is not possible to belong permanently in the ideal. So the metaphorical excursion concludes with a descent back to reality.

I have diagramed this structure of excursion and return many times in the classroom:

In print, back in the critical dark ages of the 1960s (see the second section of chapter 3), I used it to help inculcate a simplified view of what I thought was the principal moral and philosophical content of the poet's work taken altogether:

> [Keats's] significant poems center on a single basic problem, the mutability inherent in nature and human life, and openly or in disguise they debate the pros and cons of a single hypothetical solution, transcendence of earthly limitations by means of the visionary imagination. . . . Keats came to learn that this kind of imagination was a false lure, inadequate to the needs of the problem, and in the end he traded it for the naturalized imagination, embracing experience and process as his own and [humanity's] chief good. His honesty in treating the problem and his final opting for the natural world, where all the concrete images of poetry come from and where melodies impinge on "the sensual ear" or not at all, are what, more than anything else, guarantee his place "among the English Poets." (*Hoodwinking* 100)

I would not any longer seriously propose so simple a description to cover so complex a body of thinking, feeling, and writing as Keats and his poetry represent. But still (as on the present occasion) the diagram and the map can be used to make a point about the poet's authorial complexity.

The map, in my more recent understanding of the matter, is a frame for pairs of oppositions that, intentionally or not, Keats never in fact resolves in the poems. They do not cancel one another, and one of a pair does not finally win a conflict at the expense of the other. In every case, they are not so much ambiguities of an *either/or* division, where the meaning at first is uncertain but later is cleared up, as they are disparate elements in a continual *both/and* impingement and jostling of contraries. They constitute, to refer back to the beginning of this chapter, a sustained incongruity, a misfittingness that, as represented by the map, is cosmic as well as comic. And Keats manages to keep these components steadily in conflict while at the same time creating a sense that somehow the tensions are resolved.

These statements are admittedly quite abstract, and acceptable documentation would take much more space than I have available. I shall select two shorter pieces, *La Belle Dame sans Merci* and *Ode on a Grecian Urn*, to exemplify the typical conflicting spatial deployments in Keats's mature poems.

La Belle Dame is a narrative with a beginning ("I met a lady"), a middle ("And there she lulled me asleep"), and an end ("And I awoke and found me here") in which we are never actually told what happens.[8] It is cast in the form of a ballad, with a questioner who speaks the first three stanzas and then presumably stays to hear the protagonist's reply, which fills the remaining nine stanzas. The crucial question of the poem—and of anybody's individual reading of the poem—is posed at the beginning and then repeated in the fifth line: "O what can ail thee, knight at arms." The knight's well-detailed response, concluding "And this is why . . . ," seems at first a reasonable answer to the question. But it turns out to be no answer at all, because the events of the knight's story are entirely symbolic and the poem never explains the symbolism. Here, then, is another famous instance when the reader must supply significant meaning and the critical closure.

In his encounter with la Belle Dame, the clearly mortal knight crosses a boundary into a different world from his own. La Belle Dame is of another order: a "fairy's child," who sings a "fairy's song," provides exotic food ("roots of relish sweet . . . honey wild, and manna dew"), speaks "in language strange," and dwells in an "elfin grot." The two are mutually captivated; the knight provides gifts, sets her on his horse, "And nothing else saw all day long," while she responds with looks of love, moans, sighs, and a tender "I love thee true." In her "elfin grot," they make love—a reasonable interpretation of the "kisses four" followed by sleep. But then, "Ah! woe betide," the knight has a dream of "horrid warning": a company of death-pale kings, princes, and warriors declare to him, "La belle dame sans merci / Hath thee in thrall." At this point he awakens and finds himself on "the cold hill's side," the initial setting of the question-and-answer dialogue (though not, presumably, the setting of the knight's story, since he originally met la Belle Dame, he says, "in the meads," a different kind of topography).

We have, in terms of the Keats map, an actuality of the knight's mortality, his solitariness and inactivity, and a barren autumn landscape (the withered sedge, with no birds singing, at both the beginning and the end of the poem), and then a contrasting world of strange beauty, enticement, lovemaking, but also nightmare and, if we can believe the kings and princes, thralldom. One common

understanding of the story is that the knight is another of Keats's visionary protagonists who opted for the practically unattainable—union with a beautiful
creature from another world—and now suffers the consequences. In this reading, la Belle Dame is the antagonist, a merciless enchantress who will add him—
perhaps already has added him—to her collection of ruined kings, princes, and
warriors. It would seem better, on the Keats map, to stay below the line.

But what basis, exactly, is there in the poem for such a reading? Illustrators
of the poem, rather than focus on the wretched knight "alone and palely loitering," most often depict a handsome young man and a beautiful woman gazing
adoringly into each other's eyes. Can the artists be getting their idea of the story
from some other source? Actually many of the details of the knight's condition—
"alone," "palely loitering," "haggard," "woe-begone"—come from the questioner
in the first three stanzas, as do the description of the barren surroundings (no
sedge, no birds) and the knight's deathly complexion, pictured in terms of a lily,
"anguish moist and fever dew," and a fading rose. Perhaps it is the speaker of
these lines rather than the knight who is having a problem with reality; perhaps
the crucial question should be not what ails the knight but, instead, what ails
the questioner.[9]

Similarly, the notion that the knight is "in thrall" comes not from the knight's
own experience of thralldom but from the utterance of the kings, princes, and
warriors of the knight's "latest dream." This dream, which vaguely parallels the
"Ancestral voices prophesying war" in *Kubla Khan* in providing critics with
grounds for discovering a political theme (something about the demise of chiv-
alry and feudal aristocracy), is a hideous spectacle of "Pale warriors, death pale"
and "starv'd lips . . . With horrid warning gaped wide." It is not, at face value, a
reliable source concerning the knight's relationship with the lady. In the knight's
own account, which occupies most of the poem, it was a beautiful and promising love match, and the only problem is that he fell asleep, had a nightmare, and
woke up alone. Perhaps he hopes for another meeting with his lady. Perhaps his
experience has been a dream from beginning to end (and the nightmare a "dream
within a dream," as in *Endymion* 1.633). Perhaps, in his "loitering," he will make
up a story for any questioner who happens by!

Old-school biographical critics—those who read Lycius, Lamia, and Apollonius as standing for Keats, Fanny Brawne, and Charles Brown—have interpreted *La Belle Dame* as an allegory involving Keats and Fanny Brawne (or, more
abstractly, Keats and love), and also as being about Keats and tuberculosis (Keats
and death). Later writers have tended to focus on categorical differences between
the knight as mortal and la Belle Dame as nonmortal, and between the real world
of the cold hill's side and the romance world of the lady's "elfin grot," sometimes
taking la Belle Dame as a symbol of visionary imagination and the knight as a
Keatsian hoodwinked dreamer. But there are (and have been) many other interpretive possibilities.

The point here, in connection with the Keats map as an illustration of Keatsian
complexity, is that the two sides of the opposition—real world, fairy world—are
presented as having both positive and negative qualities almost simultaneously.
In the present real world of the poem (regardless of who is reporting), the knight

is alone, loitering, woebegone, apparently ill, and the surroundings are bleak and unmusical (though an oddly countering sense of autumnal fulfillment—a separate critical problem in itself—is conveyed in the references to the squirrel's granary and the completed harvest). But it is also in the real world—"in the meads"—that the knight met and fell in love with la Belle Dame, and where there were flowers, not withered sedge, for him to fashion into the garland and bracelets that he mentions. The fairy world into which he is drawn—at some (conveniently) unspecified point in the proceedings—seems, for a while at least, to be totally pleasurable, a matter of songs, strange food, strange language, and lovemaking. The knight's pleasure comes to an abrupt end with his bad dream and subsequent awakening. But the dream, which is never explained, does not really negate the romantic experience. It would be perfectly reasonable (and not just visionarily romantic) for the knight to wish to repeat it, just as Keats's readers in fact repeat it every time they read the poem.

In *Ode on a Grecian Urn*, the hypothetical romance world above the line is the ancient Greece of "Tempe or the dales of Arcady," separated from the speaker of the ode by even more miles and centuries than Byzantium is from Yeats's speaker. It stands in obvious and pointed contrast to the speaker's own modern world of process and mortality. On the painted surface of one side of the urn, the piper's melodies are imagined to be unheard and therefore sweeter; the piper never tires; the lovers, pursuing and pursued, never age or lose their beauty ("She cannot fade . . . For ever wilt thou love, and she be fair!"); the "happy" trees never shed their leaves (it is eternal spring); everything is "far above" the passionate experiences of living humans like the speaker, who are subject to "a heart high-sorrowful and cloy'd, / A burning forehead, and a parching tongue." On the other side of the urn, a sacrificial procession of priest, heifer, and townspeople is stopped forever en route to some green altar; they will neither reach their destination nor go back to whatever town they came from (though the heifer will be saved from sacrifice, and the people, just like the lovers earlier in the poem, will not age or die). These latter images, too, are different from life in the real world, where such a procession would continue to its destination, and then everybody would return home.

There is perhaps a greater density of opposites in this poem than in any other of comparable length in all of British literature. The first image, "still unravish'd bride," immediately evokes the unstated counternotions of violence and sexual fulfillment in "ravished" bride; "quietness" implies a contrary noisiness; "foster-child" makes one think of natural child. Pairings of this sort are a principal element of the ode's structure and very shortly are made explicit in such phrases as "deities or mortals," "men or gods," "pursuit . . . escape," "Heard . . . unheard," "sensual . . . spirit," and so on to the paired abstractions brought together in the urn's message of the final two lines, "Beauty is truth, truth beauty. . . ." What is important, for present purposes, is the near balance of pluses and minuses accorded to both sides of these pairs. Throughout the poem, in the phrases just quoted and in the larger oppositions connected with time (below the line) and timelessness (above), they tend to get the speaker's, and the poem's, approval and disapproval almost equally.

Older critics—for example, the American New Humanists of the 1920s—tended to read the poem as an unequivocal celebration of the timeless world of art, and they censured Keats for the supposed Romantic escapism that such celebration implied. Then the New Criticism exerted its influence, and readers began to notice (just as the speaker, being a clever reader, had noticed all along in perhaps half the lines of the poem) that the art world has its drawbacks as a hypothetical alternative to the human world: the piper cannot stop playing; the lovers can never finally kiss or make love; the trees are confined to a single season; the permanent halting of the sacrificial procession leaves an unseen "little town" forever "desolate." Some critics took these misgivings, especially the speaker's somber comments concerning the silence and desolateness of the abandoned town in the last three lines of the fourth stanza, to signify the poet's rejection of the ideal: the urn in the final stanza, now a "Cold Pastoral," is only a work of art after all, a "tease" just like eternity itself, somehow "a friend to man," but not of much practical help, for the concluding aphorism about beauty and truth really makes very little sense.

But both kinds of critical rendering—pro-ideal (therefore escapist), pro-reality (therefore skeptical of the ideal)—are necessarily one-sided, the products of the selection and unifying processes that I described in chapter 4. Rather, the urn, like the ideal that it represents, is both admired and gently pitied throughout the speaker's musings. Readers do not keep returning to the ode to learn that life in the real world is preferable to life on an urn (or vice versa). Rather, they are repeatedly drawn to the spectacle of the sensitive speaker's uncertainties in the face of these oppositions. At any point, a resolution could go either way, and they read and reread, I think, to see how the conflict will conclude each time anew. There is also, in all these poems (not just the Grecian urn ode), the attraction that, although both worlds on the Keats map always have serious shortcomings—the problems of the real world can never be made to go away, and the ideal alternative is never finally a solution—Keats continues to strike readers as upbeat rather than pessimistic in his attitudes toward both life and art, the real and the ideal, in his poetry. It would be a nice piece of criticism to explain how, as an artist, he manages to do this.

It should by now be obvious how *The Eve of St. Agnes* can fit on the Keats map. Madeline's dream sets her apart, Beadsman-like, from the reality of her surroundings, and her associations with religion, superstition, and chastity and her beauty and delicacy are further connections with some kind of ideal above the line. Her bedchamber is on an upper floor, literally as well as symbolically above the lower part of the castle where Porphyro and Angela are working out the details of a stratagem. And that stratagem, with the rest of the action that proceeds from it, puts Porphyro, through much of the narrative, in a realm of reality below the line and contrasts with the saintly purity of Madeline above. How this works out at the end—whether Madeline raises Porphyro to her upper world or Porphyro brings Madeline down to his lower, and whether (in either case) the result is a happy or a less happy outcome—is left finally, as I have been arguing all along, to the individual reader. Most of the fifty-nine readings surveyed in chapter 3 represent opinions that can be put on the map, one way or another.

So the individual reader determines the indeterminate, as it were. But Keats is the genius who created these complexities of contradictory materials out of which reader after reader constructs the meanings. In the case of *The Eve of St. Agnes*, he produced a poem about love, sex, marriage, magic, imagination that works, imagination that does not work, poetry, religion, language problems, and several kinds of politics; a poem about a young man whose ardor is tinged with selfishness and deceit; a poem about a young woman whose saintly qualities are mixed up with silly behavior; a happy poem that is framed by bitter cold and death and has a conclusion in which we are not sure what is concluded. These are some of the superabundant starting materials of many different ways of reading *The Eve of St. Agnes*. They add up, in the various reckonings, to a poem that readers cannot stop reading and that seems a little different each time a reader reads it, even if the reader has been reading and teaching it for forty years. It is no insignificant achievement for a poet who stopped writing entirely at the age of twenty-three.

CONCLUSION

Keats "among the English Poets"

WHAT HAPPENS WHEN THE TWO SIDES, author and reader, are brought together by the text? On one side, we have Keats's whimsical incongruities and more serious disjunctions, contraries, and mystic oxymorons: surely a complex multiple authorship, even if it resides almost entirely in the single historical entity, John Keats, born more than two hundred years ago. On the other side, we have an incredibly complex readership: all those thousands of individual readers discussed in chapter 4. And we of course have multiple interpretations, the inevitable outcome when complex authorship and complex readership connect at a specific site, in this case a text of *The Eve of St. Agnes*.

The practical results of this combination—nothing less than a canonical work and a canonical author—are just what Keats and his friends hoped for all along. In this final chapter I shall consider the history and then some bases of the canonicity that I think Keats had in mind. Keats has been "among the English Poets" for at least the last 150 years,[1] and his reputation has never been better than it is right now. I wish to suggest, in the course of expounding a notion of "canonical complexity," how this came about.

The Origins of Canonicity

Near the beginning of his first journal letter to his brother and sister-in-law in America, in a section now editorially dated 14 October 1818, Keats briefly describes the unfavorable reception of *Endymion* and puts it in long-range perspective with a remark that has been quoted repeatedly and with increasing admiration ever since the letter first appeared in print, in Milnes's *Life* of 1848: "This is a mere matter of the moment—I think I shall be among the English Poets after my death" (*Letters* 1:394).

Outwardly, Keats might have seemed to his friends to have little reason for such a prediction. The *Blackwood's* issue containing John Gibson Lockhart's fourth tirade against the "Cockney School of Poetry," savaging both Keats's *Poems* of 1817 and the more recent *Endymion*, was published just six weeks earlier. Within a month, John Wilson Croker's infamous attack on *Endymion* in the *Quarterly Review* appeared. Keats's only substantial poem since *Endymion* was *Isabella*, drafted in the spring, which was but one-eighth the length of *Endymion* and of questionable quality. He would later condemn it as mawkish, overly simple, "weak-sided" (*Letters* 2:162, 174). He had no new major work under way and not even any very clear idea of how to support himself. His friend Woodhouse described him about this time as "unknown[,] unheeded, despised [by] one of our archcritics, neglected by the rest" (*Letters* 1:384). Immediate personal problems included the breakup of his family of siblings. His brother Tom was dying of tuberculosis. His brother George, with his new bride, had not only been out of the country, four thousand miles away in southeastern Illinois, but had not been heard from for several months. His fifteen-year-old sister, Fanny, had been living separately with a guardian who made visits with her brothers difficult and unpleasant. Within three months after October 1818, Keats would begin *The Eve of St. Agnes* and continue into the nine-month "living year" of the major odes and narratives, produced one after another in an astonishing spate of sustained creativity. But in October, his situation and prospects were not at all promising.

His remark about being "among the English Poets" is all the more amazing, therefore, when we see it in context and imagine Keats imagining himself immortalized in a Mount Rushmore tableau of "laurel'd peers":[2] Shakespeare, Milton, Spenser—and Keats and how many others? The Mount Rushmore reference is of course anachronistic, the monument dating from more than a century after Keats's death, but so perhaps is our modern idea of who "the English Poets" were in Keats's time. Let us consider, for a moment, what he might have envisioned.

There is no universal agreement on when the idea of a national canon, a select group constituting the most highly regarded poets of the nation, first took hold. Since the Renaissance at least, there had been lists of writers for one occasion or another and, starting with Richard Tottel's landmark *Songes and Sonettes* in 1557, miscellanies that brought together poems by different authors from various sources. Through much of the eighteenth century, Shakespeare, Milton, and Spenser were routinely acknowledged as a trio of unsurpassed achievement. But the preponderance of evidence and current critical opinion suggests that the idea of identifying a larger group of the "best" writers and presenting them as "the British Poets" or "the English Poets" materialized as recently as two decades before Keats's birth—in effect, at the beginning of what we now call the Romantic period—as miscellanies developed into anthologies and publishers for the first time began producing, at a great rate, multivolume editions of poetry for increasing numbers of middle-class consumers who had, or wished to appear to have, the money to afford them and the taste and leisure to appreciate them.[3]

I want to focus specifically on those multivolume editions of poets, which I think are the most immediate and obvious embodiments of what Keats had in mind when he referred to "the English Poets." In his day, just as in ours, the publishers and booksellers played an important part in the *business* (that is, trade as well as activity) of canon formation. "Tremors began upon Scottish soil early in the 1770s," writes Thomas Bonnell ("Bookselling" 55), whose two essays on John Bell are the most authoritative accounts in print of the Edinburgh and London publishers' competitive activities during the decade. First, the distinguished Edinburgh firm of Kincaid and Creech—the booksellers Alexander Kincaid and his successor William Creech, acting together with a third Edinburgh bookseller, John Balfour—startled the London publishing establishment, or a piece of it, by issuing a 44-volume collection titled *The British Poets* between 1773 and 1776. Opening with four volumes of Milton (in a two-volumes-in-one format), the collection presented original works and translations by twenty-two poets of the seventeenth and eighteenth centuries: Milton, Samuel Butler, Abraham Cowley, Sir John Denham, Edmund Waller, Dryden, Sir Samuel Garth, Matthew Prior, Pope, Gay, and a dozen others, concluding with James Beattie, who was a fellow Scotsman, the only living writer among the group, and one of Creech's regular authors.

Ultimately not distributed in London, this Edinburgh edition was followed almost immediately by a much more ambitious and influential project, John Bell's *The Poets of Great Britain Complete from Chaucer to Churchill*, which consisted, all told, of 109 volumes published between 1777 and 1783 (the dates of the London imprints run from 1776 to 1782). This massive undertaking included works of no fewer than fifty poets: Chaucer, Spenser, and Donne in the first twenty-five volumes (when the series is arranged in its final numbering) and forty-seven later writers from Milton—occupying volumes 28–31, the first actually issued—to two authors who had died as recently as 1773 and 1779, John Cunningham and John Armstrong, in volumes 106 and 102, respectively. Attractively printed by the Apollo Press in Edinburgh, "Bell's Edition" featured (as Bell highlighted in his advertising) authoritative texts, biographical and critical prefaces—some of considerable length, again from reputable sources—and engraved portraits of all but a handful of the authors.[4] One of Bell's aims, as he wrote in a prospectus to the edition, was to issue the "English classics" in the same kind of "general and uniform" format that had long been used for Greek and Roman classics and was now being adopted for French and Italian writers as well. It was "high time," said Bell, for Great Britain to "pay her worthies that tribute to which their distinguished genius ha[d] so justly entitled them" (Bonnell, "Bookselling" 57).[5]

In almost instant reaction to Bell's audacious enterprise, thirty-six of his fellow London booksellers banded together as proprietors to inaugurate a rival edition, *The Works of the English Poets*, consisting of sixty-eight volumes that appeared between 1779 and 1781. Fifty-six of the volumes contained the works of fifty-two poets from the seventeenth and eighteenth centuries, including ten writers whom Bell omitted or was not allowed to print. The last two volumes were an index to the edition. And the ten volumes before the index were taken up with Samuel Johnson's *Prefaces, Biographical and Critical, to the Works of the English Poets* (each preface individually paged so that it could be bound up with the appropriate volume of poetry), a series that immediately became a separate canonical work in its own right as Johnson's *Lives of the Poets*. Much to Johnson's dismay—

because he was the hired preface-writer, and had virtually nothing to do with the selection of writers included in the edition—the publishers printed "Johnson's Poets" on the spine of each volume. Thus, that is the name by which the edition was known for many decades afterward.

These editions of the 1770s were the earliest examples for English poets of a type of "general and uniform" collection that has been a staple of book publishing ever since and is practically ubiquitous in the twentieth century in such series as the Oxford World Classics, the Oxford Standard Authors, the Oxford English Texts, the Everyman Library, the Penguin Classics, Random House's Modern Library, Houghton Mifflin's Riverside Editions, the Norton Critical Editions, the Library of America, and a great many others, all inevitably carrying on the work of forming and reforming our canons of classical and approved literary works.

Because these multi-author standard editions have for so long been commonplace, we probably do not give much thought to their social and political origins. But in the 1770s—the decade of the American Revolution and the one preceding the beginning of the French Revolution—the Edinburgh and London publishers' activities reflected (and of course took advantage of) widespread social changes. These are not my main topic, but I should like to noted a few of the general causes that helped produce the readers and purchasers of the multi-volume editions of poets and, in the process, produced the first British and English national canons.[6] Some were the result of Enlightenment valuing of the human individual, surfacing in the democratizing tendencies that led to the revolutions and also, in another direction, in an accelerated interest in biographical matters such as authorship, creativity, genius, and single-handed achievement (an interest represented most prominently, among the materials at hand, by the popularity and influence of Johnson's *Lives of the Poets*). Enlightenment-inspired educational reform and a consequent rise in the literacy of the population (along with, obviously, an increase in the population itself) resulted in more people who could read. A new aesthetics of valuing art and literature "as such" (in Abrams's phrase) played a part, manifested in the development of "connoisseurship" and the idea of reading for pleasure as opposed to strictly moral and utilitarian ends. People had more leisure in which to read and more disposable income for the purchase of books. And the (perpetually!) rising middle class, associating literature with gentility, acquired a connection with "high" culture when they bought the new English classics. John Bell even made a selling point of the portable size of his octodecimo volumes: the collection would fit into two folio-size boxes, and thus the purchasers could carry their culture with them wherever they traveled (Bonnell, "Bookselling" 64).

Both Bell's edition and "Johnson's Poets" were reissued, the latter many times. "Most eminent," with its further nudge toward modern canonizing, was incorporated into the title of Johnson's prefaces from 1781 on: *Lives of the Most Eminent English Poets*.[7] Numerous other multivolume collections followed. Bonnell describes a series called *The Poetical Magazine: or, Parnassian Library*, published by the London bookseller Joseph Wenman around 1780, that according to Wenman's advertisement would include "the Whole of the Poetical Works of all the justly celebrated Poets" and would be issued in "Volumes of the same Size, and printed in the same Manner, as Mr. Bell's Edition of the Poets, and therefore . . . very portable and convenient for the Pocket" ("John Bell's *Poets*" 151). Robert Anderson organized and wrote prefaces for a thirteen-volume *Complete Edition of the Poets of Great Britain*, published in London by John and Arthur Arch and others from 1792 to 1795 (a fourteenth volume was added in 1807). This edition, beginning with Chaucer, Surrey, Wyatt, and Sackville in volume 1, offered from three or four to as many as twenty writers per volume and some 120 poets and translators in the entire array.

Thomas Park edited an elaborate collection, in forty-five or more volumes, of *The Works of the British Poets, Collated with the Best Editions*, published in London by John Sharpe between 1805 and 1808. This project, according to Park's prospectus in the first volume, would provide "the Poetical Works included in the editions of Dr. Johnson and Mr. Bell, excepting a few of inferior merit, by whose exclusion, room will be obtained for such ancient Authors as are thought more worthy, or such modern Writers as the lapse of time since those publications renders essential to the completion of the work." Johnson's prefaces were incorporated, and Park supplied new ones for the additional authors. Again, as with Bell's project, much was made of the authoritativeness of the texts and the inclusion of high-quality engraved portraits. The volumes, sold by subscription as well as by the individual issue, appeared at the rate of one every two weeks, and more than a hundred authors were included, though they were all, in spite of Park's remark about "ancient Authors" in the prospectus, from the seventeenth and eighteenth centuries.

Park's edition was followed later in the same decade by the better-known "Chalmers's English Poets," an expanded reissue of "Johnson's Poets" edited by the indefatigable Alexander Chalmers. ("No man," says his biographer in the *Dictionary of National Biography*, "ever edited so many works as Chalmers for the booksellers.") This was *The Works of the English Poets, from Chaucer to Cowper*, published in 1810 by a consortium of forty-six London booksellers headed by Joseph Johnson. It was a major undertaking: twenty-one volumes amounting to 13,550 large, double-column pages of poetry and including 130 authors from Chaucer (who occupies all of the 724 pages of volume 1) to James Beattie and William Cowper from the 1770s and 1780s. The index of titles and subjects at the end of volume 21 runs to seventy-three pages.

Three shorter editions of the same period—late eighteenth century and the first two decades of the nineteenth—also deserve mention for their part in the construction and reinforcement of a national canon. George Ellis's *Specimens of the Early English Poets*, in three volumes, first published in 1790 and reissued in 1801 and 1803, anthologized the writings of 161 poets ranging from Robert of Gloucester (in the thirteenth century) to Sir Francis Fane (in the seventeenth). Robert Southey continued Ellis's work with *Specimens of the Later British Poets*, published in 1807, again a three-volume collection that presents the work of 223 poets beginning (where Ellis had left off) with Thomas Otway and ending with Cowper. Samuel Pratt's compilation, *The Cabinet of Poetry, Containing the Best Entire Pieces to Be Found in the Works of the British Poets*, came out in six thick volumes in 1808, containing Milton alone in volume 1 and eighty-one other writers, from Cowley to Beattie, in volumes 2–6. And then, to round out this background for Keats's remark about "the English Poets" in October 1818, one might add the circumstance that Thomas Campbell was just then putting together a seven-volume *Specimens of the British Poets; with Biographical and Critical Notices* that would be published by John Murray a year later, in 1819. Campbell's first volume consists mainly of a three-part "Essay on English Poetry"; volumes 2–7, amounting to 2,600 pages, present "specimens" of no fewer than 240 poets, from Chaucer to Beattie and Christopher Anstey (who had died in 1805).

This background of publishing history illuminates Keats's remark about being "among the English Poets after my death" in at least three ways. First, Keats was not, at this point in his career, showing any morbid premonition of his early death. The fact is that, apart from the single inclusion of James Beattie (1735–1803) in Creech's *British Poets* of 1773–1776, none of the writers in any of these editions from the 1770s to 1819 was alive when the work was published. Keats's "after my death" simply acknowledges that only dead poets could qualify.[8]

Second, "the English Poets," unlike the handful of distinguished persons in the Mount Rushmore tableau, were a sizable group. Creech's *British Poets* (1773–1776) included twenty-two writers; Bell's *Poets of Great Britain* (1776–1782) had fifty; the London proprietors' *Works of the English Poets* ("Johnson's Poets," 1779–1781) had fifty-two; and in Anderson's *Complete Edition* (1792–1795) the number had more than doubled to 120. Park's *Works* (1805–1808) also contained more than one hundred poets, and "Chalmers's English Poets" (1810), which for Keats's time would have been the most standard of all these editions, had 130 writers. Ellis and Southey together included 384 poets in their complementary sets of early and later *Specimens* (1790, 1807). Campbell's *Specimens* in the year following Keats's letter of October 1818 represented 240 poets. Especially from our modern vantage point, we might think that Keats was quite modest in his expectations.

Third, despite these large numbers of "English Poets" at the end of the eighteenth century and the early years of the nineteenth, Keats was clearly conscious of canonicity in the modern sense, entailing all the diverse arguments concerning what constitutes "most eminent" or "best" and who decides such matters that continue today through the latest meeting of the Modern Language Association and the latest meeting of the editors of one or another of the Norton anthologies. (Perhaps the directness of progress would be clearer if we imagined Keats thinking he would be in the *Norton Anthology of English Literature* after his death!) Keats was of course right about his future place among the poets. Let us speculate about how he and his readers, necessarily working together (there is no such thing as canonicity without readers), have elevated him, perhaps permanently, to inclusion in this canonical group.

Canonical Complexity

The bases for attaining canonicity in literature—what it takes to be a "classic," to get into an authoritative anthology or series, to be included on somebody's approved list—are usually obscure and sometimes totally mysterious. The problem arose, just as one might expect, almost simultaneously with the earliest editions of English and British poets described in the preceding section and became a frequent topic in prefaces and advertisements around the time Keats was starting to read poetry. We have already seen Thomas Park, in the prospectus for his 1805–1808 *Works of the British Poets*, mentioning "a few [poets] of inferior merit" included in Bell's and Johnson's editions and promising his subscribers that he would substitute "more worthy" ancients and some "essential" moderns in their place. Robert Southey, in his preface to *Specimens of the Later English Poets* (1807), speaking of the "many worthless versifyers" whom he has been obliged to admit among the selections, offers a justification on historical grounds: "My business was to collect specimens as for a *hortus siccus* [a collection of dried botanical samples]; not to collect flowers as for an anthology." Samuel Pratt's advertisement at the beginning of the first volume of his *Cabinet of Poetry* (1808) announces, "The present Work is compiled on the principle of rejecting all the worthless and uninteresting parts of [the poets'] compositions, and retaining only the best and most exquisite pieces. It is in regard to the mass of English Poetry, strictly a CABINET OF GEMS"—in other words, a canonizing not just of poets but of selections from their works.

Alexander Chalmers's preface to his 21-volume *Works of the English Poets* (1810) is the most thoughtful of the early musings on the selection process:

> The fate of the few collections which have been made of this kind readily pointed out that the objections of critics would be directed, either against redundancy, or defect, and it is as likely that I shall be blamed for admitting too many, as for admitting too few, into a work professing to be a BODY OF THE STANDARD ENGLISH POETS....
>
> There are perhaps but two rules by which a collector of English poetry can be guided. He is either to give a series of the BEST poets, or of the most POPULAR, but simple as these rules may appear, they are not without difficulties, for whichever we choose to rely upon, the other will be found to interfere. In the first instance, the question will be perpetually recurring "who *are* the best poets?" and as this will unavoidably involve all the disputed points in poetical criticism, and all the partialities of individual taste, an editor must pause before he venture on a decision from which the appeals will be numerous and obstinately contested.
>
> On the other hand, he will not find much more security in popularity, which is a criterion of uncertain duration, sometimes depending on circumstances very remote from taste or judgment, and, unless in some few happy instances, a mere fashion....

Chalmers has solved his dilemma, he says, with the guidance of a "mixed rule" combining the standards of "abstract merit" and "popular reception." His work will "illustrate the progress and history of the art [of poetry] from the age of Chaucer to that of Cowley," but in a selection that is, in part at least, based on his estimate of the taste and endurance of the modern audience: "It would be in vain to attempt to revive authors whom no person would read, and to fill thousands of pages with discarded prolixities, merely because they characterized the dulness of the age in which they were tolerated."

Two centuries later—with or without the benefit of Matthew Arnold and the pseudoscientificism of his famous touchstones ("infallible . . . for detecting the presence or absence of high poetic quality, and also the degree of that quality")[9]—we have still not progressed much beyond Chalmers in our explanations of how or why canonical authors and works are in the canon. Obviously, aesthetic quality plays a part (canonical works, someone may say, just before running out of the room, are "well written"), but it is next to impossible to describe and evaluate aesthetic quality objectively. A hundred years ago, a lecturer on literature would fill an hour with anecdotes of author biography, skirting the texts entirely, and then, just as the campus clock was tolling the end of the session, might pat his midsection (in ancient times the principal locus of literary appreciation) and utter something like "But ah, gentlemen, the poetry!" No doubt some of our current rhetoric about the aesthetic quality of writing amounts to the same thing. Politics certainly enters into the winnowing and gatekeeping processes, especially, as feminist critics have repeatedly pointed out, the sexual and gender politics that for so long made both literature and scholarly criticism an almost exclusively male concern.[10] Commercial considerations are, of course, a factor, just as they were at the beginning of canonicity in the late eighteenth century. No publisher makes a business of trying to sell authors and works that people do not want to read. At any given time and place, canonicity results from a combination of aesthetic, ideological, and commercial interests that are constantly in motion and continually changing in the ways in which they interact with one another.

It is interesting, though, that in every imaginable category we do always have canons. The revision or overturning of one canon inevitably puts another in its place, and every canon, whatever the category, always signifies "best" in some sense—best at giving the reader pleasure, best at inculcating moral virtue, most effective as political propaganda, and so on. To represent British Romantic poetry, we used to teach (and some continue to teach) just the six standard males, from Blake through Keats. We now usually add women writers to the group—most often, Anna Barbauld, Charlotte Smith, Mary Robinson, Joanna Baillie, Felicia Hemans, and Letitia Landon.[11] But these newcomers, who themselves have already become a canonical cluster of additions to the canon, are a mere handful of the nine hundred women poets whom J. R. de J. Jackson lists in his *Romantic Poetry by Women: A Bibliography, 1770–1835*. We have, that is, created a new canon consisting of less than one percent of the pool. The same process operates in every other category: on any given occasion, we have a small number of "best" among the members of this or that racial or ethnic minority, religious denomination, social class, occupation, nationality, locale, period, genre, and so on. The overriding question is why some writers and works are better than others in *whatever* group one designates by class, type, or purpose.

Surely part of an answer concerns an author's or a work's *style* in the old-fashioned sense of "mode of expression"—its specific words, images, and figures of speech, the way the sentences are constructed, the rhythms, the sound patterns, and any other language matters that can be considered separately from the ideas and structures of a work. Critics in general have not been successful in describing or explaining the effects of such homely components as vocabulary and syntax in a text (for example, why one word or phrase is more pleasing or telling than another), but that does not make them any less effective. To put it as broadly (and vaguely) as possible, a certain level of stylistic competence is an absolute requisite for canonicity.

But works that keep their authors "among the English Poets" long after their deaths obviously have more than just stylistic competence. What they typically have most of all, I suggest, is the capacity to stimulate multiple and contrary meanings like those I described in chapters 4 and 5 as the basis for the interpretive inexhaustibility of complex works such as *The Eve of St. Agnes*. This idea is at the heart of the most serviceable definition of canonicity that I have seen in print, a description written not by a literary theorist but by an intellectual historian, David Harlan, in an essay published in the *American Historical Review*:

> Canonical works are those texts that have gradually revealed themselves to be multi-dimensional and omni-significant, those works that have produced a plenitude of meanings and interpretations, only a small percentage of which make themselves available at any single reading. Canonical texts . . . generate new ways of seeing old things and new things we have never seen before. No matter how subtly or radically we change our approach to them, they always respond with something new; no matter how many times we reinterpret them, they always have something illuminating to tell us. Their very indeterminacy means that they can never be exhausted. . . . Canonical works are multi-dimensional, omni-significant, inexhaustible, perpetually new, and, for all these reasons, "permanently valuable."[12]

Harlan's definition, emphasizing multiple meanings and inexhaustibility, pinpoints salient qualities of the most uncontestably canonical poems of the Romantic period. I offer three quick examples—*The Tyger, Kubla Khan*, and *Tintern Abbey*—each of which, to underscore the point, could be the center of a separate book on multiple reading (with an appendix headed "Fifty-nine Ways of Looking at . . ."). In the latest survey conducted by the publisher (in 1997), teachers using the *Norton Anthology of English Literature* rated *The Tyger* the most nearly indispensable of Blake's poems. Everybody knows that *The Tyger* is in some way about the origin of evil, with the implied question of how a God who is both all-good and all-powerful can allow evil to exist. But in its separate particulars, Blake's text is full of difficulties, starting with "burning bright" in the first line (is the tiger somehow on fire? Blake's accompanying illustration shows a puffy animal that not only is not burning but looks rather like a friendly stuffed toy that a child might cuddle up with) and "forests of the night" in the second line (what could *they* be?). The "framer" of the animal's "fearful symmetry" is a winged creature working in "deeps or skies," one who "dares" and "aspires" (lines

4–8)—very likely the aspiring rebel Satan, one might think—but then why would a benevolent omnipotent deity allow Satan to make the tiger? The middle of the poem has subjects with no verbs (lines 12, 13, 15) and a series of blacksmith images that turn the tiger into something forged out of iron. The penultimate stanza begins with "the stars" either hurling down their spears on the world below or else dropping them as a sign of surrender (line 17)—these are two quite different ways of looking at the image—and ends with what might be considered the central question posed by the poem, "Did he who made the Lamb make thee?" (line 20), to which the reply ought to be "no" but might instead be "yes" or "maybe." There are of course answers to all these (and other) questions concerning the details and several ways to resolve each difficulty. My point is that the interpretive answers will differ, and can be connected in many different combinations, not only from one reader to the next, but even, for an individual reader, from one reading to the next.

Kubla Khan and *Tintern Abbey*, rated the single most essential pieces by Coleridge and Wordsworth in the Norton survey, are longer and more difficult than *The Tyger*, and they both (accordingly?) get even higher percentages of "always teach" responses from users of the anthology. After an initial reading, interpretive problems in *Kubla Khan* begin with the title and subtitle ("Kubla Khan: or, A Vision in a Dream") and the heading of the prose introductory note that appears beneath these in the latest lifetime printing of 1834 but in modern texts more often is joined with the title so as to become a second subtitle ("A Fragment"). Is this work really a "vision in a dream" (as the introductory note goes on to claim)? Is it really a fragment (as opposed to a finished work in the "fragment" genre)? And then the note itself, telling about Purchas's *Pilgrimage*, the opium dream, and the "person on business from Porlock," raises numerous additional questions, including whether the note is to be read as an integral component of the work (making *Kubla Khan* a piece partly in prose, partly in verse), whether any of the events described in the note really happened, and whether the speaker of the note is the same persona as the narrator of lines 1–36 and/or the lyric speaker of lines 37–54. This last poses the further question of the number of speakers in the work. There could be three (the voices of the note, lines 1–36, and lines 37–54), two (the voices of the note and the verse, or else one voice in the note and lines 37–54 and a second, intermediate voice, as it were, in lines 1–36), or a single voice throughout.

These are just preliminaries. In the verse of *Kubla Khan*, nearly every detail—and there are several hundred of them in the fifty-four lines—is symbolic but with no explanation of the symbolism. The Kubla Khan who decreed the stately pleasure-dome may be read as a creative genius, working miracles of unification out of the various opposed images of lines 1–36. He may also, or instead, be read as a political tyrant, famous for his Ozymandian arrogance, a violator of nature at the very least, and perhaps of much more, depending on what the "sacred river" (line 3) stands for. He appears headed for trouble—suggested by the "Ancestral voices prophesying war" in line 30—but maybe the ancestors are on his side, and the war is just what he is looking forward to. The abrupt shift in line 37 to the lyric speaker's vision of an Abyssinian maid and the question of whether he can revive her song complicates the reading still further. What has she to do with Kubla Khan? Why would a revival of her song enable the speaker to recreate Kubla Khan's "dome in air" (line 46)? At the end, does he succeed (as Kubla Khan seems to have succeeded) or fail (in the manner of the persona of the introductory note)? And more specific questions concerning the individual details, including the sexual images that abound in the original printed text's second stanza or verse paragraph (lines 12–30), could occupy hours of class discussion after some of these larger problems had been worried over.[13]

Tintern Abbey—another several hours' worth of class subject matter—is a tourist poem in which the center of attraction, the famous ruined abbey, is out of sight "a few miles" downstream; a nature poem in which, after the opening paragraph, there are almost no images of nature; a political poem in which most of the speaker's political, social, and economic beliefs lie unexpressed between the lines; a religious poem in which what seems to be unmediated contact with a pantheistic deity (for example, "we are laid asleep / In body, and become a living soul . . . [and] see into the life of things," lines 45–49) is soberly, even logically, explained in terms of tourist postcard chitchat ("How oft, in spirit, have I turned to thee, / O sylvan Wye," lines 55–56; "Therefore am I still / A lover of the meadows and the woods," lines 102–3).

The poem is a texture of contradictions from beginning to end: simultaneously a celebration and a lament over the speaker's maturing, a depiction of both the harmony and the disharmony of humans and nature, an alternately successful and unsuccessful attempt to reconcile the "two consciousnesses" of the opening lines of book 2 of *The Prelude*, and a view of the speaker's and his sister's future that is at once tenderly optimistic and funereal. Three decades ago, I remarked that "it is sometimes difficult, even after many readings, to decide what the poem is primarily about" (*William Wordsworth: Selected Poems* 516). Wordsworth criticism in the intervening years has not simplified the business. We know that *Tintern Abbey* is about nature, time, mortality, memory, imagination, society, the city, humanity, and God (to list a few of the more frequently mentioned possibilities). But it remains the individual reader's task to sort out the combinations and emphases among these, and this still leaves, just as with *Kubla Khan*, innumerable problems concerning specific details (as in lines 95–96, "a sense sublime / Of something far more deeply interfused," where the question "more deeply than what?" has no apparent answer).

I offer *The Tyger, Kubla Khan,* and *Tintern Abbey* as exemplary illustrations of what I wish to call, for short, canonical complexity. These poems abound in multiple and conflicting possibilities for interpretation—in Harlan's definition that I quoted earlier, they are "multi-dimensional, omni-significant, inexhaustible, perpetually new"—and they also, in very practical terms, get the highest ratings from teachers using the *Norton Anthology* (a distinction they share with *The Eve of St. Agnes, Ode to a Nightingale,* and *Ode on a Grecian Urn*). It is the nature of canonical works to have, or to provide the basis for, more meanings than any reader can process at a reading and therefore to be, in a manner of speaking, infinitely readable. In literature courses having a seminar or lecture-discussion format, these works elicit more discussion because of their greater density, ambiguity, and self-contradiction. They are, above all, the works that are more *interesting* to read, teach, and talk about. Indeed, it might be an improvement in everyone's thinking about canonicity to drop the notion of "best" altogether and substitute in its place "most interesting." "Good," "better," and "best" among literary works are too often determined by putting a hand on one's poetry bump or looking at a corner of the ceiling. The extent to which a work is "interesting" can be described and even quantified.

Concerning this last point, one might consider that in physics and other sciences these days, the complexity of a phenomenon is frequently defined by the number of words (or propositions or equations) required to describe it: the simpler the entity, the shorter the description; the more complex, the longer the description.[14] My "Fifty-nine Ways"—an approach applicable to *The Tyger*, *Kubla Khan*, and *Tintern Abbey*, and here applied at length to *The Eve of St. Agnes*—is just a tip-of-the-iceberg representation of what it would take to describe the "meaning" of such works.

The Union of Complex Authorship and Complex Readership

There is a tendency to associate the valuing of ambiguity, density of meanings, and internal contradiction especially with the New Critics of the 1930s, 1940s, and 1950s—I. A. Richards, William Empson, and Cleanth Brooks, to name three of the most influential, but also, specifically in connection with Keats, Kenneth Burke and Earl Wasserman, whose notions of Keatsian "mystic oxymoron" and "oxymoronic fusion" I invoked at the end of the second section of chapter 5. Since canonicity is always in one way or another reader-dependent, this association invites the question of whether complexity of the sort I have been describing is strictly a twentieth-century, or even a roughly mid-twentieth-century, standard for distinguishing the better, or the more interesting, from the rest when discriminations are called for (in making a course syllabus, for example, or revising the contents of an anthology, or sorting out entries submitted in a poetry contest).

If the answer is yes—that is, if complexity as a criterion for canonicity strictly coincides with the influence of the New Critics—then Keats's place "among the English Poets" for the last 150 years needs further explanation. We might, in such a case, construct a notion of Keats's "chameleon canonicity" (parallel with his character as chameleon poet) in which his life and works have been so variously appealing that he has suited whatever standard anyone cared to apply. In the middle of the nineteenth century, when biographical interest in writers was at an all-time high, Keats's posthumous fame got an enormous boost from the publication of R. M. Milnes's *Life, Letters, and Literary Remains*, in which many readers learned for the first time about the liveliness of the poet's personality, his heroic struggle to achieve something lasting in literature, the cruelty of the reviewers, and the tragic shortness of his life. Not long afterward, when first the Pre-Raphaelites and then the art-for-art's-sake enthusiasts made much of him, Keats represented their ideals on two counts: he filled poems like *Isabella* and *The*

Eve of St. Agnes with gorgeous, exquisitely detailed pictures that could be transferred, as it were, directly onto the painters' canvases, and he seemed to act as a theorist as well as a practitioner of aestheticism—in the famous exclamation to Benjamin Bailey, "O for a Life of Sensations rather than of Thoughts," for example, and his numerous affirmations of the importance of beauty over all other things (*Letters* 1:185, 194, 266, 388, 403, 404, 2:19, 263).

In the early decades of the twentieth century, when the philosophical and moral ideas of a writer were considered of prime importance (an era marked in Keats studies by the 1926 publication of Clarence Thorpe's *The Mind of John Keats*), the poet could again provide what was wanted, this time in the thematic seriousness of the *Hyperion* fragments and especially, again, in statements in his letters concerning such concepts as negative capability, life as a mansion of many apartments, and the world as a vale of soul-making. In the mid-century heyday of the New Criticism, Keats was at the top of everybody's list, supplying poem after poem for "close readings" in classrooms and journals. Today politics and social concerns are among the prime critical desiderata, and again Keats has come through, in Modern Language Association symposia on "Keats and Politics" and a spate of recent books and articles on the topic by Daniel Watkins, Nicholas Roe, and others. It would seem that Keats's life, letters, and poems taken together are rich and varied enough to satisfy every idea of what a poet and poetry should be.

Even so, I think the complexity of Keats's poems has been affecting readers from the beginning—a full century before the advent of the New Critics—and winning him admirers and canonical status even when readers and critics were unaware of what they were responding to. The New Critics did not, after all, *invent* the canon of major writers in place for most of the twentieth century. William Empson begins *Seven Types of Ambiguity* with an example from one of Shakespeare's sonnets. He illustrates his most radical type, the seventh—which "occurs when the two meanings of the word, the two values of the ambiguity, are the two opposite meanings defined by the context, so that the total effect is to show a fundamental division in the writer's mind" (192)—by analyzing texts from, among others, Shakespeare, Crashaw, Hopkins, Herbert, and Keats. He could have written the entire book using authors in the *Norton Anthology* (had it then been available), and no doubt had in hand some comparable anthology of the 1920s. In *The Well Wrought Urn*, Cleanth Brooks's principal examples to show that "the language of poetry is the language of paradox" (3) are poems by Milton, Herrick, Pope, Gray, Wordsworth, Keats, Tennyson, and Yeats. At the end, in an appendix headed "Criticism, History, and Critical Relativism," Brooks says that his "preceding chapters obviously look forward to a new history of English poetry" (215), but he is talking about a new way of looking at old authors, not about revising the canon. It is sometimes said that T. S. Eliot is responsible for bringing Donne and the metaphysicals into the canon with his 1921 *Times Literary Supplement* essay on "The Metaphysical Poets." Undoubtedly he raised their status, but it should not be forgotten that he was reviewing an Oxford University Press edition titled *Metaphysical Lyrics and Poems of the Seventeenth Century: Donne to Butler* and that Donne and the rest were, in fact, already in the canon.

What the New Critics did, with a collective brilliance unequaled in earlier criticism, is give the now-familiar names—irony, paradox, tension, seven types of ambiguity, the Freudian "fundamental division in the writer's mind"—to complexities that had been registering their effects all along. "Complexity" does not, as such, figure significantly in eighteenth- or nineteenth-century pronouncements on literature. Its putative opposite, "simplicity," has been a literary ideal from the time of Plato, but as Raymond Havens remarks in "Simplicity, a Changing Concept," it has been a cloudy notion at best and "like other catchwords . . . [has] meant all things to all men" (10). As the eighteenth century progressed, the idea of complexity shows up, Havens suggests, when critics begin to speak of intricacy, variety, irregularity, and obscurity, and it underlies the growing admiration in later decades for Gothicism and the picturesque (21–23), and ultimately for nature itself.[15]

Complexity also probably underlies several of Samuel Johnson's 1765 remarks about Shakespeare, whose style, he says, "was in itself ungrammatical, perplexed and obscure" ("Preface" 93). Consider, for example, this Keats-like list of opposites with which Johnson sets forth "the real state of sublunary nature" exhibited in Shakespeare's plays:

> . . . good and evil, joy and sorrow, mingled with endless variety of proportion and innumerable modes of combination; and expressing the course of the world, in which the loss of one is the gain of another; in which, at the same time, the reveller is hasting to his wine, and the mourner burying his friend; in which the malignity of one is sometimes defeated by the frolick of another; and many mischiefs and many benefits are done and hindered without design . . . [a] chaos of mingled purposes and casualties. (66)

A similar list of contraries appears in a subsequent paragraph describing (as one of Shakespeare's defects) the abrupt changes of emotion paraded before the audience:

> The admirers of this great poet have most reason to complain when he approaches nearest to his highest excellence, and seems fully resolved to sink them in dejection, and mollify them with tender emotions by the fall of greatness, the danger of innocence, or the crosses of love. What he does best, he soon ceases to do. He is not long soft and pathetick without some idle conceit, or contemptible equivocation. He no sooner begins to move, than he counteracts himself; and terrour and pity, as they are rising in the mind, are checked and blasted by sudden frigidity. (74)[16]

Shakespeare's perplexity and obscurity, the "chaos of mingled purposes and casualties," and the abrupt motions and counteractions are kindred to the rapid changes, incongruities, and self-divisions that I described in the "Multiple Keats" section of the preceding chapter.

Nothing is provable in such a matter, but let us entertain the idea
ing Keats's complexity, just like valuing Shakespeare's, was for a long t
unconscious on the part of readers and critics. In such a view (t
the poet's imagined "chameleon canonicity"), Keats over the years has bee
biographically fascinating, has been a focal point of late-nineteenth-century
aestheticism, has been a seemingly profound and original thinker, has been an
ardent champion of political and social causes—*and* has continued, decade
after decade, to be the author of *The Eve of St. Agnes, Hyperion, La Belle Dame,
Lamia,* and the great odes. Admiring the complexity of the poems and explaining the admiration in terms of some other quality can be documented only specu-
latively. But consider, as a single famous illustration, offered here to represent the
hypothesized experience of many thousands of less famous readers, Matthew
Arnold's praise of the twentieth line of *Ode on a Grecian Urn*: "When Keats con-
soles the forward-bending lover on the Grecian Urn, the lover arrested and presented in immortal relief by the sculptor's hand before he can kiss, with the line,
'For ever wilt thou love, and she be fair'—he utters a moral idea" (*Complete Prose
Works* 9:45). Investing massively in a literature of high moral seriousness, Arnold
at the same time is tremendously moved by something quite different, having very
little to do with Arnoldian morality, in the impossible complexity of the lovers'
situation. He resolves himself on the spot: the beautiful permanence of the never-
fulfilled love qualifies canonically as a "moral idea."

But, as all these examples show—Arnold, the New Critics, and others in this
chapter, the devisers of the token fifty-nine ways of reading *The Eve of St. Agnes*
in chapter 3, the several hundred thousand other readers who have kept their
interpretations of Keats's texts to themselves—complexity on the author's side
is not in itself a sufficient condition for canonicity. From the beginning, it has
required complexity on both sides of the transaction to put Keats "among the
English Poets." Undoubtedly the first indispensable element is the author. The
reader's constructions and reconstructions, however infinite and inexhaustible,
must start with materials already in the text, and it is the author who put them
there. I think it is above all because Keats provided so many, and such complicated, details—the starting materials of the fifty-nine ways (or fifty-nine *hundred*
ways) of reading *The Eve of St. Agnes* and the rest of the poems—that we made
so much of him in the celebrations of his two-hundredth birthday in 1995. But
it was of course the readers who held the celebrations, and they (and we) continue to be a second indispensable complexity in the interactive process as well.

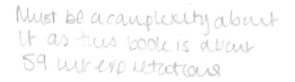
Must be a complexity about
It as this book is about
59 interpretations

APPENDIX A

Text and Apparatus

T HE TEXT OF *The Eve of St. Agnes* in the Harvard edition (Poems [1978] 299–319) is a slightly emended version of the 1820 printing, and the apparatus there gives a complete record of variants and manuscript cancellations and alterations from the surviving leaves of Keats's draft, the two extant Woodhouse copies, and George Keats's transcript. The text of this appendix reproduces the wording and accidentals of the 1820 printing exactly (including three clear errors: the lack of a closing quotation mark in line 144, the absence of punctuation at the end of line 301, and the inclusion of a closing quote in line 342), and the apparatus is, by comparison with that in the Harvard edition, much simplified in order to make the differences between the three principal versions of the poem—draft, revised manuscript, and 1820—more readily apparent.

In the present apparatus, readings of the draft version, taken from W^2 (the earlier of Woodhouse's two extant transcripts) for the missing leaf containing lines 1–63 and from the latest text of the surviving leaves of the holograph for the rest, are recorded simply as D, and those of the revised manuscript version, reconstructed from Woodhouse's notes in W^2 and the text of George Keats's transcript, are recorded as R. Where Woodhouse's variants from the now-lost revised holograph and George Keats's manuscript differ (or where George Keats shows a variant and there is no corresponding "correction" noted by Woodhouse), I have sometimes resorted to $R1$ and $R2$, with parenthetical explanation, to represent the possibility of successive stages of revision. I have not included alterations and cancellations as such from the draft manuscript, but occasionally have recorded deleted text (within angle brackets) when it is an essential part of a draft variant.

THE
EVE OF ST. AGNES.

I.

St. Agnes' Eve—Ah, bitter chill it was!
The owl, for all his feathers, was a-cold;
The hare limp'd trembling through the frozen grass,
And silent was the flock in woolly fold;
5   Numb were the Beadsman's fingers, while he told
His rosary, and while his frosted breath,
Like pious incense from a censer old,
Seem'd taking flight for heaven, without a death,
Past the sweet Virgin's picture, while his prayer he saith.

II.

10   His prayer he saith, this patient, holy man;
Then takes his lamp, and riseth from his knees,
And back returneth, meagre, barefoot, wan,
Along the chapel aisle by slow degrees:
The sculptur'd dead, on each side, seem to freeze,
15   Emprison'd in black, purgatorial rails:
Knights, ladies, praying in dumb orat'ries.
He passeth by; and his weak spirit fails
To think how they may ache in icy hoods and mails.

III.

Northward he turneth through a little door,
20   And scarce three steps, ere Music's golden tongue
Flatter'd to tears this aged man and poor;
But no—already had his deathbell rung;
The joys of all his life were said and sung:
His was harsh penance on St. Agnes' Eve:
25   Another way he went, and soon among
Rough ashes sat he for his soul's reprieve,
And all night kept awake, for sinners' sake to grieve.

Title The . . . Agnes] Saint Agnes' Eve *D, R*
1 chill] cold *D*
4 woolly] sheltered *D*
7 from] in *D*
9 while] as *R*
9, 10 prayer] prayers *D*
25 went] turn'd *D*
26 Rough] Black *D*
27 sake] souls *D*

IV.

That ancient Beadsman heard the prelude soft;
And so it chanc'd, for many a door was wide,
30   From hurry to and fro. Soon, up aloft,
The silver, snarling trumpets 'gan to chide:
The level chambers, ready for their pride,
Were glowing to receive a thousand guests:
The carved angels, ever eager-eyed,
35   Star'd. where upon their heads with cornice rests,
With hair blown back, and wings put cross-wise on their breasts.

V.

At length burst in the argent revelry,
With plume, tiara, and all rich array,
Numerous as shadows haunting fairily
40   The brain, new stuff'd, in youth, with triumphs gay
Of old romance. These let us wish away,
And turn, sole-thoughted, to one Lady there,
Whose heart had brooded, all that wintry day,
On love, and wing'd St. Agnes' saintly care,
45   As she had heard old dames full many times declare.

27/28   But there are ears may hear sweet melodies,
And there are eyes to brighten festivals,
And there are feet for nimble minstrelsies,
And many a lip that for the red wine calls.—
Follow, then follow to the illumined halls,
Follow me youth—and leave the Eremite—
Give him a tear—then trophied banneral,
And many a brilliant tasseling of light,
Shall droop from arched ways this high Baronial night. *D (apparently canceled*
before the draft was completed)
   30 fro . . . up] fro:—and now *D*
   32 The level] The high-lamp'd *R1 (RW)*; High-lamped *R2 (GK)*
   33 Were glowing] Seem'd anxious *D*
   37 burst . . . revelry] step . . . revelers *D*
   38 plume . . . all] tiara, and plume, and *R*
   39–42 Numerous . . . there]
       Ah what are they? the idle pulse scarce stirs,
       The muse should never make the spirit gay,
       Away, bright dulness, laughing fools, away,—
       And let me tell of one sweet lady there *D*
   45 times] time *R*

VI.

> They told her now, upon St. Agnes' Eve,
> Young virgins might have visions of delight,
> And soft adorings from their loves receive
> Upon the honey'd middle of the night,
50   If ceremonies due they did aright;
> As, supperless to bed they must retire,
> And couch supine their beauties, lily white;
> Nor look behind, nor sideways, but require
> Of Heaven with upward eyes for all that they desire.

VII.

55   Full of this whim was thoughtful Madeline:
> The music, yearning like a God in pain,
> She scarcely heard: her maiden eyes divine,
> Fix'd on the floor, saw many a sweeping train
> Pass by—she heeded not at all: in vain
60   Came many a tiptoe, amorous cavalier,
> And back retir'd; not cool'd by high disdain,
> But she saw not: her heart was otherwhere:
> She sigh'd for Agnes' dreams, the sweetest of the year.

VIII.

> She danc'd along with vague, regardless eyes,
65   Anxious her lips, her breathing quick and short:
> The hallow'd hour was near at hand: she sighs
> Amid the timbrels, and the throng'd resort
> Of whisperers in anger, or in sport;
> 'Mid looks of love, defiance, hate, and scorn,

48 from] of D
48 loves] love R2 (*GK, probably in error*)
52 couch] lay D
54/55 'Twas said her future lord would there appear
        Offering, as sacrifice—all in the dream—
        Delicious food, even to her lips brought near,
        Viands, and wine, and fruit, and sugar'd cream,
        To touch her palate with the fine extreme
        Of relish: then soft music heard, and then
        More pleasures follow'd in a dizzy stream
        Palpable almost: then to wake again
    Warm in the virgin morn, no weeping Magdalen. R
57 She . . . heard] Touch'd not her heart D
64 regardless] uneager D, R
68 or] and R

70   Hoodwink'd with faery fancy; all amort,
        Save to St. Agnes and her lambs unshorn,
        And all the bliss to be before to-morrow morn.

IX.

        So, purposing each moment to retire,
        She linger'd still. Meantime, across the moors,
75   Had come young Porphyro, with heart on fire
        For Madeline. Beside the portal doors,
        Buttress'd from moonlight, stands he, and implores
        All saints to give him sight of Madeline,
        But for one moment in the tedious hours,
80   That he might gaze and worship all unseen;
        Perchance speak, kneel, touch, kiss—in sooth such things have been.

X.

        He ventures in: let no buzz'd whisper tell:
        All eyes be muffled, or a hundred swords
        Will storm his heart, Love's fev'rous citadel:
85   For him, those chambers held barbarian hordes,
        Hyena foremen, and hot-blooded lords,
        Whose very dogs would execrations howl
        Against his lineage: not one breast affords
        Him any mercy, in that mansion foul,
90   Save one old beldame, weak in body and in soul.

XI.

        Ah, happy chance! the aged creature came,
        Shuffling along with ivory-headed wand,
        To where he stood, hid from the torch's flame,
        Behind a broad hall-pillar, far beyond
95   The sound of merriment and chorus bland:
        He startled her; but soon she knew his face,
        And grasp'd his fingers in her palsied hand,
        Saying, "Mercy, Porphyro! hie thee from this place;
        "They are all here to-night, the whole blood-thirsty race!

70 all amort] a la mort *R*
75 Porphyro] Lionel *D*
75 on fire] afire *D, R*
82 buzz'd] damn'd *D*
88 one breast] a soul *D*
91 creature] Beldam *D*
93 torch's] Torches *D, R*
98 Porphyro] Jesu *D, R*

XIII.

100   "Get hence! get hence! there's dwarfish Hildebrand;
        "He had a fever late, and in the fit
        "He cursed thee and thine, both house and land:
        "Then there's that old Lord Maurice, not a whit
        "More tame for his gray hairs—Alas me! flit
105   "Flit like a ghost away."—"Ah, Gossip dear,
        "We're safe enough; here in this arm-chair sit,
        "And tell me how"—"Good Saints! not here, not here;
    "Follow me, child, or else these stones will be thy bier."

XIII.

        He follow'd through a lowly arched way,
110   Brushing the cobwebs with his lofty plume,
        And as she mutter'd "Well-a—well-a-day!"
        He found him in a little moonlight room,
        Pale, lattic'd, chill, and silent as a tomb.
        "Now tell me where is Madeline," said he,
115   "O tell me, Angela, by the holy loom
        "Which none but secret sisterhood may see,
    "When they St. Agnes' wool are weaving piously."

XIV.

        "St. Agnes! Ah! it is St. Agnes' Eve—
        "Yet men will murder upon holy days:
120   "Thou must hold water in a witch's sieve,
        "And be liege-lord of all the Elves and Fays,
        "To venture so: it fills me with amaze
        "To see thee, Porphyro!—St. Agnes' Eve!
        "God's help! my lady fair the conjuror plays
125   "This very night: good angels her deceive!
    "But let me laugh awhile, I've mickle time to grieve."

103 that] *not in D*
111 mutter'd] utter'd *R2 (GK, probably in error)*
113 lattic'd, chill] latticed high *D*
113 a] the *D*
115 Angela] Goody *D, R*
116 secret] holy *D*
119 holy days] holidays *D*
122 so . . . amaze] so about these thorny ways *R*
123 To . . . Porphyro] <Young Signor Porphyro> (*the words deleted and nothing substi-tuted*) *D*; A-tempting Beelzebub *R*

XV.

Feebly she laugheth in the languid moon,
While Porphyro upon her face doth look,
Like puzzled urchin on an aged crone
130   Who keepeth clos'd a wond'rous riddle book,
As spectacled she sits in chimney nook.
But soon his eyes grew brilliant, when she told
His lady's purpose; and he scarce could brook
Tears, at the thought of those enchantments cold,
135   And Madeline asleep in lap of legends old.

XVI.

Sudden a thought came like a full-blown rose,
Flushing his brow, and in his pained heart
Made purple riot: then doth he propose
A stratagem, that makes the beldame start:
140   "A cruel man and impious thou art:
"Sweet lady, let her pray, and sleep, and dream
"Alone with her good angels, far apart
"From wicked men like thee. Go, go!—I deem
"Thou canst not surely be the same that thou didst seem.

XVII.

145   "I will not harm her, by all saints I swear,"
Quoth Porphyro: "O may I ne'er find grace
"When my weak voice shall whisper its last prayer,
"If one of her soft ringlets I displace,
"Or look with ruffian passion in her face:
150   "Good Angela, believe me by these tears;

129 Like] As *D*
132 But soon] Sudden *R*
134 Tears] Sighs *R*
135 And] Sweet *D, R*
136 thought . . . rose] rosy thought <more rosy than the rose> (*the undeleted* rosy *added above the line, and nothing substituted for the deleted words*) *D*; thought came full blown like a rose *R*
137 Flushing] Heated *D, R*
137 pained] painful *D*
143 Go, go] O Christ *D, R*
145 by . . . swear] by the great St Paul *D, R*
146 Quoth] Swear'th *D, R*
147 whisper . . . prayer] unto heaven call *D, R*
148 displace] misplace *D*

"Or I will, even in a moment's space,
"Awake, with horrid shout, my foemen's ears,
"And beard them, though they be more fang'd than wolves and bears."

XVIII.

"Ah! why wilt thou affright a feeble soul?
155   "A poor, weak, palsy-stricken, churchyard thing,
"Whose passing-bell may ere the midnight toll;
"Whose prayers for thee, each morn and evening,
"Were never miss'd."—Thus plaining, doth she bring
A gentler speech from burning Porphyro;
160   So woful, and of such deep sorrowing,
That Angela gives promise she will do
Whatever he shall wish, betide her weal or woe.

XIX.

Which was, to lead him, in close secrecy,
Even to Madeline's chamber, and there hide
165   Him in a closet, of such privacy
That he might see her beauty unespied,
And win perhaps that night a peerless bride,
While legion'd fairies pac'd the coverlet,
And pale enchantment held her sleepy-eyed.
170   Never on such a night have lovers met,
Since Merlin paid his Demon all the montrous debt.

XX.

"It shall be as thou wishest," said the Dame:
"All cates and dainties shall be stored there
"Quickly on this feast-night: by the tambour frame
175   "Her own lute thou wilt see: no time to spare,
"For I am slow and feeble, and scarce dare
"On such a catering trust my dizzy head.
"Wait here, my child, with patience; kneel in prayer

154 Ah . . . affright] How canst thou terrify *R*
159 Porphyro] Lionel *D*
160 woful] gentle *D*
161 Angela . . . do] the old Dame <promises to do> (*nothing substituted for the deleted text*) *D*
162 wish] say *D*
165 of . . . privacy] if such one there be *D, R2 (GK)*
167 And] Or *D, R*
178 Wait . . . patience] But wait an hour's passing *D*

"The while: Ah! thou must needs the lady wed,
180   "Or may I never leave my grave among the dead."

XXI.

So saying, she hobbled off with busy fear.
The lover's endless minutes slowly pass'd;
The dame return'd, and whisper'd in his ear
To follow her; with aged eyes aghast
185   From fright of dim espial. Safe at last,
Through many a dusky gallery, they gain
The maiden's chamber, silken, hush'd, and chaste;
Where Porphyro took covert, pleas'd amain.
His poor guide hurried back with agues in her brain.

XXII.

190   Her falt'ring hand upon the balustrade,
Old Angela was feeling for the stair,
When Madeline, St. Agnes' charmed maid,
Rose, like a mission'd spirit, unaware:
"With silver taper's light, and pious care,
195   She turn'd, and down the aged gossip led
To a safe level matting. Now prepare,
Young Porphyro, for gazing on that bed;
She comes, she comes again, like ring-dove fray'd and fled.

XXIII.

Out went the taper as she hurried in;
200   Its little smoke, in pallid moonshine, died:
She clos'd the door, she panted, all akin
To spirits of the air, and visions wide:

179   Ah] Sooth *R*
182   slowly] quickly *D, R*
186   many . . . gallery] lonely oaken Galleries *D*
186   gain] reach *D*
188   Porphyro . . . amain] he in panting covert will remain *D*
189   His . . . brain] <I[n] purgatory sweet or what may he attain> (*canceled and noth-*
ing substituted) *D*
193   mission'd spirit] spirit to her *R*
194   taper's] taper *R*
194   pious] gentle *D*
197   Porphyro] Lionel *D*
197   for] a *D, R*
199   hurried] floated *R*

No utter'd syllable, or, woe betide!
But to her heart, her heart was voluble,
205   Paining with eloquence her balmy side;
As though a tongueless nightingale should swell
Her throat in vain, and die, heart-stifled, in her dell.

XXIV.

A casement high and triple-arch'd there was,
All garlanded with carven imag'ries
210   Of fruits, and flowers, and bunches of knot-grass,
And diamonded with panes of quaint device,
Innumerable of stains and splendid dyes,
As are the tiger-moth's deep-damask'd wings;
And in the midst, 'mong thousand heraldries,
215   And twilight saints, and dim emblazonings,
A shielded scutcheon blush'd with blood of queens and kings.

XXV.

Full on this casement shone the wintry moon,
And threw warm gules on Madeline's fair breast,
As down she knelt for heaven's grace and boon;
220   Rose-bloom fell on her hands, together prest,
And on her silver cross soft amethyst,
And on her hair a glory, like a saint:
She seem'd a splendid angel, newly drest,
Save wings, for heaven:—Porphyro grew faint:
225   She knelt, so pure a thing, so free from mortal taint.

XXVI.

Anon his heart revives: her vespers done,
Of all its wreathed pearls her hair she frees;
Unclasps her warmed jewels one by one;

213 are] is *D*
213 damask'd] sunset *D*
214 And . . . midst] In midst whereft [= whereof] *D*
218 warm] rich *D*
219 knelt] kneel'd *D*
223 a splendid] [a] silvery *D*
224 Porphyro] Lionel *D*
225 knelt] pray'd *R2 (GK)*
225 so . . . so] too . . . too *D, R*
226 vespers] praying *D*
227 pearls] pearl *D*

Loosens her fragrant boddice; by degrees
230   Her rich attire creeps rustling to her knees:
Half-hidden, like a mermaid in sea-weed,
Pensive awhile she dreams awake, and sees,
In fancy, fair St. Agnes in her bed,
But dares not look behind, or all the charm is fled.

XXVII.

235   Soon, trembling in her soft and chilly nest,
In sort of wakeful swoon, perplex'd she lay,
Until the poppied warmth of sleep oppress'd
Her soothed limbs, and soul fatigued away;
Flown, like a thought, until the morrow-day;
240   Blissfully haven'd both from joy and pain;
Clasp'd like a missal where swart Paynims pray;
Blinded alike from sunshine and from rain,
As though a rose should shut, and be a bud again.

XXVIII.

Stol'n to this paradise, and so entranced,
245   Porphyro gazed upon her empty dress,
And listen'd to her breathing, if it chanced
To wake into a slumberous tenderness;
Which when he heard, that minute did he bless,
And breath'd himself: then from the closet crept,
250   Noiseless as fear in a wide wilderness,
And over the hush'd carpet, silent, stept,
And 'tween the curtains peep'd, where, lo!—how fast she slept.

XXIX.

Then by the bed-side, where the faded moon
Made a dim, silver twilight, soft he set
255   A table, and, half anguish'd, threw thereon
A cloth of woven crimson, gold, and jet:—
O for some drowsy Morphean amulet!

230 rich] sweet *D*
232 Pensive . . . awake] She stands awhile in dreaming thought *D*
233 in her] on her *D*
234 fled] <fl> dead *D*
252 where] and *D*
253 faded] fading *D*
254 a . . . silver] an illumed *D*
255 half . . . threw] with anguish spread *D*

The boisterous, midnight, festive clarion,
The kettle-drum, and far-heard clarionet,
260   Affray his ears, though but in dying tone:—
The hall door shuts again, and all the noise is gone.

XXX.

And still she slept on azure-lidded sleep,
In blanched linen, smooth, and lavender'd,
While he from forth the closet brought a heap
265 Of candied apple, quince, and plum, and gourd;
With jellies soother than the creamy curd,
And lucent syrops, tinct with cinnamon;
Manna and dates, in argosy transferr'd
From Fez; and spiced dainties, every one,
270 From silken Samarcand to cedar'd Lebanon.

XXXI.

These delicates he heap'd with glowing hand
On golden dishes and in baskets bright
Of wreathed silver: sumptuous they stand
In the retired quiet of the night,
275 Filling the chilly room with perfume light.—
"And now, my love, my seraph fair, awake!
"Thou art my heaven, and I thine eremite:
"Open thine eyes, for meek St. Agnes' sake,
"Or I shall drowse beside thee, so my soul doth ache."

XXXII.

280 Thus whispering, his warm, unnerved arm
Sank in her pillow. Shaded was her dream
By the dusk curtains:—'twas a midnight charm
Impossible to melt as iced stream:
The lustrous salvers in the moonlight gleam;

258 midnight] braying *R2 (GK)*
259 The] And *D*
259 clarionet] clarinet *D, R*
260 dying] faintest *D*
264 from . . . brought] brought from the cabinet *R*
266 creamy] creamed *D*
272 dishes] salvers *D*
274 In . . . of the] Amid the quiet of Sᵗ Agenes' *D*
281 Sank] Sunk *D, R*

285   Broad golden fringe upon the carpet lies:
         It seem'd he never, never could redeem
         From such a stedfast spell his lady's eyes;
         So mus'd awhile, entoil'd in woofed phantasies.

XXXIII.

         Awakening up, he took her hollow lute,—
290   Tumultuous,—and, in chords that tenderest be,
         He play'd an ancient ditty, long since mute,
         In Provence call'd, "La belle dame sans mercy:"
         Close to her ear touching the melody;—
         Wherewith disturb'd, she utter'd a soft moan:
295   He ceased—she panted quick—and suddenly
         Her blue affrayed eyes wide open shone:
         Upon his knees he sank, pale as smooth-sculptured stone.

XXXIV.

         Her eyes were open, but she still beheld
         Now wide awake, the vision of her sleep:
300   There was a painful change, that nigh expell'd
         The blisses of her dream so pure and deep
         At which fair Madeline began to weep,
         And moan forth witless words with many a sigh;
         While still her gaze on Porphyro would keep;
305   Who knelt, with joined hands and piteous eye,
         Fearing to move or speak, she look'd so dreamingly.

XXXV.

         "Ah, Porphyro!" said she, "but even now
         "Thy voice was at sweet tremble in mine ear,
         "Made tuneable with every sweetest vow;
310   "And those sad eyes were spiritual and clear:

288 So] And *D*
296 affrayed] half-frayed *D*
297 sank] sunk *D, R*
297 smooth] fair *R*
303 moan] mourn *R2* (*GK, probably in error*)
305 knelt . . . hands] with an aching brow *D*
306 Fearing] Feared *D*
307 "Ah . . . but] she speaks, "Ah Porpyro but *D*
309 Made tuneable] And tun'd devout *R*
309 with] by *D*
309 sweetest] softest *R*
310 those sad] thy kind *D*

"How chang'd thou art! how pallid, chill, and drear!
"Give me that voice again, my Porphyro,
"Those looks immortal, those complainings dear!
"Oh leave me not in this eternal woe,
315   "For if thou diest, my Love, I know not where to go."

XXXVI.

Beyond a mortal man impassion'd far
At these voluptuous accents, he arose,
Ethereal, flush'd, and like a throbbing star
Seen mid the sapphire heaven's deep repose;
320   Into her dream he melted, as the rose
Blendeth its odour with the violet,—
Solution sweet: meantime the frost-wind blows
Like Love's alarum pattering the sharp sleet
Against the window-panes; St. Agnes' moon hath set.

XXXVII.

325   'Tis dark: quick pattereth the flaw-blown sleet:
"This is no dream, my bride, my Madeline!"
'Tis dark: the iced gusts still rave and beat:
"No dream, alas! alas! and woe is mine!
"Porphyro will leave me here to fade and pine.—
330   "Cruel! what traitor could thee hither bring?
"I curse not, for my heart is lost in thine,
"Though thou forsakest a deceived thing;—
"A dove forlorn and lost with sick unpruned wing."

311 thou art] art thou *D*
311 chill] cold *R*
314–22 Oh . . . blows]
    See, while she speaks his arms encroaching slow,
    Have zoned her, heart to heart,—loud, loud the dark winds blow!

    For on the midnight came a tempest fell;
    More sooth, for that his quick rejoinder flows
    Into her burning ear: and still the spell
    Unbroken guards her in serene repose.
    With her wild dream he mingled, as a rose
    Marrieth its odour to a violet.
    Still, still she dreams, louder the frost wind blows *R1* (*RW*); *R2* (*GK*) *has
the same revised text but with* close *for* quick *in the second line of the new stanza*
315 For] Ah *D*
322 Solution sweet] *deleted in D and nothing substituted*
324 Against . . . panes] Against the windows dark *D*
324 hath] had *D*
325 quick] still *D, R*

XXXVIII.

       "My Madeline! sweet dreamer! lovely bride!
335   "Say, may I be for aye thy vassal blest?
       "Thy beauty's shield, heart-shap'd and vermeil dyed?
       "Ah, silver shrine, here will I take my rest
       "After so many hours of toil and quest,
       "A famish'd pilgrim,—saved by miracle.
340   "Though I have found, I will not rob thy nest
       "Saving of thy sweet self; if thou think'st well
    "To trust, fair Madeline, to no rude infidel."

XXXIX.

       "Hark! 'tis an elfin-storm from faery land,
       "Of haggard seeming, but a boon indeed:
345   "Arise—arise! the morning is at hand;—
       "The bloated wassaillers will never heed:—
       "Let us away, my love, with happy speed;
       "There are no ears to hear, or eyes to see,—
       "Drown'd all in Rhenish and the sleepy mead:
350   "Awake! arise! my love, and fearless be,
    "For o'er the southern moors I have a home for thee."

XL.

       She hurried at his words, beset with fears,
       For there were sleeping dragons all around,
       At glaring watch, perhaps, with ready spears—
355   Down the wide stairs a darkling way they found.—
       In all the house was heard no human sound.
       A chain-droop'd lamp was flickering by each door;
       The arras, rich with horseman, hawk, and hound,
       Flutter'd in the besieging wind's uproar;
360   And the long carpets rose along the gusty floor.

XLI.

       They glide, like phantoms, into the wide hall;
       Like phantoms, to the iron porch, they glide;

    339 A . . . miracle] Pale feautred and in weeds of Pilgrimage *D*
    340 I will] but can *D*
    341–42 Saving . . . infidel] Soft Nightingale, I'll keep thee in a cage / To sing to me—
but hark! the blended tempests' rage *D*
    350 Awake . . . love] Put on warm cloathing, sweet *D*
    351 For . . . moors] Over the dartmoor blak *D*

Where lay the Porter, in uneasy sprawl,
With a huge empty flaggon by his side:
365   The wakeful bloodhound rose, and shook his hide,
But his sagacious eye an inmate owns:
By one, and one, the bolts full easy slide:—
The chains lie silent on the footworn stones;—
The key turns, and the door upon its hinges groans.

XLII.

370   And they are gone: ay, ages long ago
These lovers fled away into the storm.
That night the Baron dreamt of many a woe,
And all his warrior-guests, with shade and form
Of witch, and demon, and large coffin-worm,
375   Were long be-nightmar'd. Angela the old
Died palsy-twitch'd, with meagre face deform;
The Beadsman, after thousand aves told,
For aye unsought for slept among his ashes cold.

364 huge] large *D*
364 flaggon] beaker *D, R*
366 sagacious] unangerd *D*
368 lie] lay *D, R*
371 away] *not in D*
372 night] Morn *D*
375 long] all *D, R2 (GK)*
375–78 Angela . . . cold]
                                    Angela went off
              Twitch'd by the palsy:—and with face deform
              The Beadsman stiffen'd—'twixt a sigh and laugh,
                  Ta'en sudden from his beads by one weak little cough *R1 (RW); R2 (GK) has*
      the same revised text but with with the Palsy *for* by the palsy *in the second line*

APPENDIX B

Fifty-nine Ways of Looking at The Eve of St. Agnes

LOVE, SEX, MARRIAGE

1. Human love (celebration of love over all obstacles)
2. Keats's love life
3. Keats's love specifically for Fanny Brawne
4. Celebration of sexual love
5. Celebration of Christian marriage
6. Erotic love versus religious purity
7. Sexual politics I: Porphyro the peeping Tom/rapist, Madeline the victim
8. Sexual politics II: Madeline the seducer, Porphyro the victim (husband caught at last!)

MAGIC, FAIRY TALE, MYTH

9. Romance, enthrallment, enchantment
10. Sleeping Beauty
11. Porphyro as liberator of Madeline
12. Porphyro as vampire
13. The triumph of Fairy over Christian religion
14. Initiation and transformation of maiden into mother
15. A version of Joseph Campbell's monomyth
16. The Fortunate Fall
17. Masturbatory ritual

IMAGINATION

18. Authenticity of dreams
19. The visionary imagination succeeding (celebration)

20. The visionary imagination failing miserably (skepticism)
21. Porphyro's creative (seizing, adaptive) imagination
22. Contrast (or conflict) of two kinds of imagination
23. The hoodwinking of *everyone* (Beadsman, Angela, Madeline, Porphyro, the kinsmen and revelers)

WISH-FULFILLMENT (SUBHEAD OF THE PRECEDING)

24. Narrative of desire
25. Fantasy of wish-fulfillment
26. Successful merging of romance and reality, or of beauty and truth

POETRY, ART, CREATIVITY

27. Parable (allegory) of literary creativity
28. Antiromance; illustration of the limitations of romance
29. Remake of *Romeo and Juliet* I: imitation
30. Remake of *Romeo and Juliet* II: modernization ("tough-minded 'modern' recasting" as in *Isabella*)
31. Exercise in Gothicism
32. Satire on (parody of) Gothicism
33. Completion of Coleridge's *Christabel*
34. Rich Romantic tapestry
35. Pure aestheticism: art is the only thing that matters

RELIGION

36. Religion of experience
37. Religion of beauty
38. Love as a religious sacrament
39. Keats's attack on religion
40. Ironic version of the Annunciation
41. Parody of a saint's life
42. Paganism versus religion; the triumph of old religion over Christianity

HUMAN EXPERIENCE MORE GENERALLY

43. Mortality and Madeline's fall from innocence
44. Tragedy
45. The inconsequentiality of human life (death takes all)

EPISTEMOLOGY, AMBIGUITY

46. Uncertainty of the phenomenal world
47. The semiotics of vision (looking, gazing); scopophilia
48. Ambiguity of idealism and reality

49. Poem of disjunctions, equivocation—open-endedness in the extreme
50. Poem about speech, language, communication (and their unreliability)
51. Poem about the weather, the seasons, day and night, and so on (phenomenological reading)

POLITICS

52. Family politics (the *Romeo and Juliet* situation, with emphasis on social conflict)
53. The rottenness of aristocratic society (*Hamlet* theme)
54. The crisis of feudalism (feudal decay, mercantile ascendancy, disruption of the class system)
55. Dynastic oppression (Madeline the victim)
56. Patriarchal domination of women (ditto)
57. Keats's disparagement of women (characters and readers alike)
58. Poem about escape—from the castle, from family and/or society, from reality
59. Politics of interpretation: who gets to say what things mean (Madeline? Porphyro? the narrator? the critic? the teacher? the reader?)

APPENDIX C

Paintings and Book Illustrations

THOUGH A PAINTING REFERRING TO *Ode to the Nightingale* was exhibited at the Royal Academy as early as May 1821, three months after Keats's death, and another based on *Endymion* was shown in 1828, the serious activity of illustrating the poems began in the 1840s, following the appearance of the first English collected edition (by William Smith, 1840), and accelerated with the publication of R. M. Milnes's *Life* of Keats in August 1848, the formation of the Pre-Raphaelite Brotherhood in September, and the establishment of Keats's place "among the English Poets" shortly thereafter. Mid-nineteenth-century interest in his life, together with the pictorialism of his poetry, his many associations with art and artists both in life and in his writings, and a growing interest in (and market for) literary paintings of all kinds, rapidly made Keats one of the most frequently painted and illustrated poets in recent English literature. *Endymion, Isabella,* and *The Eve of St. Agnes* were the works most often featured, and Richard Altick reports that twenty or more pictures were made from each of the three (*Pictures from Books* 447). The first illustrated edition of Keats's poems was published by Edward Moxon in 1854 (containing "120 Designs, Original and from the Antique, Drawn on Wood by George Scharf, Jun., F.S.A., F.R.S.L."). The *National Union Catalogue* and J. R. MacGillivray's *Keats: A Bibliography and Reference Guide* record scores of illustrated editions thereafter from the 1850s on into the third decade of the twentieth century.

This appendix lists a handful of the most frequently mentioned paintings based on *The Eve of St. Agnes*, with references to descriptions, commentary, and reproductions where they are available, and then the principal illustrated editions of the poem, most of which can be examined in the Harvard Keats Collection. For general discussion of the paintings and illustrations, see Altick (especially 231–33, 445–48); Helen Haworth, "'A Thing of Beauty Is a Joy Forever?'

Early Illustrated Editions of Keats's Poetry"; Wayne Cook, "John Keats and the Pre-Raphaelite Brotherhood"; and Julie Codell, "Painting Keats." Haworth comments at length (89–91) on George Scharf's engravings in the Moxon 1854 edition and reproduces (following 96) one of his four illustrations of *The Eve of St. Agnes*.

PAINTINGS

Charles Hutton Lear, *Porphyro Discovered in the Hall of Madeline*, 1842. Exhibited at the Royal Academy, 1842, Lear's first appearance there. Present whereabouts of the painting unknown.

William Holman Hunt, *The Flight of Madeline and Porphyro during the Drunkenness Attending the Revelry* (*The Eve of St. Agnes*), 1848. Guildhall Art Gallery, London. Exhibited at the Royal Academy, 1848. Color reproductions in *The Pre-Raphaelites* (1984) 57 (with commentary by Judith Bronkhurst, 57–58) and Mary Bennett, *Artists of the Pre-Raphaelite Circle* plate 2 (following 64). Black and white reproductions in *William Holman Hunt* (Walker Art Gallery exhibition catalogue, 1969) plate 10; Hilton 113; Altick 446; Barlow 72 (with commentary, 70–75); Codell 343; and elsewhere.

———, *The Eve of St. Agnes*, 1847–1857. Walker Art Gallery, Liverpool. This is a study in oils for the preceding, begun earlier but finished some years afterward. Color reproduction in Codell 344. Black and white reproductions in *William Holman Hunt* plate 12; Bennett, *Artists* 65; Grant Scott, *The Sculpted Word* 88.

    The Walker Gallery catalogue of 1969 (*William Holman Hunt*) also has reproductions of a pencil sketch and a study for the drunken porter (plates 11 and 13) plus descriptive entries (nos. 90–92) for several sketches and studies not reproduced.

Arthur Hughes, *The Eve of St. Agnes* (triptych), 1856. Tate Gallery, London. Exhibited at the Royal Academy, 1856. Black and white reproductions in Hilton 114–15 and with commentary in Altick 448; Codell 353; Turner's *Dictionary of Art* 14:850.

James Smetham, *The Eve of St. Agnes*, watercolor, 1858. Tate Gallery, London. Turner's *Dictionary of Art* mentions this as an example of Smetham's "intense religious mysticism that marked all his mature work and brought him close to William Blake, an artist he much admired" (28:869). Morchard Bishop, who reports that the picture was titled "Flight of Porphyro and Madeline" in a contemporary Liverpool sale catalogue (and priced there at 3 guineas), says it is "now in the Tate Gallery as The Eve of St. Agnes, pen and ink drawings touched with colour, 3 ¼" x 4", and dated 1858" (Malins and Bishop 39).

John Everett Millais, *The Eve of St. Agnes*, 1862–1863. Collection of Her Majesty Queen Elizabeth, the Queen Mother (Clarence House, London). Exhibited at the Royal Academy, 1863. Black and white reproductions in *The Pre-Raphaelites* (1984) 199 (with commentary by Malcolm Warner, 199–200, who also mentions two pencil studies in the Birmingham City Art Gallery and a private collection, as well as the two studies listed just below); Oliver Millar, *Victorian Pictures* plate 416 (with description and commentary at 1:185–86); Codell 344. Commentary also in Altick 231–33.

———, study in watercolor and chalk (?) for *The Eve of St. Agnes*, 1862–1863. Collection of Her Majesty Queen Elizabeth, the Queen Mother (Clarence House, London). Black and white reproduction in Millar plate 417.

————, study in watercolor and oil for *The Eve of St. Agnes*, 1862–1863. Victoria
and Albert Museum, London. Black and white reproduction in Scott 94.
Daniel Maclise, *Madeline after Prayer*, 1868. Walker Art Gallery, Liverpool. Exhibited at the Royal Academy, 1868. Black and white reproductions in *The Bookman*,
supplement to vol. 42, June 1912 (45), and Altick 448 (with commentary at
232–33).

ILLUSTRATED EDITIONS

The Eve of St. Agnes. Illustrated by Edward H. Wehnert. London: Sampson Low, 1855.
Issued again by Sampson Low in 1858, c. 1860, and 1875, and published in
New York by D. Appleton in 1855, 1859, and 1866 and by Cassell, Petter, and
Galpin in 1856 and c. 1880. Twenty engravings, including five elves hurling
snowballs (to illustrate the "elfin-storm from faery land") and, after the final
stanza, a family portrait of Porphyro, Madeline, two children, and a dog.
The Eve of Saint Agnes. Illustrated by Charles O. Murray. London: Sampson Low,
Marston, Searle, and Rivington, 1880. Published in New York by Dodd, Mead,
also 1880. Nineteen pictures engraved on thirteen plates.
The Eve of St. Agnes. Illustrated by Edmund H. Garrett. (Some of the title pages specify
"Edmund H. Garrett under the supervision of Geo. T. Andrew.") Boston: Estes
and Lauriat, 1885. Reissued in Boston by Estes and Lauriat in 1886, 1887, and
c. 1893. Also published in Troy, N.Y., by H. B. Nims, 1885, and in London by
John Bumpus, 1885 and 1887. Sixteen engravings.
The Eve of St. Agnes and Other Poems. Illustrated by E. A. Abbey. London: The Gold
Medal Library, c. 1910. Four undistinguished illustrations.
The Eve of St. Agnes. Illustrated by E. M. Craig. London: John Lane, 1928. Four wood-
cuts, in the first of which (the frontispiece) Porphyro and Madeline are leaving
the castle dressed in a clown suit and a flowered kimono and in the third of
which (32) it is revealed that Madeline has nothing on under her kimono.

NOTES

1. INTRODUCTION: THE LITERARY TRANSACTION

1. The full range of scholarly discussion of the place of authorial intention in interpretation and editing would take several pages to document. For a quick summary, with the most important references, see my *Multiple Authorship* 188–201 and notes.

2. Hyder E. Rollins, *Keats Circle* 1:128–29 (with Woodhouse's draft account of his conversation with Keats somewhat cleaned up here for the sake of readability). I have discussed the poet's initial intentionlessness in "Keats's Extempore Effusions" and again, comparing Keats with Coleridge, in *Coleridge and Textual Instability* 100–7.

3. The classical statement of this position is E. D. Hirsch's *Validity in Interpretation*, especially 3–5, 26–27. For another example of the meaningless closed book, in this instance *Moby-Dick*, see Shillingsburg, *Resisting Texts* 50.

4. Some writers distinguish between reader-response and reception theories, reserving "reception" for strict application to Hans Robert Jauss and the German school of *Receptionkritik*. But Jauss and his colleagues at Constance have been only intermittently interested in actual readers, giving their main attention to history and politics. In the present study, I have followed the more common practice of using "reader-response" and "reception" interchangeably.

5. Rosenblatt has another thing in common with the famous French writers: the fact that her books are constantly in use in the research libraries. When I first became interested in Rosenblatt's work, belatedly, only a few years ago, I found that every copy of both *Literature as Exploration* and *The Reader, the Text, the Poem* was either charged out or else missing or "withdrawn" not only from my own library at the University of Illinois but from all forty of the other institutions in the Illinois library consortium system—a clear sign of especially heavy demand over the years.

6. I have culled these terms mainly from Stanley Fish ("Literature in the Reader" and *Is There a Text*), Jonathan Culler (*Pursuit*), and Umberto Eco (*Interpretation*).

7. This is true, however, only in a conventional view that insists on "authoritative" authorship and versions. In a broader (or merely different) view, every new printing of the poem is yet another version, and anyone responsible for changes

from whatever went before—for example, emendation of wording, standardizing of punctuation and spelling, the editorial embellishments of introduction, commentary, critical and historical appendixes, the inclusion of graphic illustrations —represents added authorship (in which case, at the very least, each of Keats's editors—I, Miriam Allott, John Barnard, Elizabeth Cook, Nicholas Roe, and the rest— is part-author of a version of *The Eve of St. Agnes*). If the poem is presented in a different form from ordinary print, as in a movie, a cartoon, a musical setting, an opera, or hypertext, there will be, even more obviously, further new versions. The "validity" of authorship and versions depends entirely on the rules one establishes in the first place. For a practical theory of versions, see my *Coleridge and Textual Instability* 118–40, especially 132–37. For a broader view of the extent to which versions can multiply, see Joseph Grigely's *Textualterity*.

2. THE STARTING MATERIALS:
TEXTS AND CIRCUMSTANCES

1. The frequently repeated "living year" was introduced into Keats criticism more than four decades ago by Robert Gittings, in *John Keats: The Living Year*, referring to a twelve-month span beginning toward the end of September 1818. But the evidence for the composition of *Hyperion*, the one major work formerly assigned to the closing months of 1818, now seems to point mainly to March and April 1819, and this reduces the "year" to January through September 1819, from *The Eve of St. Agnes* through the ode *To Autumn* and Keats's final efforts with the unfinished *Fall of Hyperion*.

2. I have published three successive accounts of the textual relationships among the manuscripts and the first printed text of the poem—revising and correcting myself in the process—in "The Text of 'The Eve of St. Agnes'" (1963), *The Texts of Keats's Poems* 214–20 (1974), and the textual note in *Poems* (1978) 625–31. This last gives the most accurate information, and I draw on it freely in this and the next section. Complete facsimiles of three of the four extant manuscripts are available— the draft in *John Keats: Poetry Manuscripts at Harvard* 94–131, Woodhouse's first longhand transcript in *The Woodhouse Poetry Transcripts at Harvard* 197–225, and George Keats's transcript in *Manuscript Poems in the British Library* 119–21, 131–60 (the three books are listed in the Bibliography under my name). The fourth manuscript, Woodhouse's second longhand transcript, has not been reproduced in facsimile, but its substantive variants and some other peculiarities are recorded in the foot-of-the-page apparatus in *Poems* (1978) 299–318.

3. It is a certainty that Woodhouse wrote his first copies of Keats's manuscripts of *Isabella* and *The Eve of St. Mark* in shorthand and then made longhand copies from the shorthand, because in both cases the intervening shorthand versions are extant (at the Morgan Library and Bryn Mawr, respectively). For the evidence that Woodhouse used the same method in copying Keats's draft of *The Eve of St. Agnes*, see *Poems* (1978) 626–27.

4. It is also possible, perhaps even likely, that Keats is referring to Woodhouse's W^1 collection when he asks Fanny Brawne, sometime in the spring of 1820, to return by messenger a manuscript that he has lent her—"my or rather Taylor's manuscript" (*Letters* 2:216). If so, Keats, preparing his work for the 1820 volume and, as he tells Fanny, "clear[ing] up my arrears in versifying," would have been reviewing his poems via Woodhouse's copies of them. The W^1 transcripts of *Isabella* and *Hyperion* served as printer's copy for the volume.

5. In addition to the lengthy extracts given in the text of my chapter, there are several elided matters in these letters by Woodhouse and Taylor that deserve notice as well: Woodhouse's notion that *Isabella* would be more pleasing to readers than

The Eve of St. Agnes (and Keats's counterassertion of the relative "mawkishness" of his earlier narrative); the suggestion that Keats might have been affecting "the 'Don Juan' style of mingling up sentiment & sneering" in his revised ending of *St. Agnes*, except that the poet, while interested in Byron's latest work, had not yet actually seen it; Keats's characteristic manner of reciting his poems ("badly"); and several further statements by Taylor concerning Keats's attitude toward the "opinion of the World" and what Taylor viewed as Keats's questionable morality (*Letters* 2:162–64, 182–83).

6. I was wrong, in *The Texts of Keats's Poems* 66, 216–17, to suggest that the 1820 text of *The Eve of St. Agnes* may have been set from a now-lost transcript by Charles Brown. The direct source is much more likely to have been Keats's own revised manuscript.

7. See Magnuson's "'The Eolian Harp' in Context," "The Politics of 'Frost at Midnight,'" and *Reading Public Romanticism*. The discussion here is partly based on my section headed "The Ubiquity of Versions" in *Coleridge and Textual Instability* 121–24. See also note 7 to the preceding chapter.

8. Keats's draft of *Ode to a Nightingale*, now in the Fitzwilliam Museum, Cambridge, has 188 of the 199 words that appeared in the final text, amounting to 94.5% (see my "Keats's Extempore Effusions" 312). The proportion of final words in the *St. Agnes* draft would be even greater.

9. In Appendix A, giving the text of 1820 and an apparatus of variants from the manuscripts, the readings of the revised holograph are the same as 1820 where no variant is cited, or where the apparatus records a variant for *D* alone. Revised holograph readings different from 1820 appear in the apparatus with the siglum *R*. The wording of the lost revised manuscript cannot be reconstructed exactly in every line, because Woodhouse's notes in W^2 and George Keats's transcript differ from one another in a number of particulars (see *Poems* [1978] 627–28), and some of these—though we do not know which ones for sure—may represent further changes by Keats after Woodhouse made his notes. Full texts of George Keats's manuscript have been published in M. R. Ridley, *Keats' Craftsmanship* 180–90, and in Elizabeth Cook's Oxford Authors edition, *John Keats*, Appendix I, 544–54. Ridley discusses Keats's revisions in detail in his chapter on the poem, 96–190.

10. In his letter to Taylor of 19 September 1819, quoted at length in the preceding section, Woodhouse says that Keats's revision of this passage is an "alteration of about 3 stanzas" (*Letters* 2:163). Actually it affects no more than the final couplet of one stanza and the first seven lines of the next (stanzas 35 and 36 as they are numbered in the 1820 text). But Woodhouse had merely heard, not read, the revised poem when he wrote to Taylor about it, and his worry over the "unfitness" of the passage could have made it seem longer than it actually was.

11. I am here speculating partly on the basis of the contributions that Woodhouse and Taylor made to the 1820 text of *Isabella*, for which we have reliable evidence in a series of altered documents, including Keats's revised holograph and three transcripts by Woodhouse, the last of which (W^1) was used as printer's copy. See my *Multiple Authorship*, chapter 2, "Keats and His Helpers: The Multiple Authorship of *Isabella*," 25–49.

12. The arrangement of text and apparatus in Appendix A similarly elevates 1820 to single-text status, relegating the draft and revised holograph readings to the subordinate status of variants. I had the same problem in my Coleridge book, where I argued at length for the validity of each of the multiple versions of *The Ancient Mariner* and the other major poems and then, in order to provide texts and apparatuses for reference in an appendix, had to choose a single version of each poem as a main text and represent the rest of the versions in fragmentary notes.

13. See *Poems* (1978) 15, 629. This sort of eclecticism—in effect, the editor hypothesizing what an author *would have* preferred in the text—was a standard feature of 1960s and 1970s editorial projects based on the "copy-text" principles of W. W. Greg and Fredson Bowers. The Pennsylvania Dreiser *Sister Carrie* (1981) and the Northwestern-Newberry *Moby-Dick* (1988) are two of the more prominent examples. See Peter Shillingsburg, "The Three *Moby-Dicks*" and *Resisting Texts*, chapter 8, "Textual Ethics: The Meaning of Editorial Work."

14. There is one exception to this, in Keats's letter to Taylor, c. 11 June 1820, correcting "an alteration . . . very much for the worse" in lines 57–58. "My meaning is quite destroyed in the alteration," Keats says, and then goes on to explain what he meant instead (*Letters* 2:294–95).

15. Wordsworth interprets his poems in prefaces, notes, and letters ("I wished to draw attention to the truth that . . ."; "my intention was to point out . . ."; "It was my wish in this poem to show . . ."; "The Poem . . . was composed under a belief that . . ."), perhaps most elaborately in the detailed comments on 350 of his poems that he dictated to his friend Isabella Fenwick in 1843—comments in print since 1850 and closely associated with the poems for more than a century (see Jared Curtis, *Fenwick Notes*). Unlike Keats, Wordsworth lived a long life and thus had numerous occasions on which to issue such directives. But his most fundamental difference from Keats as an authorial presence was a matter of personality. Keats, though he was much influenced by the older poet, did not admire Wordsworth's conspicuous self-assertiveness, both as a poet and as a person, for which, in a letter to Woodhouse of 27 October 1818, he coined the term "wordsworthian or egotistical sublime" (*Letters* 1:387).

3. THE MULTIPLE READINGS

1. Wordsworthian "silent poets" view the world imaginatively but cannot, or at least do not, write about it in poetry. See Wordsworth's *The Excursion* 1.77–91, *When, to the attractions of the busy world* lines 77–83, and *The Prelude* (1850 version) 10.234–35, 13.265–75.

2. Reviewing Keats's 1820 volume in the *Indicator*, 2, 9 August 1820, Hunt described the poem as "rather a picture than a story" (Matthews, *Keats: The Critical Heritage* 172). The idea gets general support from Keats's own comments in his letter to John Taylor of 17 November 1819 concerning "colouring" and "drapery" in the poem (*Letters* 2:234).

3. One of my graduate seminars a few years ago, studying graphic representations of Keats's Isabella weeping over her pot of basil and observing that it makes a considerable difference whether the viewer knows (what is never *shown* in any of the pictures) that Lorenzo's severed head lies rotting inside the pot beneath the luxuriant greenery, invented a "Lorenzo's Head School of Contextualist Criticism." Initially just a class joke, this developed into something more serious when we found that we could, for almost any complex work on the syllabus, find something hidden from sight that, even though invisible, has significant explanatory power for what we see on the surface and can be put to use as an interpretive key. More recently, new historicist critics of Wordsworth, expounding a "metaphysics of absence," have been making much of things seemingly hidden, because not specifically mentioned, in *The Prelude*, *Tintern Abbey*, the Intimations Ode, and other works (see Marjorie Levinson and Alan Liu in particular; "metaphysics of absence" is Levinson's phrase in *Wordsworth's Great Period Poems* 99). Lorenzo's head really is buried in the pot of basil; there is still considerable argument among the Wordsworthians about the existence of things not mentioned in the works of the older poet.

4. Critics do not usually distinguish between the more explicit version of the consummation in the revised manuscript and the vaguer descriptions in the draft and the 1820 text. Notable exceptions are John Barnard (*John Keats*) and, before him, John Bayley.

5. The most enthusiastic defense of Porphyro against the moral censure that this kind of close reading usually produces is Norman Talbot's "Porphyro's Enemies," which reads the poem as a combination of "Christian faithful hope," "pagan magic," and "unsmokeable Boccaccio seduction-yarn" (222). "Those who conceive of the story as the hoodwinking of a virgin must see this as an ornately written orgasm, and it undoubtedly includes orgasm. Such matters are more unselfconsciously dealt with when the girl, however inexperienced, can respond with the freedom of Faery, and the boy is flushed with the double thrill of trespass and welcome" (226–27). "Porphyro's major dangers come from opposed versions of himself; the opportunistic young blood, the over-reverent, immobilised worshipper, and the immortal lover of Madeline's dream-world. It is yet to be seen whether the lovers and their poem . . . will survive the many-headed scepticism of the anti-Romantic critics" (230–31). In other words, as people used to say, boys will be boys.

6. The plot proceeds from more than just Endymion's dream, of course. In addition to his mythological sources in Lemprière's *Classical Dictionary*, Keats was following Percy Shelley's *Alastor*, published a year earlier, in which the protagonist's similar dream of an unknown beloved woman turns out to be a false lure: the love-vision is self-created out of the protagonist's own sensations, and he is shown to be pursuing something that in fact does not exist outside himself. In bringing Endymion and his goddess together at the finale, Keats's poem in effect rewrites Shelley's with a happy ending.

7. Of necessity, critics quote this long letter only in part, extracting the most telling sentences (just as I have here) and avoiding a great many complications that lurk in the passages thus elided. For discussion of the problems, see James Caldwell 100–2, 134–35, 153–58; Newell Ford 20–38; Earl Wasserman 102–4; Stillinger, *Hoodwinking* 151–57; Robert Ryan 129–40; and A. D. Nuttall. It is worth noting, as illustration of the poet's negative capability, that Keats wrote this affirmation of imagination and dreaming to Bailey around the same time (possibly even the very same week) he was drafting his hero's fervent renunciation of dreaming in *Endymion* 4.615–69.

8. In an essay forthcoming in *Keats-Shelley Journal*, Nancy Rosenfeld proposes that Keats was also influenced by Eve's dream in *Paradise Lost* (books 4–5) and that it is a better analogy than Adam's dream for the depiction of imagination in *The Eve of St. Agnes*. "The central parallel between Madeline's and Eve's dreams . . . is that both are prophetic of confusion and disappointment. The two dreams . . . illustrate the way in which reality falls short of what imagination anticipates."

9. These are all one-sided readings to illustrate what can be done (if one wishes) with author intertextuality. Each of the poems has been read in many different ways over the years.

10. For a detailed reading of *The Eve of St. Agnes* as a Pre-Raphaelite painting, see Grant Scott, *The Sculpted Word* 86–95. The poem, says Scott, "provided a rich source of vibrant and colorful images for these artists [the Pre-Raphaelites], but more importantly . . . it showed them that Keats was doing in words what they so desperately wanted to achieve in paint—luxuriating in the texture of the medium itself" (87).

11. Rhonda Kercsmar could also serve as spokesperson: "*The Eve of St. Agnes* uses the violation of the female body and of the romance structure that frames it to affirm gender inequality and female powerlessness" ("Keats's Violation of Romance"

25). But she is also interested in several other issues, including Keats's manipulations of both traditional and Gothic romance conventions.

12. This is the final engraving in the edition illustrated by Edward Wehnert, published by Sampson Low in 1856 and reprinted several times thereafter. See Appendix C for particulars.

4. WHY THERE ARE SO MANY MEANINGS (I): COMPLEX READERSHIP

1. Keats's current status at or near the top of the standard academic canon in this country is undisputed. In a 1990 survey conducted by the publisher, and again in 1997, English teachers using the *Norton Anthology of English Literature* ranked Keats, Coleridge, and Wordsworth the three most "essential" writers in the two-century span covered by volume 2, 1780 to the present. Harriet Kramer Linkin's survey published in *College English* in 1991, narrowing the focus to "The Current Canon in British Romantics Studies," has Keats and Coleridge in first place, taught in 99 percent of all courses in Romantic literature. Even the most revisionist of recent Romantic anthologies, Anne Mellor and Richard Matlak's *British Literature, 1780–1830*, calls Keats's *Lamia* volume "perhaps the single greatest volume of poetry in the nineteenth century" (1255).

2. For a quick overview of materials concerning Keats's first readers and the development of his reputation and influence, see my bibliographical essay ("John Keats") in Jordan 712–16. The most useful collections of the earliest reviews and other nineteenth-century comments are Lewis Schwartz's *Keats Reviewed by His Contemporaries*, Donald Reiman's *The Romantics Reviewed*, and G. M. Matthews's *Keats: The Critical Heritage*. Concerning the readers and reviews of Keats's *Poems* of 1817, see Donald Goellnicht, "The Politics of Reading."

3. These are representative of the better responses that I get (from students who will receive an A or B in the course) and not of the class as a whole. The authors of the comments are, in order, Helen H. Son, Ken Tatarelis, Bryan Rasmussen, Yeon Sook Koo, Sean Butler, Victoria Lopez, Amy Kovarick, and Mark Johnston. I have lightly edited the passages for presentation here, but no more than copyeditors have edited my own sentences over the years.

4. For the idea of chaos in this context, I am initially indebted to Louise Smith's "Writing on 'Isabella,'" the most sensible short account of reading Keats that I know of. Smith cites Ann Berthoff's rhetoric textbook, *Forming, Thinking, Writing*. On the topic of reading more generally—the different ways that people read, how meaning is registered, how separate details are constructed into overall understanding, and many other aspects of the subject—there has been enormous research activity over the past three decades. Richard Beach's *A Teacher's Introduction to Reader-Response Theories* concludes (before the index) with a 33-page bibliography listing more than seven hundred books and articles—and this is just a practical introduction written for schoolteachers. Most of the work has been done in schools of education (as opposed to departments of English) and is published in journals with titles such as *Reading Improvement, Reading Research Quarterly*, and *Journal of Reading Behavior* (all of which began in the 1960s); the journals *Research in the Teaching of English* and *Reader: Essays in Reader-Oriented Theory, Criticism, and Pedagogy* attempt to appeal more widely to the interests of teaching, reading research, and literary theory all at once. The most helpful items for literary scholars and theorists who have little or no background in the day-to-day concerns of schools of education are the two volumes of *Handbook of Reading Research* (1984, 1991). The first of these (edited by P. David Pearson) includes essays on "The History of Reading Research," "Current Traditions of Reading Research," and "Models of the Reading Process"; the second

(edited by Rebecca Barr et al.) contains eleven essays in Part 3 on the topic "Constructs of the Reader Process." My own account of the reading process in the present section is purposely simpler than any of these research materials and mainly highlights the two-part process of selection and unifying that produced the readings of *The Eve of St. Agnes* described in chapter 3 and underlies those that I observe in my teaching. Nothing in this section is meant to conflict with the more ambitious work of the educational researchers.

5. In my introduction to *John Keats: Complete Poems*, discussing Keats's ability to identify with an object and communicate that inner identification to the reader, I suggested that the line conveys "a sense of what it is like . . . to be limping and to put tender feet down, one at a time, on frozen grass; and there may be a further sensation of how frozen grass itself feels when it is walked upon" (xxvii).

6. I was helped to this passage by Mark Jones's *The "Lucy Poems,"* where it appears (in a longer version) as an epigraph preceding the first chapter.

7. Let us suppose, to construct a hypothetical case, that each of the thirty-seven items in my list for stanza 1 could be read in five different ways (a purely arbitrary number, since for some of the images the range of variations would be very great). The possibilities from which the reader could make a selection in this stanza would then number 185 (37×5). If the remaining forty-one stanzas averaged out to be similarly rich in potential variation of response, the total for the poem would be 7,770 (185×42). My hypothetical case may seem silly, but it is sillier still to imagine that *everything* in so complicated a poem as *The Eve of St. Agnes* would (or should) have exactly the same meaning for all readers alike.

8. This topic is further developed in the "Multiple Keats" section of chapter 5.

9. See my *Coleridge and Textual Instability* 111–16, 247, for a thumbnail sketch of the critical ideal of Coleridgean unity and the accompanying notion, based in part on my dozen years of editing the *Journal of English and Germanic Philology*, that "a major critical industry has grown up in this century concerned to discover Coleridgean unity in works of every period of literature."

10. The best work on Keats's own ideas of the author-reader transaction and the reading process has been done by Donald Goellnicht in "Keats on Reading" and "Re(:)reading Keats." Goellnicht analyzes this letter to Reynolds at length, calling it "Keats's most extensive description of the act of reading" and relating it to ideas of Iser, Jauss, Barthes, and Poulet ("Keats on Reading" 193–201).

11. Brian Gibbons's *Shakespeare and Multiplicity* centers on this very quality: "There is a sense of great abundance in Shakespeare's plays—so much so, indeed, that in every generation there are interpreters who cut and simplify, unable to cope with the wealth of ideas and experiences in the plays, or supposing their audiences incapable of doing so. . . . Shakespeare's plays . . . promote as multiple an awareness as possible of differing facets of a story" (1). In his concluding chapter, Gibbons mentions "multiple aspects of . . . theme," increasing complexity, and a "sense of instability of perspective" among Shakespeare's virtues; the plays "are so charged with matter that they can seem just as full of unrealised potential after a fine performance as before one" (208–11).

12. In Evert and Rhodes's volume on teaching Keats, the proportion of authoritarian to open approaches is roughly two to one, in spite of the senior editor's introductory remark that "If there is any single characteristic that mediates the diversity of these essays, it is clearly the abhorrence of interpretive closure in teaching" (37). In Richard Matlak's companion volume on teaching Coleridge, virtually all the essays are intent on dictating "the meaning" to students—for example, concerning *Kubla Khan*, "The poem *is* about the creative process, but in a peculiar and quite unsymbolic way. To see this, one must ignore the preface and read the poem as one would any other" (94).

13. The same point is made by Joseph Harris in a review of several recent works on teaching, including Karolides's collection: "A common tactic in writing about teaching at the college level is for the writer to present his or her own reading of a text as a classroom 'discussion' . . . :

Our discussion begins with . . .
I then ask . . .
We are next ready to look at . . .
I then explain . . .
I outline . . .
Finally, students begin to see . . .

These are all typical signposts in loose classroom narratives of this sort. The voices of students do sometimes enter into such accounts, but usually only briefly and anonymously" (788).

14. The most provocative work on these questions is still, after three decades, Hirsch's *Validity in Interpretation*, which equates "objective interpretation" with recovery of the author's intention but never confronts the inherent problem that authorial intention when separated from a text is for all practical purposes unrecoverable. Earlier notable attacks on subjectivity in reading, interpretation, and evaluation include Wimsatt and Beardsley's "The Affective Fallacy" (which of course takes a quite different view from Hirsch's concerning authorial intention) and Matthew Arnold's paragraph on the "fallacy" of "the personal estimate" in "The Study of Poetry" (*Complete Prose Works* 9:163–64).

15. Kernan's Coriolanian contempt for the "extreme democratic view" in these and many other passages makes his work a straw book for anyone who wishes to emote to the contrary. Numerous better-tempered attacks against theory (deconstruction in particular) have appeared in the interim—for example, among the most recent, Wendell Harris's *Literary Meaning*, which proposes that the "first goal to be pursued by English departments should . . . be the accurate interpretation of literary texts of all genres" (198). Right—but then which of the fifty-nine shall we decide is the most "accurate"?

16. Formerly such comprehensiveness was valued as the best means of recovering or approximating the author's intention in a work. In a reader-oriented scheme, comprehensiveness simply produces the better reading. The criterion of validity is supplanted by the criteria of richness and complexity.

17. There are of course other meanings and effects here besides those I have mentioned in the four principal clusters. One might, for example, point to the hovering pun on "vain"/"vein" in the final line of the stanza, producing the additional physiological detail of swelling in (a) vein. The last three words, "in *her* dell," perhaps carry the implication that each nightingale has its assigned place and responsibility in the world—to fill its particular dell with song—and that Keats's tongueless nightingale has failed in its responsibility. There is also the fact that the nightingale in these lines is one more in a series of bird images associated with Madeline. The others are "ringdove" (line 198), "dove forlorn" (333), and "Soft Nightingale" (in the draft version at 341–42), and most of them are connected to Porphyro's character as hunter, nestrobber, and cager (188, 340, and the draft at 340, 341–42).

5. WHY THERE ARE SO MANY MEANINGS (II): COMPLEX AUTHORSHIP

1. Charles H. Webb, "Byron, Keats, and Shelley." I am much obliged to the author for permission to quote from the version read at Los Angeles.

2. Some of this is recorded in *John Keats, 1795–1995, with a Catalogue of the Harvard Keats Collection*; the Grolier Club's *John Keats: Bicentennial Exhibition, September 19–November 22, 1995*; and the Grasmere catalogue by Robert Woof and Stephen Hebron.

3. See in particular Wolfson's "Feminizing Keats" and "Keats and the Manhood of the Poet" and Levinson's *Keats's Life of Allegory*.

4. The most useful criticism on this topic is Martin Halpern's "Keats and the 'Spirit that Laughest.'" One of the earliest pieces on the poet's comic spirit is Ferdinand Reyher's 1915 tribute, "The Humor of Keats."

5. Compare especially, for likenesses in tone, Chaucer's stanzas recounting the lovers' first sexual union (*Troilus and Criseyde* 3.1303 ff.), which include the tender question that they repeatedly ("ful ofte") address to one another: "O swete, / Clippe ich yow thus, or elles I it meete?" (1343–44)—"O sweet, do I embrace you thus, or am I dreaming?" In "Keats and Chaucer," F. E. L. Priestley is mainly concerned to point out Chaucerian echoes in *Isabella* and *The Eve of St. Agnes*, but he cites several parallels between *Troilus* and *Endymion*.

6. One could append here a lengthy note on the pervasiveness of grotesque, even slapstick, humor in serious poetry. For a handful of examples specifically involving animals from the work of two of Keats's most serious contemporaries, consider Wordsworth's "horse that thinks," the smartest character in *The Idiot Boy*, who plays an important role in the joyful reunion at the end of the poem (Johnny's mother almost knocks him over); the "rough terrier of the hills" in the early lines of the fourth book of *The Prelude*, who helps Wordsworth compose his poetry; and Coleridge's "toothless mastiff bitch" at the beginning of *Christabel*, who with uncanny chronometrical precision utters four short howls for each of the preliminary quarter hours and sixteen howls (four for the final quarter plus twelve for the hour) at the stroke of midnight. Each of these is pointedly linked with serious thematic matter— Betty Foy's love for her idiot son, one of the *Prelude*-speaker's epiphanic experiences in nature (concluding with "a breath-like sound, / Quick as the pantings of the faithful dog, / The off and on companion of my walk," 4.185–87 in the 1850 text), and the first of several significant references to Christabel's dead mother.

7. The Keats map originated in a graduate seminar a decade ago as the by-product of an attempt to create a Keats lexicon listing recurring words and phrases in the major poems and sorting them into five categories: ideas, events, images, characters, and places. The ideas category—themes, motifs, concerns, matter— included most of the oppositions of abstractions that critics repeatedly refer to (time versus permanence, mortality versus immortality, pain versus pleasure, and so on). The events category—plots, situations, narrative structures—highlighted the various journeys, quests, and encounters in the poems. The images section—tropes, figures, symbols—was packed with terms having to do with visions, dreams, nightmares, fairies, magic, narcotics, religion, nature (and much else). The most interesting feature of the characters category (heroes, enchantresses, dreamers, gods, goddesses, priests, and so on) was the recurrence of mismatches between a mortal, usually male, and some kind of immortal, usually female (a goddess or a fairy). The places category, which included the medieval or classical past, hidden sites such as the nightingale's forest, and ideal realms, led us on to the Keats map.

8. I am here reading and quoting the earlier of the two basic versions of *La Belle Dame*, that of the extant manuscripts by Keats, Brown, and Woodhouse, but my comments apply as well to the later version published in Leigh Hunt's *Indicator*, 10 May 1820. In this and the next six paragraphs, I draw on parts of my brief discussion of *La Belle Dame* in "Reading Keats's Plots" (de Almeida, *Critical Essays* 88–102).

9. Wolfson (*Questioning Presence* 296–300) relates *La Belle Dame* to Wordsworth's technique of "a perplexed questioner and a voice trying to answer" in the *Lyrical*

Ballads, especially *The Thorn*. The question-answer situation in *We Are Seven* may be an even better example, if we do not wholly accept the adult questioner's account of the reality debated in that poem. In *La Belle Dame*, it is true that the knight repeats some of the questioner's words almost verbatim in the final three lines; but this can be read, if one wishes, as an ironical, perhaps even taunting, echo. There is a substantial literature on the open-endedness of *La Belle Dame*. Along with Wolfson's discussion, I especially recommend Anne Mellor's three pages in *English Romantic Irony* 93–95.

6. CONCLUSION: KEATS "AMONG THE ENGLISH POETS"

1. Keats's emergence from obscurity is usually connected with the publication of the first full-scale biography, Richard Monckton Milnes's *Life, Letters, and Literary Remains, of John Keats*, in 1848. But a cluster of significant events in the late 1820s helped initiate the process two decades earlier: the appearance of an extended biographical sketch of Keats in Leigh Hunt's *Lord Byron and Some of His Contemporaries* (first and second eds. both 1828), the first English printing of Percy Shelley's *Adonais* in 1829 (an edition sponsored by the so-called Cambridge Apostles—Milnes, Alfred Tennyson, and A. H. Hallam—and set from a copy of the 1821 Pisa edition that Hallam had brought back from Italy), and the issue of a pirated *Poetical Works of Coleridge, Shelley, and Keats* in Paris, also in 1829. Joseph Grigely, urging the importance of (usually neglected) *non*authorized texts in our historical and cultural studies, makes an interesting point concerning this last: "One could argue . . . that Keats's most compelling moment of critical recognition in the early nineteenth century was not Richard Monckton Milnes's *Life* . . . but Galignani's piracy of 1829" (*Textualterity* 31–32).

2. *Ode to Apollo* line 20 and *To My Brother George* (sonnet) line 3. Toward the end of book 2 of *Endymion*, Keats's narrator expresses fear that there may be no room for additions to the group: "Aye, the count / Of mighty Poets is made up; the scroll / Is folded by the Muses; the bright roll / Is in Apollo's hand: . . . The world has done its duty . . . the sun of poesy is set" (723–29).

3. "Preponderance of evidence" in academic discourse is frequently translatable as "I too have some thoughts on this matter." Theorists on canonicity—Wendell Harris ("Canonicity"), John Guillory ("Canon" and *Cultural Capital*), and Jonathan Kramnick ("The Making of the English Canon"), to mention two canonical examples and a newcomer to the group—are not very precise concerning the history of the topic, and literary historians tend to shy away from theory. The works that I have found most helpful as background for this brief discussion are three pieces by Laura Mandell—"Romantic Canons," "Canons Die Hard" (both on the Web), and an unpublished draft tracing the development of miscellanies into anthologies ("The Monstrosity of Minimal Difference")—and two superbly researched articles by Thomas Bonnell on John Bell's *Poets of Great Britain*. Aileen Ward has collected and analyzed Keats's various references to (poetic) fame in his poems and letters ("'That Last Infirmity'"), and I have profited as well from M. H. Abrams's "Art-as-Such," Douglas Patey's "The Eighteenth Century Invents the Canon," and Trevor Ross's "The Emergence of 'Literature.'"

4. Keats's friend Brown owned at least four of the Spenser volumes from this edition, and several kinds of circumstantial evidence suggest that the underlinings and marginal markings in these volumes, now at the Keats House, Hampstead, may be in the poet's own hand. See Greg Kucich, "A Lamentable Lay" especially 7–12 and *Keats, Shelley, and Romantic Spenserianism* 230–34.

5. Bonnell remarks, "If one considers Bell's explicit design, the great size of his undertaking, and his pointed and persistent advertising, then the significance of

the *Poets* becomes clear: it was the first serious attempt to publish a comprehensive English literary canon" ("John Bell's *Poets*" 130). One wants to agree, but there is a great unevenness about the available information on these early editions. Bonnell knows everything, and relays most of what he knows, about Bell's edition of 1776–1782. But Creech's Edinburgh edition just preceding it in 1773–1776 is relatively obscure (I have taken most of my details from the description in the *National Union Catalogue* 76:557), and in Samuel Johnson studies there is widespread misinformation, originating in Boswell's *Life*, concerning the relation of "Johnson's Poets" of 1779–1781 to Bell's edition.

6. See in particular Alan Richardson's *Literature, Education, and Romanticism* and Barbara Benedict's *Making the Modern Reader* for authoritative explanations and comprehensive references to the considerable scholarship on these large social and cultural changes in Britain toward the end of the eighteenth century.

7. Subsequently, "most eminent" became a stock phrase in the titles of collections and anthologies, as in *The Poetical Bouquet, Selected from the Works of the Most Eminent British Poets* in 1810 and the subtitle of a new edition of Vicesimus Knox's much reprinted *Elegant Extracts* around the same time: *Being a Copious Selection . . . from the Most Eminent British Poets*.

8. William Hazlitt's *Lectures on the English Poets*, most of which Keats heard when they were delivered in London in January–March 1818 and undoubtedly read after they were published as a book by Taylor and Hessey in May, would have been another influence on Keats's idea of "the English Poets." The eighth lecture, "On the Living Poets"—eleven writers from Anna Barbauld to Southey and Coleridge—might be thought evidence to the contrary concerning the notion that only dead poets could qualify. But Hazlitt addresses this very point in the opening pages of the lecture: "Genius is the heir of fame; but the hard condition on which the bright reversion must be earned is the loss of life. Fame is the recompense not of the living, but of the dead." He makes quite clear that the living poets, while they may have "popularity," "reputation," and "praise," are in an altogether different category from those who have earned "everlasting renown . . . the honours which time alone can give" (*Complete Works* 5:143–45).

9. "The Study of Poetry," *Complete Prose Works* 9:168. Arnold's general position (if I may apply a touchstone of my own) exemplifies an extreme degree of the elitism that some theorists object to in the idea of a canon of any sort. He was, like Thomas Carlyle in *Heroes, Hero-Worship, and the Heroic in History*, a believer in the notion of universal history as a record of the works of "great men," and among his publications are an edition of *Johnson's Chief Lives of the Poets* (1878)—representing a sort of crème de la crème, a "chief" six chosen out of Johnson's "most eminent" fifty or so—and a short introduction to the first volume of *The Hundred Greatest Men: Portraits of One Hundred Greatest Men of History Reproduced from Fine and Rare Steel Engravings* (1880).

10. See, for example, Nina Baym's "Melodramas of Beset Manhood: How Theories of American Fiction Exclude Women Authors" and "Early Histories of American Literature: A Chapter in the Institution of New England," in *Feminism and American Literary History* 3–18, 81–101.

11. Sometimes Hannah More, Dorothy Wordsworth (as poet), and Mary Tighe are added or substituted, but the number of women Romantic poets regularly taught and written about has not, so far, exceeded nine or ten.

12. Harlan, "Intellectual History" 598. Harlan draws on, among others, Frank Kermode (*Forms of Attention* 75) and Wolfgang Iser (*The Act of Reading* 7, 8), but his own definition is more useful, because it is clearer and more comprehensive than the statements he quotes.

13. The shifting stanza or paragraph divisions in successive versions of *Kubla Khan*—there are two stanzas in Coleridge's extant fair copy of the poem, four in the original printing of 1816, three in the collected editions of 1828 and 1829, and either three or four (depending on the significance of a page-break between lines 36 and 37) in the collected edition of 1834—are either an aid or a further confusion in interpretation but in any case probably ought to be a consideration for a reader who is consulting more than one authorial text. See my *Coleridge and Textual Instability* 73–77.

14. See, for example, Murray Gell-Mann, *The Quark and the Jaguar*, especially 27–32. Gell-Mann's explanations of complex adaptive and complex evolving systems (9, 16–21) are at least metaphorically descriptive of the model of reading that I am developing. The authorship side of the literary transaction can be considered a complex adaptive system: authors do read in the process of writing, interpret in the process of reading, and constantly interact with the works they are creating. The text, in the middle of the scheme, is not complexly adaptive; it just sits there (in a manner of speaking) and is acted upon. But obviously it can be considered a complex *evolving* system, in the sense that it undergoes change every time somebody does something to it. The readership side is an infinitely expanding activity of further complex adaptive systems: each individual reader is a center of virtually infinite possibilities for imaginative response in the process of reading—and then there is an infinite number of individual readers (past, present, and future), each responding differently from all the others. For the history and theories of complexity in literature itself, Frederick Garber's concise "Simplicity and Complexity" is an excellent starting point. Handily for my purposes, Garber uses *The Eve of St. Agnes* to exemplify complexity!

15. Wordsworth's expression in *The Prelude*, book 5, "the great Nature that exists in works / Of mighty Poets" (1850 text, lines 594–95), with its implication that the reader's mind operates creatively upon poetry in the same way that the spectator's mind acts creatively upon nature, can be read as an early hint of the "ennobling interchange" that takes place between reader and author (via the text) in a literary transaction.

16. Johnson can sound amazingly modern for a critic writing more than two centuries ago. There is a straight line from his description of metaphysical wit as "a kind of *discordia concors*; a combination of dissimilar images, or discovery of occult resemblances in things apparently unlike" ("Cowley," *Lives* 1:20) to Coleridge's equally memorable statement that the imagination "reveals itself in the balance or reconciliation of opposite or discordant qualities" (*Biographia Literaria* chapter 14), and thence to the twentieth-century New Critics via T. S. Eliot's essays (in which he cites both of these passages by Johnson and Coleridge) and I. A. Richards's *Coleridge on Imagination* (which also refers to Johnson).

BIBLIOGRAPHY

Abrams, M. H. "Art-as-Such: The Sociology of Modern Aesthetics" (1985). Reprinted in Abrams's *Doing Things with Texts: Essays in Criticism and Critical Theory*, ed. Michael Fischer, 135–58, 400–2. New York: W. W. Norton, 1989.

Adelman, Clifford. "The Dangers of Enthrallment." In Danzig, 99–115.

Allott, Miriam. "'Isabella', 'The Eve of St. Agnes' and 'Lamia.'" In Muir, 39–62.

Altick, Richard D. *Paintings from Books: Art and Literature in Britain, 1760–1900*. Columbus: Ohio State University Press, 1985.

Alwes, Karla. *Imagination Transformed: The Evolution of the Female Character in Keats's Poetry*. Carbondale: Southern Illinois University Press, 1993.

Arcana, Judith. "Midwinter Night's Dream: 'The Eve of St. Agnes' as Sacred Ritual in the Old Religion of the Britons." *Journal of Ritual Studies* 1, no. 2 (Summer 1987): 43–57.

Arnold, Matthew. *The Complete Prose Works of Matthew Arnold*, ed. R. H. Super. Vol. 9: *English Literature and Irish Politics*. Ann Arbor: University of Michigan Press, 1973.

Arseneau, Mary. "Madeline, Mermaids, and Medusas in 'The Eve of St. Agnes.'" *Papers on Language and Literature* 33 (1997): 227–43.

Aske, Martin. "Magical Spaces in 'The Eve of St. Agnes.'" *Essays in Criticism* 31 (1981): 196–209.

Atkins, G. Douglas. "*The Eve of St. Agnes* Reconsidered." *Tennessee Studies in Literature* 18 (1973): 113–32.

Babbitt, Irving. *Rousseau and Romanticism*. Boston: Houghton Mifflin, 1919.

Baker, Jeffrey. "Aphrodite and the Virgin: A Note on Keats's 'Eve of St. Agnes.'" *Antigonish Review* 47 (Autumn 1981): 99–108. Revised and expanded in Baker's *John Keats and Symbolism*, 48–61. Brighton: Harvester; New York: St. Martin's, 1986.

Banerjee, Jacqueline. "Mending the Butterfly: The New Historicism and Keats's 'Eve of St. Agnes.'" *College English* 57 (1995): 529–45.

Barlow, Paul. "Pre-Raphaelitism and Post-Raphaelitism: The Articulation of Fantasy and the Problem of Historical Space." In *Pre-Raphaelites Re-Viewed*, ed. Marcia Pointon, 66–82. Manchester: Manchester University Press, 1989.

Barnard, John. *John Keats*. Cambridge: Cambridge University Press, 1987.

Barr, Rebecca, Michael L. Kamil, Peter B. Mosenthal, and P. David Pearson, eds. *Handbook of Reading Research*. Vol. 2. New York: Longman, 1991. (For vol. 1, see Pearson, below.)

Barthes, Roland. "The Death of the Author" (originally in French in *Mantéia*, 1968). In Barthes's *Image—Music—Text*, ed. and trans. Stephen Heath, 142–48. New York: Hill and Wang, 1977.

Bate, Jonathan. "Living with the Weather." *Studies in Romanticism* 35 (1996): 431–47.

———. *Shakespeare and the English Romantic Imagination*. Oxford: Clarendon Press, 1986.

Bate, Walter Jackson. *John Keats*. Cambridge: Harvard University Press, 1963.

Bayley, John. *The Uses of Division: Unity and Disharmony in Literature*. London: Chatto and Windus; New York: Viking, 1976.

Baym, Nina. *Feminism and American Literary History: Essays*. New Brunswick: Rutgers University Press, 1992.

Beach, Richard. *A Teacher's Introduction to Reader-Response Theories*. Urbana: National Council of Teachers of English, 1993.

Bell, Arthur H. "'The Depth of Things': Keats and Human Space." *Keats-Shelley Journal* 23 (1974): 77–94.

———. "Madeline's House Is Not Her Castle." *Keats-Shelley Journal* 20 (1971): 11–14.

Benedict, Barbara M. *Making the Modern Reader: Cultural Mediation in Early Modern Literary Anthologies*. Princeton: Princeton University Press, 1996.

Bennett, Andrew J. "'Hazardous Magic': Vision and Inscription in Keats's 'The Eve of St. Agnes.'" *Keats-Shelley Journal* 41 (1992): 100–21. Revised in Bennett's *Keats, Narrative and Audience: The Posthumous Life of Writing*, 96–112. Cambridge: Cambridge University Press, 1994.

Bennett, Mary. *Artists of the Pre-Raphaelite Circle: The First Generation*. London: Lund Humphries, 1988.

Berthoff, Ann E. *Forming, Thinking, Writing: The Composing Imagination*. Rochelle Park, NJ: Hayden, 1978.

Bérubé, Michael. *Public Access: Literary Theory and American Cultural Politics*. London: Verso, 1994.

Blackstone, Bernard. *The Consecrated Urn: An Interpretation of Keats in Terms of Growth and Form*. London: Longmans, Green, 1959.

Bleich, David. *Readings and Feelings: An Introduction to Subjective Criticism*. Urbana: National Council of Teachers of English, 1975.

———. *Subjective Criticism*. Baltimore: Johns Hopkins University Press, 1978.

Bloom, Harold. *The Visionary Company: A Reading of English Romantic Poetry*. Garden City, NY: Doubleday, 1961.

Boehm, Alan D. "Madeline's Castle: Setting and Visual Discrepancy in John Keats's 'The Eve of St. Agnes.'" In *Spectrum of the Fantastic: Selected Essays from the Sixth International Conference on the Fantastic in the Arts*, ed. Donald Palumbo, 21–27. Westport, CT: Greenwood Press, 1988.

Bonnell, Thomas F. "Bookselling and Canon-Making: The Trade Rivalry over the English Poets, 1776–1783." *Studies in Eighteenth-Century Culture* 19 (1989): 53–69.

———. "John Bell's *Poets of Great Britain*: The 'Little Trifling Edition' Revisited." *Modern Philology* 85 (1987): 128–52.

Boulger, James D. "Keats' Symbolism." *ELH* 28 (1961): 244–59.

Bronk, William. "Skeptic." In Bronk's *The Shaker Chair*. New Rochelle: James L. Weil, 1993.

Brooks, Cleanth. *The Well Wrought Urn: Studies in the Structure of Poetry*. New York: Harcourt, Brace, 1947.

Burgess, C. F. "'The Eve of St. Agnes': One Way to the Poem." *English Journal* 54 (1965): 389–94.

Burke, Kenneth. "Symbolic Action in a Poem by Keats." *Accent* 4 (1943): 30–42. Reprinted in Burke's *A Grammar of Motives*, 447–63. New York: Prentice-Hall, 1945.

Bush, Douglas. *John Keats: His Life and Writings*. New York: Macmillan, 1966.

Byron, Lord. *Byron's Letters and Journals*, ed. Leslie A. Marchand. 12 vols. Cambridge: Harvard University Press, 1973–1982.

Caldwell, James Ralston. *John Keats' Fancy: The Effect on Keats of the Psychology of His Day*. Ithaca: Cornell University Press, 1945.

Campbell, Joseph. *The Hero with a Thousand Faces*. New York: Bollingen, 1949.

Carr, Arthur. "John Keats' Other 'Urn.'" *University of Kansas City Review* 20 (1954): 237–42.

Codell, Julie F. "Painting Keats: Pre-Raphaelite Artists between Social Transgressions and Painterly Conventions." *Victorian Poetry* 33 (1995): 341–70.

Coleridge, Samuel Taylor. *Biographia Literaria*, ed. James Engell and W. Jackson Bate. 2 vols. Princeton: Princeton University Press, 1983.

Colglazier, Lyndel P. "'The Eve of St. Agnes' and the Seductive Mystery of Imagination." *University of Mississippi Studies in English*, new ser. 10 (1992): 1–11.

Collick, John. "Desire on 'The Eve of St. Agnes.'" *Critical Survey* 3 (1991): 37–43.

Colvin, Sidney. *Keats*. English Men of Letters Series. London: Macmillan, 1887.

Cook, Wayne. "John Keats and the Pre-Raphaelite Brotherhood: Pictorial Poetry and Narrative Painting." *University of Hartford Studies in Literature* 20, no. 3 (1988): 1–23.

Culler, Jonathan. *The Pursuit of Signs: Semiotics, Literature, Deconstruction*. Ithaca: Cornell University Press, 1981.

Curtis, Jared, ed. *The Fenwick Notes of William Wordsworth*. London: Bristol Classical Press, 1993.

Cusac, Marian H. "Keats as Enchanter: An Organizing Principle of *The Eve of St. Agnes*." *Keats-Shelley Journal* 17 (1968): 113–19.

Damon, S. Foster. *Amy Lowell: A Chronicle*. Boston: Houghton Mifflin, 1935.

Danzig, Allan, ed. *Twentieth Century Interpretations of "The Eve of St. Agnes": A Collection of Critical Essays*. Englewood Cliffs: Prentice-Hall, 1971.

de Almeida, Hermione, ed. *Critical Essays on John Keats*. Boston: G. K. Hall, 1990.

———. *Romantic Medicine and John Keats*. New York: Oxford University Press, 1991.

Dunbar, Georgia S. "The Significance of the Humor in 'Lamia.'" *Keats-Shelley Journal* 8 (1959): 17–26.

Eaves, Morris. "'Why Don't They Leave It Alone?' Speculations on the Authority of the Audience in Editorial Theory." In Ezell and O'Keeffe, 85–99.

Eco, Umberto, with Richard Rorty, Jonathan Culler, and Christine Brooke-Rose. *Interpretation and Overinterpretation*, ed. Stefan Collini. Cambridge: Cambridge University Press, 1992.

———. *The Limitations of Interpretation*. Bloomington: Indiana University Press, 1990.

———. *The Role of the Reader: Explorations in the Semiotics of Texts*. Bloomington: Indiana University Press, 1984.

Eliot, T. S. "The Metaphysical Poets" (1921). Reprinted in *Selected Essays, 1917–1932*, 241–50. New York: Harcourt, Brace, 1932.

Empson, William. *Seven Types of Ambiguity* (1930). Rev. ed. New York: New Directions, 1947.

Enscoe, Gerald. *Eros and the Romantics: Sexual Love as a Theme in Coleridge, Shelley and Keats*. The Hague: Mouton, 1967.

Evert, Walter H., and Jack W. Rhodes, eds. *Approaches to Teaching Keats's Poetry*. New York: Modern Language Association, 1991.

Ezell, Margaret J. M., and Katherine O'Brien O'Keeffe, eds. *Cultural Artifacts and the Production of Meaning: The Page, the Image, and the Body*. Ann Arbor: University of Michigan Press, 1994.

Farnell, Gary. "'Unfit for Ladies': Keats's *The Eve of St Agnes*." *Studies in Romanticism* 34 (1995): 401–12.

Fields, Beverly. "Keats and the Tongueless Nightingale: Some Unheard Melodies in 'The Eve of St. Agnes.'" *The Wordsworth Circle* 14 (1983): 246–50.

Finney, Claude Lee. *The Evolution of Keats's Poetry*. 2 vols. Cambridge: Harvard University Press, 1936.

Fish, Stanley. *Is There a Text in This Class? The Authority of Interpretive Communities*. Cambridge: Harvard University Press, 1980.

———. "Literature in the Reader: Affective Stylistics." *New Literary History* 2 (1970): 123–62. Reprinted in Fish's *Is There a Text*, 21–67, 373–76.

Fogle, Richard Harter. "A Reading of Keats's 'Eve of St. Agnes.'" *College English* 6 (1945): 325–28.

———. "Reading Recommended by the Book Committee." *Key Reporter* 38, no. 1 (Autumn 1972): 5.

Ford, Newell F. *The Prefigurative Imagination of John Keats: A Study of the Beauty-Truth Identification and Its Implications*. Stanford: Stanford University Press, 1951.

Foucault, Michel. "What Is an Author?" (originally in French in *Bulletin de la société française de philosophie*, 1969). In Foucault's *Language, Counter-Memory, Practice: Selected Essays and Interviews*, ed. Donald F. Bouchard, 113–38. Ithaca: Cornell University Press, 1977. Revised version in Foucault's *Textual Strategies: Perspectives in Post-Structuralist Criticism*, ed. and trans. Josué V. Harari, 141–60. Ithaca: Cornell University Press, 1979.

Fraistat, Neil. *The Poem and the Book: Interpreting Collections of Romantic Poetry*. Chapel Hill: University of North Carolina Press, 1985.

Garber, Frederick. "Simplicity and Complexity." In *The New Princeton Encyclopedia of Poetry and Poetics*, ed. Alex Preminger and T. V. F. Brogan, 1151–53. Princeton: Princeton University Press, 1993.

Garvin, Katharine. "The Christianity of St. Agnes' Eve: Keats' Catholic Inspiration." *Dublin Review* 234 (1960–1961): 356–64.

Gell-Mann, Murray. *The Quark and the Jaguar: Adventures in the Simple and the Complex*. New York: W. H. Freeman, 1994.

Gibbons, Brian. *Shakespeare and Multiplicity*. Cambridge: Cambridge University Press, 1993.

Gibson, Gail McMurray. "Ave Madeline: Ironic Annunciation in Keats's 'The Eve of St. Agnes.'" *Keats-Shelley Journal* 26 (1977): 39–50.

Gilbreath, Marcia. "The Etymology of Porphyro's Name in Keats's 'Eve of St. Agnes.'" *Keats-Shelley Journal* 37 (1988): 20–25.

Gittings, Robert. *John Keats*. Boston: Little, Brown, 1968.

———. *John Keats: The Living Year, 21 September 1818 to 21 September 1819*. Cambridge: Harvard University Press, 1954.

Goellnicht, Donald C. "Keats on Reading: 'Delicious Diligent Indolence.'" *Journal of English and Germanic Philology* 88 (1989): 190–210.

———. "The Politics of Reading and Writing: Periodical Reviews of Keats's *Poems* (1817)." In *New Romanticisms: Theory and Critical Practice*, ed. David L. Clark and Donald C. Goellnicht, 101–31. Toronto: University of Toronto Press, 1994.

————. "Re(:)reading Keats." In Evert and Rhodes, 99–105.

Gradman, Barry. *Metamorphosis in Keats*. New York: New York University Press, 1980.

Grigely, Joseph. *Textualterity: Art, Theory, and Textual Criticism*. Ann Arbor: University of Michigan Press, 1995.

Guillory, John. "Canon." In *Critical Terms for Literary Study*, ed. Frank Lentricchia and Thomas McLaughlin, 2nd ed., 233–49. Chicago: University of Chicago Press, 1995.

————. *Cultural Capital: The Problem of Literary Canon Formation*. Chicago: University of Chicago Press, 1993.

Hagstrum, Jean H. *The Romantic Body: Love and Sexuality in Keats, Wordsworth, and Blake*. Knoxville: University of Tennessee Press, 1985.

Hall, Jean. "Romance to Ode: Love's Dream and the Conflicted Imagination." In Evert and Rhodes, 126–30.

Halpern, Martin. "Keats and the 'Spirit that Laughest.'" *Keats-Shelley Journal* 15 (1966): 69–86.

Harlan, David. "Intellectual History and the Return of Literature." *American Historical Review* 94 (1989): 581–609.

Harris, Joseph. "The Course as Text/The Teacher as Critic." *College English* 55 (1993): 785–93.

Harris, Wendell V. "Canonicity." *PMLA* 106 (1991): 110–21.

————. *Literary Meaning: Reclaiming the Study of Literature*. New York: New York University Press, 1996.

Harvey, Karen J. "The Trouble about Merlin: The Theme of Enchantment in 'The Eve of St. Agnes.'" *Keats-Shelley Journal* 34 (1985): 83–94.

Havens, Raymond D. "Simplicity, a Changing Concept." *Journal of the History of Ideas* 14 (1953): 3–32.

Haworth, Helen E. "'A Thing of Beauty Is a Joy Forever?' Early Illustrated Editions of Keats's Poetry." *Harvard Library Bulletin* 21 (1973): 88–103.

Hazlitt, William. *The Complete Works of William Hazlitt*, ed. P. P. Howe. 21 vols. London: J. M. Dent and Sons, 1930–1934.

Hilton, Timothy. *The Pre-Raphaelites*. London: Thames and Hudson, 1970.

Hirsch, E. D., Jr. *Validity in Interpretation*. New Haven: Yale University Press, 1967.

Hirst, Wolf Z. *John Keats*. Boston: Twayne, 1981.

Holland, Norman N. *The Dynamics of Literary Response*. New York: Oxford University Press, 1968.

————. *Five Readers Reading*. New Haven: Yale University Press, 1975.

————. *Laughing: A Psychology of Humor*. Ithaca: Cornell University Press, 1982.

Homans, Margaret. "Keats Reading Women, Women Reading Keats." *Studies in Romanticism* 29 (1990): 341–70.

Hunt, Leigh. *Lord Byron and Some of His Contemporaries*. London: Henry Colburn, 1828.

Iser, Wolfgang. *The Act of Reading: A Theory of Aesthetic Response*. Baltimore: Johns Hopkins University Press, 1978.

————. *The Implied Reader: Patterns of Communication in Prose Fiction from Bunyan to Beckett*. Baltimore: Johns Hopkins University Press, 1974.

Jack, Ian. *Keats and the Mirror of Art*. Oxford: Clarendon Press, 1967.

Jackson, J. R. de J. *Romantic Poetry by Women: A Bibliography, 1770–1835*. Oxford: Clarendon Press, 1993.

Jauss, Hans Robert. *Toward an Aesthetic of Reception*, trans. Timothy Bahti. Minneapolis: University of Minnesota Press, 1982.

John Keats: Bicentennial Exhibition, September 19–November 22, 1995. New York: Grolier Club, 1995.

John Keats, 1795–1995, with a Catalogue of the Harvard Keats Collection. Cambridge: Houghton Library, 1995.

Johnson, Samuel. *Lives of the English Poets,* ed. George Birkbeck Hill. 3 vols. Oxford: Clarendon Press, 1905.

———. "Preface [to Shakespeare]." In *Johnson on Shakespeare,* ed. Arthur Sherbo. *The Yale Edition of the Works of Samuel Johnson,* 7:59–113. New Haven: Yale University Press, 1968.

Jones, Elizabeth. "Keats in the Suburbs." *Keats-Shelley Journal* 45 (1996): 23–43.

———. "The Suburban School: Snobbery and Fear in the Attacks on Keats." *Times Literary Supplement,* 27 October 1995, 14–15.

Jones, Mark. *The "Lucy Poems": A Case Study in Literary Knowledge.* Toronto: University of Toronto Press, 1995.

Jordan, Frank, ed. *The English Romantic Poets: A Review of Research and Criticism,* 4th ed. New York: Modern Language Association, 1985.

Karolides, Nicholas J., ed. *Reader Response in the Classroom: Evoking and Interpreting Meaning in Literature.* White Plains, NY: Longman, 1992.

Keats, John. *The Complete Works of John Keats,* ed. H. Buxton Forman. 5 vols. Glasgow: Gowans and Gray, 1900–1901.

———. *John Keats,* ed. Elizabeth Cook. Oxford Authors. Oxford: Oxford University Press, 1990.

———. *John Keats: Complete Poems,* ed. Jack Stillinger. Cambridge: Harvard University Press, 1982.

———. *John Keats: Selected Poems,* ed. Nicholas Roe. Everyman Library. London: J. M. Dent, 1995.

———. *John Keats's Anatomical and Physiological Note Book,* ed. Maurice Buxton Forman. London: Oxford University Press, 1934.

———. *The Letters of John Keats, 1814–1821,* ed. Hyder E. Rollins. 2 vols. Cambridge: Harvard University Press, 1958.

———. *The Poems of John Keats,* ed. Miriam Allott. London: Longman, 1970.

———. *The Poems of John Keats,* ed. Jack Stillinger. Cambridge: Harvard University Press, 1978.

———. *The Poetical Works of John Keats,* ed. H. W. Garrod. Oxford: Clarendon Press, 1939. 2nd ed., 1958.

———. *The Poetical Works and Other Writings of John Keats,* ed. Harry Buxton Forman. 4 vols. London: Reeves and Turner, 1883. Reissued, with new material, 4 vols. London: Reeves and Turner, 1889.

———. *Selected Poems and Letters,* ed. Douglas Bush. Boston: Houghton Mifflin, 1959.

Kercsmar, Rhonda Ray. "Keats's Violation of Romance: Transgression in 'The Eve of St. Agnes.'" *Topic* 46 (1996): 25–35.

Kermode, Frank. *Forms of Attention.* Chicago: University of Chicago Press, 1985.

Kern, Robert. "Keats and the Problem of Romance." *Philological Quarterly* 58 (1979): 171–91. Reprinted in de Almeida, *Critical Essays,* 68–87.

Kernan, Alvin. *The Death of Literature.* New Haven: Yale University Press, 1990.

Kerrigan, John. "Keats and *Lucrece*." *Shakespeare Survey* 41 (1989): 103–18.

Kramnick, Jonathan Brody. "The Making of the English Canon." *PMLA* 112 (1997): 1087–1101.

Kucich, Greg. *Keats, Shelley, and Romantic Spenserianism.* University Park: Pennsylvania State University Press, 1991.

———. "A Lamentable Lay: Keats and the Making of Charles Brown's Spenser Volumes." *Keats-Shelley Review* 3 (1988): 1–22.

————. "Spenserian Versification in Keats's *The Eve of St. Agnes.*" *Michigan Academician* 16 (1983): 101–108.

Lau, Beth. *Keats's Reading of the Romantic Poets.* Ann Arbor: University of Michigan Press, 1991.

————. "Madeline at Northanger Abbey: Keats's Anti-Romances and Gothic Satire." *Journal of English and Germanic Philology* 84 (1985): 30–50.

Levinson, Marjorie. *Keats's Life of Allegory: The Origins of a Style.* Oxford: Basil Blackwell, 1988.

————. *Wordsworth's Great Period Poems: Four Essays.* Cambridge: Cambridge University Press, 1986.

Linkin, Harriet Kramer. "The Current Canon in British Romantic Studies." *College English* 53 (1991): 548–70.

Little, Judy. *Keats as a Narrative Poet: A Test of Invention.* Lincoln: University of Nebraska Press, 1975.

Liu, Alan. *Wordsworth: The Sense of History.* Stanford: Stanford University Press, 1989.

Lowell, Amy. *John Keats.* 2 vols. Boston: Houghton Mifflin, 1925.

MacGillivray, J. R. *Keats: A Bibliography and Reference Guide with an Essay on Keats' Reputation.* Toronto: University of Toronto Press, 1949.

Madonick, Michael David. "The Pirate Map." *Cimarron Review* 103 (April 1993): 83–85.

Magnuson, Paul. "'The Eolian Harp' in Context." *Studies in Romanticism* 24 (1985): 3–20.

————. "The Politics of 'Frost at Midnight.'" *The Wordsworth Circle* 22 (1991): 3–11. Revised in Magnuson's *Reading Public Romanticism,* 67–94.

————. *Reading Public Romanticism.* Princeton: Princeton University Press, 1998.

Maier, Rosemarie. "The Bitch and the Bloodhound: Generic Similarity in 'Christabel' and 'The Eve of St. Agnes.'" *Journal of English and Germanic Philology* 70 (1971): 62–75.

Malins, Edward, and Morchard Bishop. *James Smetham and Francis Danby: Two 19th Century Romantic Painters.* London: Eric and Joan Stevens, 1974.

Mandell, Laura. "Canons Die Hard: A Review of the New Romantic Anthologies." *Romanticism on the Net* 7 (August 1997: www-sul.stanford.edu/mirrors/romnet).

————. "The Monstrosity of Minimal Difference: Eighteenth-Century Women Poets and the Formation of the British Canon." Unpublished paper. Miami University, 1997.

————. "Romantic Canons: A Bibliography (and an Argument)." Attachment to Mandell's home page (miavx1.muohio.edu/~update/canon.htm).

Matlak, Richard E., ed. *Approaches to Teaching Coleridge's Poetry and Prose.* New York: Modern Language Association, 1991.

Matthews, G. M., ed. *Keats: The Critical Heritage.* London: Routledge and Kegan Paul; New York: Barnes and Noble, 1971.

Mayhead, Robin. *John Keats.* Cambridge: Cambridge University Press, 1967.

Mays, J. C. C. *How We Got Where We Are, as We Cease to Be There.* Inaugural Lecture Delivered at University College Dublin, 27 October 1994.

McClelland, Fleming. "Does Madeline Sleep, or Does She Wake? The Hoodwinking of Porphyro." *Keats-Shelley Review* 10 (1996): 31–34.

McGann, Jerome J. *A Critique of Modern Textual Criticism.* Chicago: University of Chicago Press, 1983.

Mellor, Anne K. *English Romantic Irony.* Cambridge: Harvard University Press, 1980.

————, and Richard E. Matlak, eds. *British Literature, 1780–1830.* Fort Worth: Harcourt Brace, 1996.

Millar, Oliver. *The Victorian Pictures in the Collections of Her Majesty the Queen.* 2 vols. Cambridge: Cambridge University Press, 1992.

Milnes, Richard Monckton, ed. *Life, Letters, and Literary Remains, of John Keats.* 2 vols. London: Edward Moxon, 1848.

Motion, Andrew. *Keats.* New York: Farrar, Straus and Giroux, 1997.

Muir, Kenneth, ed. *John Keats: A Reassessment.* Liverpool: Liverpool University Press, 1958.

Mulvey, Laura. "Visual Pleasure and Narrative Cinema." *Screen* 16, no. 3 (Autumn 1975): 6–18.

Murry, John Middleton. *Keats and Shakespeare: A Study of Keats' Poetic Life from 1816 to 1820.* London: Oxford University Press, 1925.

Nuttall, A. D. "Adam's Dream and Madeline's." In *Religious Imagination,* ed. James P. Mackey, 125–41. Edinburgh: Edinburgh University Press, 1986.

Parker, Hershel. *Flawed Texts and Verbal Icons: Literary Authority in American Fiction.* Evanston: Northwestern University Press, 1984.

Patey, Douglas Lane. "The Eighteenth Century Invents the Canon." *Modern Language Studies* 18, no. 1 (Winter 1988): 17–37.

Patterson, Charles I., Jr. *The Daemonic in the Poetry of John Keats.* Urbana: University of Illinois Press, 1970.

Pearson, P. David, ed. *Handbook of Reading Research.* Vol. 1. New York: Longman, 1984. (For vol. 2 of this work, see Barr, above.)

Peter, Brother Baldwin. "'The Eve of St. Agnes' and the Sleeping-Beauty Motif." *Keats-Shelley Memorial Bulletin* 22 (1971): 1–6.

Pettet, E. C. *On the Poetry of Keats.* Cambridge: Cambridge University Press, 1957.

The Pre-Raphaelites. London: Tate Gallery/Penguin Books, 1984.

Priestley, F. E. L. "Keats and Chaucer." *Modern Language Quarterly* 5 (1944): 439–47.

Ragussis, Michael. "Narrative Structure and the Problem of the Divided Reader in *The Eve of St. Agnes.*" *ELH* 42 (1975): 378–94. Revised in Ragussis's *The Subterfuge of Art: Language and the Romantic Tradition,* 70–84. Baltimore: Johns Hopkins University Press, 1978.

Rajan, Tilottama. *Dark Interpreter: The Discourse of Romanticism.* Ithaca: Cornell University Press, 1980.

Reiman, Donald H., ed. *The Romantics Reviewed: Contemporary Reviews of British Romantic Writers.* Part C: *Shelley, Keats, and London Radical Writers.* 2 vols. New York: Garland, 1972.

Reyher, Ferdinand. "The Humor of Keats." *New Republic,* 30 October 1915, 334–35.

Richards, I. A. *Coleridge on Imagination.* London: K. Paul, Trench, Trubner, 1934.

————. *Practical Criticism: A Study of Literary Judgment.* London: K. Paul, Trench, and Trubner, 1929.

————. *Principles of Literary Criticism.* London: Routledge and Kegan Paul, 1924.

Richardson, Alan. *Literature, Education, and Romanticism: Reading as Social Practice, 1780–1832.* Cambridge: Cambridge University Press, 1994.

Ricks, Christopher. *Keats and Embarrassment.* Oxford: Clarendon Press, 1974.

Ridley, M. R. *Keats' Craftsmanship: A Study in Poetic Development* (1933). Lincoln: University of Nebraska Press, 1963.

Roe, Nicholas. *John Keats and the Culture of Dissent.* Oxford: Clarendon Press, 1997.

————, ed. *Keats and History.* Cambridge: Cambridge University Press, 1995.

Rollins, Hyder E., ed. *The Keats Circle: Letters and Papers, 1816–1878.* 2 vols. Cambridge: Harvard University Press, 1948.

Rooke, Constance. "Romance and Reality in *The Eve of St. Agnes*." *English Studies in Canada* 4 (1978): 25–40.

Rosenblatt, Louise M. *Literature as Exploration* (1938). 5th ed. New York: Modern Language Association, 1996.

———. *The Reader, the Text, the Poem: The Transactional Theory of the Literary Work.* Carbondale: Southern Illinois University Press, 1978.

Rosenfeld, Nancy. "'Eve's dream will do here': Miltonic Dreaming in Keats's *Eve of St. Agnes*." Forthcoming in *Keats-Shelley Journal* 49 (2000).

Ross, Trevor. "The Emergence of 'Literature': Making and Reading the English Canon in the Eighteenth Century." *ELH* 63 (1996): 397–422.

Rossetti, William Michael. *Life of John Keats*. London: Walter Scott, 1887.

Ryan, Robert M. *Keats: The Religious Sense*. Princeton: Princeton University Press, 1976.

Rzepka, Charles J. *The Self as Mind: Vision and Identity in Wordsworth, Coleridge, and Keats.* Cambridge: Harvard University Press, 1986.

Schwartz, Lewis M. *Keats Reviewed by His Contemporaries: A Collection of Notices for the Years 1816–1821.* Metuchen, NJ: Scarecrow Press, 1973.

Scott, Grant F. *The Sculpted Word: Keats, Ekphrasis, and the Visual Arts.* Hanover, NH: University Press of New England, 1994.

Sharp, Ronald A. *Keats, Skepticism, and the Religion of Beauty.* Athens: University of Georgia Press, 1979.

Sharrock, Roger. "Keats and the Young Lovers." *Review of English Literature* 2, no. 1 (January 1961): 76–86.

Shillingsburg, Peter L. *Resisting Texts: Authority and Submission in Constructions of Meaning.* Ann Arbor: University of Michigan Press, 1997.

———. "The Three *Moby-Dicks*." *American Literary History* 2 (1990): 119–30.

———. "Text as Matter, Concept, and Action." *Studies in Bibliography* 44 (1991): 31–82. Revised in Shillingsburg's *Resisting Texts*, 49–103.

Slatoff, Walter J. *With Respect to Readers: Dimensions of Literary Response.* Ithaca: Cornell University Press, 1970.

Small, Robert C., Jr. "Connecting Students and Literature: What Do Teachers Do and Why Do They Do It?" In Karolides, 3–20.

Smith, Louise Z. "Writing on 'Isabella' from the Perspective of Composition Theory." In Evert and Rhodes, 92–98.

Sperry, Stuart M. *Keats the Poet*. Princeton: Princeton University Press, 1973.

———. "Romance as Wish-Fulfillment: Keats's *The Eve of St. Agnes*." *Studies in Romanticism* 10 (1971): 27–43. Revised in Sperry's *Keats the Poet*, 198–220.

Steiner, Wendy. *Pictures of Romance: Form against Context in Painting and Literature.* Chicago: University of Chicago Press, 1988.

Stephenson, William C. "The Performing Narrator in Keats's Poetry." *Keats-Shelley Journal* 26 (1977): 51–71.

Stillinger, Jack. *Coleridge and Textual Instability: The Multiple Versions of the Major Poems.* New York: Oxford University Press, 1994.

———. *The Hoodwinking of Madeline and Other Essays on Keats's Poems.* Urbana: University of Illinois Press, 1971.

———. "The Hoodwinking of Madeline: Scepticism in 'The Eve of St. Agnes.'" *Studies in Philology* 58 (1961): 533–55. Reprinted in *The Hoodwinking of Madeline*, 67–93.

———. "John Keats." In Jordan, 665–718.

———. "Keats's Extempore Effusions and the Question of Intentionality." In *Romantic Revisions*, ed. Robert Brinkley and Keith Hanley, 307–20. Cambridge: Cambridge University Press, 1992.

———. *Multiple Authorship and the Myth of Solitary Genius.* New York: Oxford University Press, 1991.

———. "The Plots of Romantic Poetry." *College Literature* 12 (1985): 97–112. Reprinted *College Literature* 15 (1988): 208–23. Revised as "Reading Keats's Plots." In de Almeida, *Critical Essays,* 88–102.

———. "The Text of 'The Eve of St. Agnes.'" *Studies in Bibliography* 16 (1963): 207–12. Reprinted in *The Hoodwinking of Madeline,* 158–66.

———. *The Texts of Keats's Poems.* Cambridge: Harvard University Press, 1974.

———. "Textual Primitivism and the Editing of Wordsworth." *Studies in Romanticism* 28 (1989): 3–28. Revised in *Multiple Authorship,* 69–95.

———, ed. *John Keats: Poetry Manuscripts at Harvard. A Facsimile Edition.* Cambridge: Harvard University Press, 1990.

———, ed. *Manuscript Poems in the British Library: Facsimiles of the "Hyperion" Holograph and George Keats's Notebook of Holographs and Transcripts.* Manuscripts of the Younger Romantics series, John Keats vol. 5. New York: Garland, 1988.

———, ed. *William Wordsworth: Selected Poems and Prefaces.* Boston: Houghton Mifflin, 1965.

———, ed. *The Woodhouse Poetry Transcripts at Harvard: A Facsimile of the W² Notebook, with Description and Contents of the W¹ Notebook.* Manuscripts of the Younger Romantics series, John Keats vol. 6. New York: Garland, 1988.

Stillinger, Tom. "Saint Madeline." Unpublished paper. Yale University, 1973.

Suleiman, Susan R., and Inge Crosman, eds. *The Reader in the Text: Essays on Audience and Interpretation.* Princeton: Princeton University Press, 1980.

Talbot, Norman. "Porphyro's Enemies." *Essays in Criticism* 38 (1988): 215–32.

Tennyson, Hallam Lord. *Alfred Lord Tennyson: A Memoir.* 2 vols. London: Macmillan, 1897.

Thomson, Heidi. "Eavesdropping on 'The Eve of St. Agnes': Madeline's Sensual Ear and Porphyro's Ancient Ditty." *Journal of English and Germanic Philology* 97 (1998): 337–51.

Thorpe, Clarence D. *The Mind of John Keats.* New York: Oxford University Press, 1926.

Tompkins, Jane P., ed. *Reader-Response Criticism: From Formalism to Post-Structuralism.* Baltimore: Johns Hopkins University Press, 1980.

Turner, Jane, ed. *The Dictionary of Art.* 34 vols. New York: Grove, 1996.

Twitchell, James B. "Porphyro as 'Famish'd Pilgrim': The Hoodwinking of Madeline Continued." *Ball State University Forum* 19, no. 2 (Spring 1978): 56–65. Revised in Twitchell's *The Living Dead: A Study of the Vampire in Romantic Literature,* 92–101. Durham: Duke University Press, 1981.

Van Ghent, Dorothy. *Keats: The Myth of the Hero,* rev. and ed. Jeffrey Cane Robinson. Princeton: Princeton University Press, 1983.

Waldoff, Leon. "Porphyro's Imagination and Keats's Romanticism." *Journal of English and Germanic Philology* 76 (1977): 177–94. Revised in Waldoff's *Keats and the Silent Work of Imagination,* 62–81. Urbana: University of Illinois Press, 1985.

———. "The Question of Porphyro's Stratagem." In Evert and Rhodes, 39–44.

Ward, Aileen. *John Keats: The Making of a Poet.* New York: Viking, 1963.

———. "'That Last Infirmity of Noble Mind': Keats and the Idea of Fame." In *The Evidence of the Imagination: Studies of Interactions between Life and Art in English Romantic Literature,* ed. Donald H. Reiman, Michael C. Jaye, and Betty T. Bennett, 312–33. New York: New York University Press, 1978.

Ward, W. S. "A Device of Doors in *The Eve of St. Agnes.*" *Modern Language Notes* 73 (1958): 90–91.

Wasserman, Earl R. *The Finer Tone: Keats' Major Poems.* Baltimore: Johns Hopkins University Press, 1953.

Watkins, Daniel P. *Keats's Poetry and the Politics of the Imagination.* Rutherford, NJ: Fairleigh Dickinson University Press, 1989.

Webb, Charles H. "Byron, Keats, and Shelley." Poem read at the conference "Celebrating Keats: 1795–1995," Clark Library, Los Angeles, 29 April 1995.

White, R. S. *Keats as a Reader of Shakespeare.* Norman: University of Oklahoma Press, 1987.

Wiener, David. "The Secularization of the Fortunate Fall in Keats's 'The Eve of St. Agnes." *Keats-Shelley Journal* 29 (1980): 120–30.

William Holman Hunt: An Exhibition Arranged by the Walker Art Gallery. Liverpool: Walker Art Gallery, 1969.

Williams, Anne. *Art of Darkness: A Poetics of Gothic.* Chicago: University of Chicago Press, 1995.

Wilson, James D. "John Keats' Self-Reflexive Narrative: 'The Eve of St. Agnes,'" *South Central Review* 1, no. 4 (Winter 1984): 44–52.

Wimsatt, W. K., Jr., and Monroe C. Beardsley. "The "Affective Fallacy." *Sewanee Review* 57 (1949): 31–55. Reprinted in Wimsatt's *The Verbal Icon: Studies in the Meaning of Poetry,* 21–39. Lexington: University of Kentucky Press, 1954.

———, and Monroe C. Beardsley. "The Intentional Fallacy." *Sewanee Review* 54 (1946): 468–88. Reprinted, in revised form, in Wimsatt's *The Verbal Icon,* 3–18.

Wolfson, Susan J. "Feminizing Keats." In de Almeida, *Critical Essays,* 317–56.

———. "Keats and the Manhood of the Poet." *European Romantic Review* 6 (1995): 1–37.

———. *The Questioning Presence: Wordsworth, Keats, and the Interrogative Mode in Romantic Poetry.* Ithaca: Cornell University Press, 1986.

———, ed. "Keats and Politics: A Forum." *Studies in Romanticism* 25 (1986): 171–229.

Woof, Robert, and Stephen Hebron. *John Keats.* Grasmere: Wordsworth Trust, 1995.

Wright, Herbert G. "Has Keats's 'Eve of St. Agnes' a Tragic Ending?" *Modern Language Review* 40 (1945): 90–94.

INDEX